Autobiography: A Reader for Writers

AUTOBIOGRAPHY
A READER FOR WRITERS
SECOND EDITION

Robert Lyons

Queens College
of the City University of New York

NEW YORK

OXFORD UNIVERSITY PRESS

1984

Copyright © 1977, 1984 by Oxford University Press, Inc.

Library of Congress Cataloging in Publication Data
Main entry under title:

Autobiography: a reader for writers.

1. College readers.   2. English language—Rhetoric.
3. Readers—Autobiography.   4. Autobiographies.
5. Biography.   I. Lyons, Robert B.
PE1417.A85   1984   808'.0427   83-22026
ISBN 0-19-503401-5 (pbk.)

Printing (last digit):   9 8 7 6 5 4 3 2 1

Printed in the United States of America

PREFACE TO THE SECOND EDITION

This edition introduces a considerable number of new selections, chosen to extend the range of themes and styles included in the anthology. Since students and teachers have found my general introductions useful, I have made relatively minor changes in most of these commentaries. However, an entirely new section on letter writing has been added as a way of emphasizing the writer's concern with audience. I have also expanded the discussion of generalization in my final chapter, in order to give further attention to the crucial transition from autobiographical writing to less personal forms of writing.

New York   R. L.
October 1983

CONTENTS

Introduction   3

I. Talking About Ourselves   9

II. Beginnings 81

III. Events 107

IV. Places 177

Autobiography: A Reader for Writers

Introduction

Everyone who is going to write autobiographically has to get beyond the first awkward moment when he may think, "I have nothing to write about." A writer seldom recognizes how common that moment is, and is only uncomfortably aware that he has nothing to say about the one subject he should know best of all. The purpose of this anthology is to help writers learn how to regard themselves as a subject for their own writing, and how to write about that subject with authority.

We have all had the experience of meeting an old friend we have not seen for a long time, and of having the friend ask "What's new?" or "What have you been doing?"—in other words, tell me something autobiographical. Usually we shrug and say "Nothing much" or "Everything's fine." Obviously many things have happened to us, but it is difficult in a moment to isolate an event and to explain why and how it was important in our lives. We hesitate because, in effect, we are being asked to choose the autobiographical subject that best sums up the quality of our life since we last saw our friend. We are always relieved if there has been some publicly significant event that could serve to answer the friend's question—I got married, I changed jobs, I'm going to a new school—the kind of information that the local newspaper might print as part of the neighborhood news. Only after we have reestablished some intimacy with our friend do we relax, express ourselves more fully, and begin to create a more personal portrait of our life for him. The sources for this portrait are varied; they may be responses to specific questions by the friend, sudden random associations, or memories of shared interests in the past. Whatever they are they lead to specific recollections which, fragment by fragment, begin to compose an autobiographical sketch.

3

Our feeling of having nothing to say about ourselves is actually based on the enormous number of potential subjects (one could say that every moment in our past life is a potential subject) that momentarily paralyze our powers to choose and discriminate. In addition, we may not be used to seeing our own behavior from the outside rather than the inside. Unless we are in the habit of cultivating a certain amount of detachment toward ourselves, we may never have interpreted our own experiences or established links between the present moment and what has shaped it in the past or what it portends for the future. Of course, our lives are lived in the first person, not the third, and too much objectivity about ourselves can be dehumanizing, but some is necessary for self-understanding. If we have not thought about our actions, feelings, and motives, we have no way of verbalizing an answer to our friend's question.

One advantage we would have in talking about ourselves to a friend rather than a stranger is that we could call upon whatever shared experiences, interests, and values created the friendship to begin with. Many things could be left unsaid or explained by referring to some common memory ("It was a day like the one when we went sailing on Long Island Sound"). Consider instead another autobiographical moment, when we are being asked about ourselves by a job interviewer. In one sense, it may be easier for us to find something interesting to say, because we are likely to be asked specific questions about our background and experience, and we will have some clear expectations about the kinds of experiences we should be prepared to talk about. To a job interviewer, for example, we would probably present moments in our lives when we showed a great deal of initiative and responsibility and we would not tell the story of a balmy day of sunning and sailing on Long Island Sound. However, the main difference in this second autobiographical situation is that we are dealing with a stranger. Some of the same problems we had with our friend would still exist—choosing what to select and how to present it—but we now would have to be much more conscious of an audience uninformed about our life and its context. We would have to include many more details in our story and we would have to make firmer and more conscious decisions about how we wanted to present ourselves. We could no longer rely on those casual kinds of shorthand communication that friendship and familiarity make available to us.

Whichever audience we have in mind, being autobiographical always forces us to select from the multitude of our minute-by-minute, day-by-day experiences, to give shape and order to our selections, and to convey to our audience some sense of why we have chosen to emphasize this particular aspect of our lives. Written autobiography follows this same process, whether it deals with private experience or public accomplishment. Moreover, written autobiography addresses an audience that is not known to us personally, one that we can imagine to be as well disposed toward us as our friend, but one that we must remember has as little information about us as does the job interviewer.

The audience for autobiography in a writing class occupies a middle ground between friend and stranger. Although most of you, as students of writing, may not know one another personally at the beginning, you will share some common traits and some common experiences (the life at the school, if nothing else). Furthermore, you will become more familiar with one another through the meetings of the class itself and, most important, you will share a common interest in the craft of writing.

Your confidence as a writer and mastery of skills are enhanced by writing autobiographically, and these gains can be transferred to various kinds of college essays. (In fact, one purpose of this book is to help you use autobiography to prepare yourself for other forms of writing.) Nevertheless, autobiography involves a different kind of writing situation from that imposed by academic subjects, since you know your own experiences differently from the way you know the material in a history course. Writing about yourself, you are usually aware of the innumerable threads of thought and feeling that connect any one experience with other experiences in your life. For that reason there is invariably some sense of frustration when you try to catch your past in words. You may be among the many students who find that a less personal subject may prove less demanding, at least to their sense of what they can achieve as writers. For example, a college freshman can approach a vast historical topic, such as the American Civil War, and, after doing some research, can develop an ordered account of the main causes of this immensely complicated series of events. The student finishes such a paper with a sense of control, based in part on the fact that a good deal of the preliminary work of organizing his subject has already been done for him. Each historian he has read while researching the topic has offered him some pattern of causation for the war, so that the student begins writing with some coherent outlines for his subject already in mind. When the same student writes about a single moment in his own life, he finds himself uneasily trying to decide what details are important and what pattern of significance he can create for them.

On the other hand, there is one great satisfaction for the autobiographical writer; he is clearly in command, the best and indeed the only authority on his subject. If we sometimes feel inadequate to deal with our experiences in words, we should remember that no one else can make the attempt with anything like our chances for success. Especially for students who have to write in college courses, where the instructor is more knowledgeable about most essay topics than they are, writing about oneself should be a potentially liberating experience. Furthermore, the very difficulties of the autobiographical process that we have been discussing do have their own rewards, for the difficulties create pressure to clarify and interpret one's past in order to present it convincingly to a reader. Through the effort to find words to communicate transient experiences, a writer starts to formulate answers to such permanent questions as who he is and what he has accomplished. In fact, the motivation for many writers of published autobiographies is as much a desire for self-definition as it is a desire to create a public record of a life.

CHAPTER ONE

TALKING
ABOUT
OURSELVES

Part One–Interviews

Introduction: From Speech to Writing

*This first chapter is intended as an introduction to the auto-*biographical process, offering some informal ways to experiment with being autobiographical. The first section of the chapter is devoted to spoken recollections directed to a listener, usually an interviewer, who with his questions prompts the speaker to remember more. Talking about ourselves is obviously less demanding than writing about ourselves, basically because we are so much more accustomed to talking than to writing. Although we may know someone whose particular form of eloquence is close to written prose, someone who we say "speaks in paragraphs," most of us feel more comfortable with speech because it is a less constrained, more improvised form of expression.

There are many reasons for this lack of constraint. First of all, speech seems a matter of the moment; in most situations, it does not involve the same kind of commitment on the part of the speaker as do words on a page for a writer. This impermanence gives us a sense of freedom, because we can elaborate upon, redirect, even contradict what we say as the flow of talk continues. Secondly, speech can always be assisted or complemented by the tone of our voice, the look on our face, the gestures of our hands, the position of our body—all additional and compelling features of our language. In addition, we have an audience present before us, who confirm or deny what we say with their reactions and who motivate our speech with their words in the give and take of conversation. Finally, because speech usually involves a far greater element of improvisation than does writing, we take pleasure in its spontaneity as a mark of its deeply personal quality, its capacity to reflect what is unique about each one of us.

This is not to say that everyone's speech has these qualities or that every situation in which we use speech calls them forth. However, when we read the record of Harry Truman's spoken recollections, we hear the colloquial ease and directness as well as the narrative energy of a lively human voice. As we can see in Heather Lamb's description of her work, speech can make positive use of repetitions of words, phrases, and grammatical structures, as well as sentence fragments and run-ons; all of these devices would be inappropriate in most kinds of writing, but they have a powerful expressive force here. The most striking characteristic of all the spoken recollections included in this section is the sense of an individual voice that in each case still exists on the page.

It may seem odd to begin work on writing by concentrating on speaking, but on the other hand it would be difficult to write convincing autobiography without having a sense of what one's own voice sounds like and how and to what degree it can be transferred to the printed page. Writing and speaking are unquestionably separate activities, rather than different versions of the same process; writing, however, is learned later and more formally than speech, so it should, as our "second language," draw as much as possible on what we have mastered of the first. Grounding our writing on the characteristic cadences and patterns of our own speech is a way of making sure that the writing will never become completely cut off from its human source, and therefore will not disappear entirely into the faceless, voiceless world of cliché and jargon.

Speaking can also lead us to writing in another way, since speaking is a more familiar and less inhibiting form of communication. When we need a starting point for our written work we should take advantage of our ability to produce words quickly and easily in speech. Our beginning forays into our past life ought to rely on the freedom of association, the opportunities for sudden digression, and the lack of formality that we associate with oral expression. In addition, the interview, a familiar source for oral autobiography today, can be a great help in making us see what kinds of questions we need to ask ourselves as we start to become autobiographical. In fact, a very useful way for students to begin working with autobiography is to trade off the roles of interviewer and interviewee with other classmates, learning both to formulate and to answer questions about personal experience. Ultimately, the procedure becomes internalized, and the writer is able to explore his own experience by interrogating himself.

A valuable first step for the writer, therefore, is to use self-questioning in order to re-create as many facets of an autobiographical event as he can. Sense impressions, feelings, actions, relationships with other persons (if others are involved in the event), causes, and results—all these elements contribute to the event and any one might prove central to an understanding of it. For example, a student knows that attending his high school graduation was somehow a memorable event in his life, but he cannot think of any way to talk about it and make it personal until he starts to re-create the event out of its many details by asking himself about those details. What did the hall look like? How did I feel as I entered the hall? Who was on the speaker's platform? How did each speaker behave and what did he say? If I can't remember those details, why not? Was I thinking of other things during the ceremony? What were they? Why did they come to my mind just at that time? In fact, questions often tend to produce other questions, or one mental image of the past will lead to another, so that if we begin actively to explore some past moment, the process itself rapidly becomes more comfortable and more rewarding.

Such a process of exploration should be attempted even when a writer feels that he can communicate his experience without any kind of self-questioning. Sometimes, of course, that may be true, but often the result is surprisingly trite and impersonal. For example, we all have some sense of what a high school graduation would be like, even apart from whatever we experienced ourselves, because we have often read accounts in newspapers or watched television coverage of such events. It then becomes very easy for a writer to rely on what he knows about the standard form of such an event in any school—walking into the auditorium, singing the school song, listening to the valedictory speech, receiving the diploma from the principal—and to transpose it into the first person. He can go ahead and write because he feels he has enough to say, but in fact he introduces virtually nothing that would represent the distinctive nature or quality of his own experience of the event. Actually exploring his memory will certainly help the writer who is unable to get started, the writer who has difficulty getting beyond conventional summaries of his experience, and even the resourceful and talented writer who may find in some previously ignored detail a new dimension to an event that he then may want to develop. A writer may produce material at this stage as simple lists of words or phrases that trigger his imagination, as ordered notecards, as paragraphs of random fragments of recollection, or as stretches of free-form associative writing. The method chosen depends on the individual's preference and on simple experiments to find out what works best and proves most congenial to his creative energies.

∽ Harry S. Truman ∽

(1884-1972)

Harry S. Truman was born in Missouri. He became involved in politics after his failure in business during the Depression. He was U.S. Senator from Missouri (1934–44) and then became Vice-President under Franklin D. Roosevelt. When Roosevelt died in 1945, Truman became the thirty-third President of the United States and won election to a full term in 1948. Merle Miller, novelist and journalist, conducted a lengthy series of interviews with Truman at his home in Independence, Missouri, in 1961 and 1962 and later published them under the title Plain Speaking *(1973).*

THE HAPPIEST CHILDHOOD*

Mr. President, tell me about your first job.

"Well, when I was ten, maybe eleven years old, I got a job at Jim Clinton's drugstore on the northeast corner of the square in Independence. I had to get there at six thirty in the morning and set up the place so that when Mr. Clinton came down, he would find everything in order. I'd mop the floor and dust off the bottles and wipe off the counters, and then I'd wake Jim Clinton at seven."

Did you ever have any early-morning customers?

"Oh, yes, a great many. The people who were church members, the high hats in town, the ones who were afraid to go into

From Merle Miller: *Plain Speaking.* Copyright © 1973, 1974 by Merle Miller. Reprinted by permission of Berkley Publishing Corporation.

* Unbracketed titles are the author's; bracketed titles have been supplied by the editor.

a saloon and buy a drink, they'd come in, and I'd have to set out a bottle of whiskey, and they'd pay a dime for a drink before most people were up and around to see them. They'd put their dimes on the counter, and I'd leave all those dimes there until Mr. Clinton came in, and he'd put them in the cash register.

"All those fancy high hats, they'd say, 'Harry, give me a drink,' and I'd do it. And that's where I got my idea of what prohibitionists and high hats are. That's the reason some of them didn't like me. Because they knew I knew their background and their history.

"There were saloons all around the square, and the tough old birds who didn't give a damn about what people think, they'd go into the saloons and buy a drink when they wanted it. But as I say, the so-called *good* people, the fancy ones, they'd come in and buy a drink behind the prescription counter from a boy who didn't have any right to sell it to them.

"But that's the way I got to . . . well, feel a lack of respect for the counterfeits, and I don't care where they are. In Washington or wherever. There's a story they tell about this high hat that got to be Postmaster General of the United States. I think Mark Twain told it on him.

"He got to be Postmaster General, and he came back to his hometown to visit, and there wasn't anybody at the station to meet him but the village idiot. And the high hat wanted to know what people in the town had said when they found out he was Postmaster General.

"And the village idiot said, 'They didn't say anything. They just laughed.'

"That's what happens if you're a high hat and start taking yourself too seriously."

Do you think you ever did that, Mr. President?

"I tried not to. I did my level best not to, and if I had, the Boss and Margaret wouldn't ever have let me get away with it."

Mr. President, I understand that when you were still a boy, you got a job working as timekeeper for the Santa Fe Railroad.

16

"I worked for an old fellow named Smith. L. J. Smith his name was, and he was head of the construction company that was building the double track for the Santa Fe Railroad down here from Eaton Falls to where the Missouri Pacific comes into the Santa Fe down at Sheffield.

"I was eighteen years old, and I'd just finished high school and knew I wasn't going to get to go to West Point. So I took this job as a timekeeper. I took it to help out at home, to keep my brother, Vivian, and my sister, Mary, in school. My father was having a hard time with finances just then.

"Old man Smith had three camps, and there were about a hundred hoboes in each camp, and I got very well acquainted with them. My job was to keep tabs on them, to keep track of how much time they put in, and then I'd write out their paychecks for them. I'd usually write those checks in a saloon on the north side of the square in Independence here, a saloon called Pogunpo's or in old man Schmidt's saloon in Sheffield. I used to sit there and pay off those hoboes. And they weren't bad fellows. They'd work for two weeks. They'd get discounted if they drew their checks before that time. So they'd work two weeks, and then they'd spend all their money for whiskey in the saloon and come back to work the next Monday morning. I'd pay them off on Saturday night.

"But they weren't bad fellows. Not in any way. Most of them had backgrounds that caused them to be hoboes. Either they'd had family troubles or they'd been in jail for some damn fool thing that wasn't a penitentiary offense. But they weren't bad citizens at all. I remember one time I told the old man that ran the saloon, he was an old Dutchman and wore whiskers, I told him, I said, 'This old bastard is the blacksmith out there on the railroad, and we need him. So try to cut out on his whiskey.'

"Well, damn old Schmidt went out and told this blacksmith what I'd said, and I never got a better cussing in my life than I did for interfering with the freedom of an American citizen. And he was right. And that taught me something.

"But after that I guess the blacksmith was grateful for it because he took a file, a regular ordinary file about that long and made a butcher knife out of it and tempered it so that the edge would never come off. He made two of them for me, and I think one of them is still around the house somewhere. . . . So he didn't hold it against me that I was trying to keep him from getting drunk."

When you said camps, what were they, houses or tents?

"Tents mostly. There were tents, and I had a tricycle car on the railroad that I went up and down on. I had to make a list of the men that were working every morning at seven thirty, and then I had to go back at one thirty in the afternoon to be sure that they were still there. So when the time came for their being paid, I had the records. No one ever doubted the records I kept."

How much did those men make?

"They made eleven dollars for two weeks' work, and as I say, they'd get paid on Saturday, and by Monday morning most of them had drunk it all up. But it was one of the best experiences that I ever had because that was when I began to understand who the underdog was and what he thought about the people who were the high hats. They felt just like I did about them. They didn't have any time for them. And neither did I. I always liked the underdogs better than the high hats. I still do."

Weren't you ever uneasy? I mean, you were a reader of books and wore glasses and, as you say, you'd been called a sissy.

"No. No. I never had any trouble with those birds. They were just as nice as they could be, and when I left, the foreman down there in Sheffield said, 'Harry's all right from the navel out in every direction.' Which when you come to think of it is just about the highest compliment I ever have been paid.

"Some of those hoboes had better educations than the president of Ha-vud University, and they weren't stuck up about it either. The average of them was just as smart as the smartest people in the country, and they'd had experiences, and a lot of them told me about their experiences. I hope I profited from it, and I think I did. I had to quit at the end of the summer, but my goodness, that was a great experience for me."

I understand you learned a few cuss words that summer.

"I did. The words some of those men knew I'd never heard before, but later when I was in the Army, there was an occasion or two when those words came in handy, and I used them.

"That experience also taught me that the lower classes so called are better than the high hats and the counterfeits, and they can be trusted more, too.

"About this counterfeit business. My Grandfather Young felt the same way. We had a church in the front yard where the cemetery is now. And the Baptists and the Methodists and all of them used it. And Grandfather Young when I was six years old, he died when I was eight, he told me that whenever the customers in any of those denominations prayed too loud in the Amen corner, you'd better go home and lock your smokehouse.

"And I found that to be true. I've never cared much for the loud pray-ers or for people who do that much going on about religion."

∽ Studs Terkel ∽

(1912-   )

Studs Terkel was born in New York City, but has lived in Chicago most of his life. Work as a radio announcer led him to develop an interest in oral history. He has published several books based on his tape-recorded interviews with a wide range of Americans, most of them not prominent or professional people. The following excerpt is from his book Working (1972) *and reflects Terkel's skill in getting people to speak for and about themselves.*

HEATHER LAMB

For almost two years she has been working as a long distance telephone operator at Illinois Bell. A naval base is nearby. She works three nights a week, split shift, during the high-school season and a full forty hours in the summertime. She is turning eighteen.

It's a strange atmosphere. You're in a room about the size of a gymnasium, talking to people thousands of miles away. You come in contact with at least thirty-five an hour. You can't exchange any ideas with them. They don't know you, they never will. You feel like you might be missing people. You feel like they put a coin in the machine and they've got you. You're there to perform your service and go. You're kind of detached.

A lot of the girls are painfully shy in real life. You get some girls who are outgoing in their work, but when they have to talk to someone and look them in the face, they can't think of what to say. They feel self-conscious when they know someone can see them. At the switchboard, it's a feeling of anonymousness.

There are about seven or eight phrases that you use and that's it: "Good morning, may I help you?" "Operator, may I help you?" "Good afternoon." "Good evening." "What number did you want?" "Would you repeat that again?" "I have a collect call for you from so-and-so, will you accept the charge?" "It'll be a dollar twenty cents." That's all you can say.

A big thing is not to talk with a customer. If he's upset, you can't say more than "I'm sorry you've been having trouble." If you get caught talking with a customer, that's one mark against you. You can't help but want to talk to them if they're in trouble or if they're just feeling bad or something. For me it's a great temptation to say, "Gee, what's the matter?" You don't feel like you're really that much helping people.

Say you've got a guy on the line calling from Vietnam, his line is busy and you can't interrupt. God knows when he'll be able to get on his line again. You know he's lonesome and he wants to talk to somebody, and there you are and you can't talk to him. There's one person who feels badly and you can't do anything. When I first started, I asked the operator and she says, "No, he can always call another time."

One man said, "I'm lonesome, will you talk to me?" I said, "Gee I'm sorry, I just can't." But you *can't*. (Laughs.) I'm a communications person but I can't communicate.

I've worked here almost two years and how many girls' first names do I know? Just their last name is on their headset. You might see them every day and you won't know their names. At Ma Bell they speak of teamwork, but you don't even know the names of the people who are on your team.

It's kind of awkward if you meet someone from the company and say, "Hi there, Jones," or whatever. (Laughs.) It's very embarrassing. You sit in the cafeteria and you talk to people and you don't even know their names. (Laughs.) I've gone to a lot of people I've been talking to for a week and I've said, "Tell me your name." (Laughs.)

You have a number—mine's 407. They put your number on your tickets, so if you made a mistake they'll know who did it. You're just an instrument. You're there to dial a number. It would be just as good for them to punch out the number.

The girls sit very close. She would be not even five or six inches away from me. The big thing is elbows, especially if she's left-handed. That's why we have so many colds in the winter, you're so close. If one person has a cold, the whole office has a cold. It's very catchy.

You try to keep your fingernails short because they break. If you go to plug in, your fingernail goes. You try to wear your hair simple. It's not good to have your hair on top of your head. The women don't really come to work if they've just had their hair done. The headset flattens it.

Your arms don't really get tired, your mouth gets tired. It's strange, but you get tired of talking, 'cause you talk constantly for six hours without a break.

Half the phones have a new system where the quarter is three beeps, a dime is two beeps, and a nickel is one beep. If the guy's in a hurry and he keeps throwing in money, all the beeps get all mixed up together (laughs), and you don't know how much money is in the phone. So it's kinda hard.

When you have a call, you fill it out on this IBM card. Those go with a special machine. You use a special pencil so it'll go through this computer and pick up the numbers. It's real soft lead, it just goes all over the desk and you're all dirty by the time you get off. (Laughs.) And sometimes your back hurts if your chair isn't up at the right height and you have to bend over and write. And keeping track. You don't get just one call at a time.

There is also the clock. You've got a clock next to you that times every second. When the light goes off, you see the party has answered, you have to write down the hour, the minute, and the second. Okay, you put that in a special slot right next to the cord light. You're ready for another one. Still you've got to watch the first one. When the light goes on, they disconnect and you've got to take that card out again and time down the hour, the minute, and the second—plus keeping on taking other calls. It's hectic.

∾ Oriana Fallaci ∾

(1930-   )

Oriana Fallaci, an international correspondent for the Italian magazine L'Europeo, *became famous during the 1970s as an interviewer of major political figures throughout the world. The texts of some of these conversations were published in her book* Interview with History *(1976). Here Fallaci is herself interviewed for* Rolling Stone *magazine by Jonathan Cott. Their talk was later republished in Cott's book* Forever Young *(1977).*

[BEING AN INTERVIEWER]

It wasn't so long ago that advice-to-the-lovelorn columnists tried to suggest that all a woman had to do to get a man interested in her was to cajole him gently into talking about himself all evening, thereby flattering him and bolstering his sense of self-importance. In your interviews you seem, almost unconsciously, to have taken this piece of folk wisdom and pushed it very far down the line, doing it in order to expose your grandiloquent subjects for what they really are.

I've never thought of that. Neither in my private nor my public life have I ever thought in terms of "seducing" somebody, using what are called the "feminine arts"—it makes me vomit just to think of it. Ever since I was a child—and way before the recent feminist resurgence—I've never conceived of . . . I'm very surprised by what you say. There might be some truth here, but you've really caught me by surprise.

What you're talking about implies a kind of psychological violence which I never commit when I interview someone. I never force a person to talk to me. If he doesn't want to talk, or if he talks without pleasure, I just walk out; I've done that many times. There's no courting or seducing involved. The main secret of my interviews lies in the fact that there's no trick whatsoever. None.

You know, there are many students who write about my interviews—in Italy, France, and America, too. And they always ask me how I go about it and if I could teach them to do it. But it's impossible, for these interviews are what they are, good or bad, because they're made by me, with this face, with this voice. They have to do with my personality, and I bring too much of myself into them to teach them.

When I was reading Interview with History, *I began thinking of the great Enlightenment author Diderot, who, it's been said, had an "instinctual" urge to expose what was concealed. And it seems to me that one of the underlying impulses of your work—along with your unmediated hatred for fascism and authoritarianism—is exactly this instinctual urge to expose. Do you feel that this is true?*

All right. You must give me a little time to answer, as I do with the people I interview. It's a difficult question, very difficult. As I told you before, I bring myself into these interviews completely, as a human being, as a personality; I bring what I know, what I don't know, what I am. Oriana is in there, as an actor. And I bring into these encounters all my choices, all my ideas, and my temperament as well. So, being at the same time very antifascist and very passionate, it's very difficult for me to interview the fascist, in the broad sense of the word. And I say it with shame, since I'm perfectly aware of how ridiculous this is. If I am, as I claim to be, a historian as much as a journalist (I claim that a journalist is a historian of his time), how can I reject at least half of humanity? Because at least half of humanity is fascist.

. . .

In a recent interview with Jean-Paul Sartre on his seventieth birthday, he stated: "I believe that everyone should be able to speak of his innermost being to an interviewer. I think that what spoils relations among people is that each keeps something hidden from the other, something secret, not necessarily from everyone, but from whomever he is speaking to at the moment. I think transparency should always be substituted for what is secret."

I don't believe it. He's not sincere, he's acting. Noble, intelligent, yes; he's playing the philosopher. But I can't conceive for a second that he means what he's saying because his daily life is the contrary of that. He's an arrogant man, often proud, and he can be very cruel and cold to people. He never forgets to be Sartre.

You want to know what I think of his idea? You cannot deny a human being his right to his privacy, to his secrets, to himself. When I speak of socialism, I don't mean that. I am mine, and to hell with the others: at a certain point I have the right to say that. What he's saying is pure intellectualism. If he had said that to me, I would have replied: "Come on, that's enough of that bullshit, you don't believe that. Come on, now."

You're obviously more Shakespearean—knowing that if you conceal something, you reveal it at exactly that moment, while letting it be known when and how this occurs.

What have you studied, politics or English literature? You studied it well, huh? Did you finish? Bravo. I'm very surprised, I'm fascinated—now I would like to interview you! But anyway . . . to get back to Sartre. I really believe so little in what he says. You know, there's always a moment during an interview, during my research into the soul of the person, when I stop. I voluntarily stop. I don't want to go on, I haven't the guts to invade further the soul of that person.

Listen, I'll give you an example. I've had two moments of great embarrassment. Not superficial embarrassment, because I'm a tough person, but here, inside. One was with Golda, when I asked her about her husband and she cried. And I felt—I'll make a confession now—a sort of shame. It was far from the vulgar way that journalists put questions, you know: "Tell me about Mr. So-and-so." I'd done it very sweetly, very elegantly, but all the same I felt ashamed of myself when she was crying. And the other moment was with Thieu, when he started crying while talking about being just a little man. And God knows, I was against everything he represented, but I saw a man, a person, and again I felt a sort of shame.

There are moments when I listen with an internal embarrassment that you'd never notice, but I have it very deep. For instance, with Kissinger—when we got to the problem of women, he was like that, he didn't want to talk about it. But I didn't want to either. Even with Hussein, when he spoke of the fear of his being killed, I felt uncomfortable, uncomfortable.

I think it's important to make a distinction between "mystification" and "mystery," and I feel that you respect the latter.

Ah, you see how coherent I am for once in my life? The way I reacted to Sartre . . . well, the explanation is here. Because I wouldn't like them to do it with me. I wouldn't.

The duty of a journalist is to reveal everything that's possible. Not to leave any interrogation point. To wipe out all curiosity. But I'm not a journalist 100 percent. I'm a writer, and I bring that into the journalism. I much prefer to have something well written, well built from a literary and a dramatic point of view, so that it can be read as a piece of literature—and this necessarily includes the *mystery*. I'm more interested in doing that than in telling everything as a good journalist should.

And when I'm asked, "What do you prefer to be, a journalist or a writer, and what is the difference between them?" I reply that there is no difference for me. And I mean that. My approach is to see the president of Angola, for example, as if he were a character in a novel rather than just an important name mentioned in *The New York Times*.

• • •

Are you going to continue doing interviews?

It's becoming more and more difficult for me and I'll tell you why. First, I've launched a fashion and now everybody does it, or tries to do it. There are more people requiring those interviews and so you see more of them around. And second, it's become more difficult because people are stupidly scared of me. They're worried. And if they decide to do an interview with me, it's because they think the moment is good for them—I'm a good vehicle for publicity. And then they act too nice. I have one to do soon, and when I telephoned yesterday, the people said: "Oh, Oriana Fallaci—we're *so* honored," and I thought: "Oh, no, *Madonna mia.*" Others like Qaddafi, for example, don't want to see me. (I accused him of having stolen my Golda Meir tapes—which is true.) Some persons really don't have the guts to see me.

∽ Frank O'Connor ∽

(1903-1966)

Frank O'Connor was born in Cork, Ireland. O'Connor's father was a day laborer, and the family lived in poverty, sometimes made worse by the father's bouts of alcoholism. O'Connor was largely self-educated and worked at a variety of jobs until he participated in the Irish Civil War and was briefly imprisoned in 1923. While in his twenties, he began to write fiction, first in Gaelic and then in English. Although he has published verse, translations, biographies, and literary criticism, he is best known as a writer of short stories, virtually all of which have a contemporary Irish setting. The following selection is from an interview with O'Connor that originally appeared in Paris Review. *That magazine regularly features interviews in which creative writers are asked about their work and their working habits. Some of these interviews were collected in* Writers at Work *(1957), from which these excerpts were taken. The interviewer was Anthony Whittier.*

[A WRITER AT WORK]

INTERVIEWER: What about working habits? How do you start a story?

O'CONNOR: "Get black on white" used to be Maupassant's advice—that's what I always do. I don't give a hoot what the writing's like, I write any sort of rubbish which will cover the main outlines of the story, then I can begin to see it. When I write, when I draft a story, I never think of writing nice sentences about, "It was a nice August evening when Elizabeth Jane Moriarty was coming down the road." I just write roughly what happened, and then I'm able to see what the construction looks like. It's the design of the story which to me is most important, the thing that tells you there's a bad gap in the narrative here and you really ought to fill that up in some way or another. I'm always looking at the design of a story, not the treatment. Yesterday I was finishing off a piece about my friend A. E. Coppard, the greatest of all the English storytellers, who died about a fortnight ago. I was describing the way Coppard must have written these stories, going around with a notebook, recording what the lighting looked like, what that house looked like, and all the time using metaphor to suggest it to himself, "The road looked like a mad serpent going up the hill," or something of the kind, and, "She said so-and-so, and the man in the pub said something else." After he had written them all out, he must have got the outline of his story, and he'd start working in all the details. Now, I could never do that at all. I've got to see what these people did, first of all, and *then* I start thinking of whether it was a nice August evening or a spring evening. I have to wait for the theme before I can do anything.

INTERVIEWER: Do you rewrite?

O'CONNOR: Endlessly, endlessly, endlessly. And keep on rewriting, and after it's published, and then after it's published in book form, I usually rewrite it again. I've rewritten versions of most of my early stories and one of these days, God help, I'll publish these as well.

INTERVIEWER: Do you keep notes as a source of supply for future stories?

O'CONNOR: Just notes of themes. If somebody tells me a good story, I'll write it down in my four lines; that is the secret of the theme. If you make the subject of a story twelve or fourteen lines, that's a treatment. You've already committed yourself to the sort of character, the sort of surroundings, and the

moment you've committed yourself, the story is already written. It has ceased to be fluid, you can't design it any longer,
you can't model it. So I always confine myself to my four lines.
If it won't go into four, that means you haven't reduced it to its
ultimate simplicity, reduced it to the fable.

INTERVIEWER: I have noticed in your stories a spareness of
physical description of people and places. Why this apparent
rejection of sense impressions?

O'CONNOR: I thoroughly agree, it's one of the things I know
I do, and sometimes when I'm reading Coppard I feel that it's
entirely wrong. I'd love to be able to describe people as he describes them, and landscapes as he describes them, but I begin
the story in the man's head and it never gets out of the man's
head. And in fact, in real life, when you meet somebody in the
street you don't start recording that she had this sort of nose—
at least a man doesn't. I mean, if you're the sort of person that
meets a girl in the street and instantly notices the color of her
eyes and of her hair and the sort of dress she's wearing, then
you're not in the least like me. I just notice a feeling from people. I notice particularly the cadence of their voices, the sort of
phrases they'll use, and that's what I'm all the time trying to
hear in my head, how people word things—because everybody
speaks an entirely different language, that's really what it
amounts to. I have terribly sensitive hearing and I'm terribly
aware of voices. If I remember somebody, for instance, that I
was very fond of, I don't remember what he or she looked like,
but I can absolutely take off the voice. I'm a good mimic; I've
a bit of the actor in me, I suppose, that's really what it amounts
to. I cannot pass a story as finished unless I connect it myself,
unless I know how everybody in it spoke, which, as I say, can
go quite well with the fact that I couldn't tell you in the least
what they looked like. If I use the right phrase and the reader
hears the phrase in his head, he sees the individual. It's like
writing for the theater, you see. A bad playwright will "pull"
an actor because he'll tell him what to do, but a really good
playwright will give you a part that you can do what you like

with. It's transferring to the reader the responsibility for acting those scenes. I've given him all the information I have and put it into his own life.

. . .

INTERVIEWER: Have you any particular words of encouragement for young writers?

O'CONNOR: Well, there's this: Don't take rejection slips too seriously. I don't think they ought to send them out at all. I think a very amusing anthology might be gotten up of rejection letters alone. It's largely a question of remembering, when you send something out, that So-and-so is on the other end of this one, and he has certain interests. To give an example of what I mean on this rejection business, I had a story accepted by a magazine. So I wrote it over again as I always do, and sent it back. Well, someone else got it and I got this very nice letter saying that they couldn't use it, but that they'd be very interested in seeing anything else I wrote in the future.

Possibilities for Writing

1. First join with other students in exchanging the roles of interviewer and interviewee. As an interviewer, try to find out about your subject's life, his background, interests, and ambitions. After participating in these interviews, write a list of questions that you now think it might be important for an autobiographical writer to try to answer.
2. Write a draft of an account of some early point in your life—your memories of the first grade, for example, or of some person, place, or event from an even earlier time. Then let yourself be interviewed by several members of the class and see to what extent their questions make you provide additional information or help you gain a new perspective on your subject.
3. Together with other students in the class, try to recall a recent experience that you have all shared—for example, the registration process, your first meal at the cafeteria, a school concert or dance. After each student in turn has presented his account of the experience, write a brief report explaining which student's recollection was most convincing for you.

Part Two – Diaries and Journals

Introduction: Writing for Oneself

Section two of this chapter consists of selections from diaries and journals; these are intended to serve as transitions to formal autobiography. With these excerpts we have moved across the line from speaking to writing, but to a type of writing that can still share some of the informality characteristic of speech. The journal writer has even greater freedom than a speaker does to decide what he will comment on, when he will suddenly shift to another subject, and how long he will continue to develop the subject before he stops entirely. While speech usually involves a participating audience, listening and responding, the writer of diaries or journals addresses either himself alone or else an imagined audience that he defines to fit his own desires. What is most important about diaries and journals is that they do encourage us to write; through them we transfer our experience to written language, a step which almost inevitably leads to greater coherence and greater detachment.

A distinction is conventionally made between a diary—a day-to-day record of the events of one's life—and a journal—a record of the intellectual or spiritual development of an individual. In practice, this distinction is often blurred, since most writers tend to mix reflection and specific recollections, and so this introduction will refer to any private record as a journal. The only consistent characteristic of a journal is the frequency of its entries; writers who keep journals like to return to them regularly, even if not on a daily basis or according to a specific timetable. Such habits are understandable, since journals are prompted by our own desire to record something about our-selves, not by any external requirement. Because journals are private, each writer sets his own rules. What he says can be long or short, personal or impersonal, grammatical or ungram-matical; it can be lyrical, analytical, satirical, or anything else within the range of the writer's expression; it can strike any tone, express any mood. Such freedom makes journal writing one of the best ways for an inexperienced writer to savor the potential pleasures of writing, since it offers the rewards of self-expression, directed to that most attentive and intuitive of audiences, oneself.

To benefit from keeping a journal, a student must under-stand and value the freedom it offers him. Too often a student thinks of his journal as simply an anonymous record of daily life, at best a jog to the memory, reminding him weeks after-ward what movie he saw on that particular Friday and what relative came visiting the day after. But such writing cannot interest a reader, even when the reader is oneself, and this type of journal is usually abandoned, a victim of its author's own boredom. The freedom of the journal needs to be seen as an opportunity, challenging us to find out more about what we see, think, and feel. True, here we can concentrate on "getting it down" without worrying about such other concerns as: am I making a fool of myself? would anyone else want to read this? am I really prepared to write about this subject? But we should make sure that we are writing about something that puzzles or provokes or intrigues us, something we actually care about. Then we can take advantage of the greater precision we can reach for in writing and use the journal as a means of self-discovery as well as self-satisfaction.

Because journals provide an opportunity for writers to stretch themselves out, the entries in this section are often com-plex and challenging. Thoreau uses his journal not just to sum-marize what he saw on a given day at Walden Pond, but to register the sounds and motions and shapes caught by his alert senses. And John Holt lets the observed moments in a classroom lead him to speculations about other children, other schools. What each writer says records a moment's impression or reflection, a fragment because it is not immediately made part of some larger plan. But each entry suggests how the writer concentrates his energies, using the journal to get beyond a facile or conventional response to his experience.

The journal, then, should function like an artist's sketchbook, where the artist records what strikes his eye, and experiments not only with a particular kind of subject, like portraiture or landscape, but also with different methods of interpreting that subject. The artist's sketchbook does not contain drawings ready to be framed and exhibited, but neither is it full of crude or sloppy approximations of his serious work. Instead, the artist uses the skechbook to draw provisionally; in it the artist concentrates on fragments, drawn and redrawn, that in one form or another may eventually find their way into a completed painting.

However skillful he may be, any writer can make good use of a journal as a verbal sketchpad to test new possibilities. Preferably his journal writing should not be limited only to recording one particular situation or one particular mood. It would then become merely a reflection of a single facet of his potential skills, lapsing into a comfortable and repetitive record of current reading, let us say, or family conversations. An inexperienced writer taking advantage of the freedom the journal provides should write about whatever catches his interest—events, ideas, feelings, passing sensations or impressions. He should also feel free to come back to a previous entry and refocus or rephrase what he has done, giving himself experience in revising his own work, by expanding or reordering or modifying some earlier passage. By using the journal in these ways, he can extend himself as a writer without having his desire to experiment inhibited by the need to persuade or impress an audience. The journal may ultimately become a useful source book for more ambitious writing projects, but it will already have served its major function if it helps to put a writer in touch with his own potentialities.

∽ Lorraine Hansberry ∽

(1930-1965)

Lorraine Hansberry achieved a major success with her first play, A Raisin in the Sun *(1959). Her very promising career was ended when she died of cancer at the age of 34. Her husband, Robert Nemiroff, compiled a selection of her writings,* To Be Young, Gifted and Black *(1969), in order to present a portrait of her life, her work, and her ideas. The selection here is not from a single journal, but was drawn together by Nemiroff from various journals, letters, and miscellaneous papers; the passages are unified by their common subject of Hansberry's childhood in Chicago.*

from *To Be Young, Gifted and Black*

1.

For some time now—I think since I was a child—I have been possessed of the desire to put down the stuff of my life. That is a commonplace impulse, apparently, among persons of massive self-interest; sooner or later we all do it. And, I am quite certain, there is only one internal quarrel: how much of the truth to tell? How much, how much, how much! It *is* brutal, in sober uncompromising moments, to reflect on the comedy of concern we all enact when it comes to our precious images!

Even so, when such vanity as propels the writing of such memoirs is examined, certainly one would wish at least to

From Lorraine Hansberry: *To Be Young, Gifted and Black: Lorraine Hansberry in Her Own Words,* ed. Robert Nemiroff. © 1969 by Robert Nemiroff and Robert Nemiroff as Executor of the Estate of Lorraine Hansberry. Reprinted by permission of Prentice-Hall, Inc.

have some boast of social serviceability on one's side. I shall set down in these pages what shall seem to me to be the truth of my life and essences . . . which are to be found, first of all, on the Southside of Chicago, where I was born. . . .

2.

All travelers to my city should ride the elevated trains that race along the back ways of Chicago. The lives you can look into!

I think you could find the tempo of my people on their back porches. The honesty of their living is there in the shabbiness. Scrubbed porches that sag and look their danger. Dirty gray wood steps. And always a line of white and pink clothes scrubbed so well, waving in the dirty wind of the city.

My people are poor. And they are tired. And they are determined to live.

Our Southside is a place apart: each piece of our living is a protest.

3.

I was born May 19, 1930, the last of four children.

Of love and my parents there is little to be written: their relationship to their children was utilitarian. We were fed and housed and dressed and outfitted with more cash than our associates and that was all. We were also vaguely taught certain vague absolutes: that we were better than no one but infinitely superior to everyone; that we were the products of the proudest and most mistreated of the races of man; that there was nothing enormously difficult about life; that one *succeeded* as a matter of course.

Life was not a struggle—it was something that one *did*. One won an argument because, if facts gave out, one invented them—with color! The only sinful people in the world were dull people. And, above all, there were two things which were never to be betrayed: the family and the race. But of love, there was nothing ever said.

If we were sick, we were sternly, impersonally and carefully nursed and doctored back to health. Fevers, toothaches were attended to with urgency and importance; one always felt *important* in my family. Mother came with a tray to your room with the soup and Vick's salve or gave the enemas in a steaming bathroom. But we were not fondled, any of us—head held to breast, fingers about that head—until we were grown, all of us, and my father died.

At his funeral I at last, in my memory, saw my mother hold her sons that way, and for the first time in her life my sister held me in her arms I think. We were not a loving people: we were passionate in our hostilities and affinities, but the caress embarrassed us.

We have changed little. . . .

4.

Seven years separated the nearest of my brothers and sisters and myself; I wear, I am sure, the earmarks of that familial station to this day. Little has been written or thought to my knowledge about children who occupy that place: the last born separated by an uncommon length of time from the next youngest. I suspect we are probably a race apart.

The last born is an object toy which comes in years when brothers and sisters who are seven, ten, twelve years older are old enough to appreciate it rather than poke out its eyes. They do not mind diapering you the first two years, but by the time you are five you are a pest that has to be attended to in the washroom, taken to the movies and "sat with" at night. You are not a person—you are a nuisance who is not particular fun any more. Consequently, you swiftly learn to play alone. . . .

5.

My childhood Southside summers were the ordinary city kind, full of the street games which other rememberers have turned into fine ballets these days, and rhymes that anticipated what some people insist on calling modern poetry:

Oh, Mary Mack, Mack, Mack
With the silver buttons, buttons, buttons
All down her back, back, back.
She asked her mother, mother, mother
For fifteen cents, cents, cents
To see the elephant, elephant, elephant
Jump the fence, fence, fence.
Well, he jumped so high, high, high
'Til he touched the sky, sky, sky
And he didn't come back, back, back
'Til the Fourth of Ju—ly, ly, ly!

I remember skinny little Southside bodies by the fives and tens of us panting the delicious hours away:

"May I?"

And the voice of authority: "Yes, you may—you may take one giant step."

One drew in all one's breath and tightened one's fist and pulled the small body against the heavens, stretching, straining all the muscles in the legs to make—one giant step.

It is a long time. One forgets the reason for the game. (For children's games are always explicit in their reasons for being. To play is to win something. Or not to be "it." Or to be high pointer, or outdoer or, sometimes—just *the winner*. But after a time one forgets.)

Why was it important to take a small step, a teeny step, or the most desired of all—one GIANT step?

A giant step *to where?*

6.

Evenings were spent mainly on the back porches where screen doors slammed in the darkness with those really very special summertime sounds. And, sometimes, when Chicago nights got too steamy, the whole family got into the car and went to the park and slept out in the open on blankets. Those were, of course, the best times of all because the grownups were invariably reminded of having been children in the South and told the best stories then. And it was also cool and sweet to be on the grass and there was usually the scent of freshly cut lemons or melons in the air. Daddy would lie on his back, as fathers must, and explain about how men thought the stars above us came to be and how far away they were.

I never did learn to believe that anything could be as far away as *that*. Especially the stars. . . .

∽ John Holt ∽

(1923-)

John Holt was born in New York City and educated at Yale. He has had experience in almost every kind of academic setting, from an elementary school to a graduate program. Holt is one of the most influential American writers on educational theory and practice, and his many books draw upon his own classroom experience as a basis for his arguments. How Children Fail *(1964) began as a series of memos recording what Holt discovered while acting as an observer and a teacher in a fifth-grade class.*

from *How Children Fail*

February 27, 1958

A few days ago Nell came up to the desk, and looking at me steadily and without speaking, as usual, put on the desk her ink copy of the latest composition. Our rule is that on the ink copy there must be no more than three mistakes per page, or the page must be copied again. I checked her paper, and on the first page found five mistakes. I showed them to her, and told her, as gently as I could, that she had to copy it again, and urged her to be more careful—typical teacher's advice. She looked at me, heaved a sigh, and went back to her desk. She is left-handed, and doesn't manage a pen very well. I could see her frowning with concentration as she worked and struggled. Back she came after a while with the second copy. This time the first page had seven mistakes, and the handwriting was noticeably worse. I told her to copy it again. Another bigger sigh, and she went back to her desk. In time the third copy arrived, looking much worse than the second, and with even more mistakes.

At that point Bill Hull asked me a question, one I should have asked myself, one we ought all to keep asking ourselves: "Where are you trying to get, and are you getting there?"

The question sticks like a burr. In schools—but where isn't it so?—we so easily fall into the same trap: the means to an end becomes an end in itself. I had on my hands this three-mistake rule meant to serve the ends of careful work and neat compositions. By applying it rigidly was I getting more careful work and neater compositions? No; I was getting a child who was so worried about having to recopy her paper that she could not concentrate on doing it, and hence did it worse and worse, and would probably do the next papers badly as well.

We need to ask more often of everything we do in school, "Where are we trying to get, and is this thing we are doing helping us to get there?" Do we do something because we want to help the children and can see that what we are doing is helping them? Or do we do it because it is inexpensive or convenient for school, teachers, administrators? Or because everyone else does it? We must beware of making a virtue of necessity, and cooking up high-sounding educational reasons for doing what is done really for reasons of administrative economy or convenience. The still greater danger is that, having started to do something for good enough reasons, we may go on doing it stubbornly and blindly, as I did that day, unable or unwilling to see that we are doing more harm than good.

October 30, 1958
Everyone around here talks as if, except for a few hopeless characters, these children know most of the math they are supposed to know. It just isn't so. Out of the twenty kids in the class, there are at least six who don't even know simple "addition facts," and many more who, whether they know the facts or not, habitually add by counting on their fingers, usually keeping them well out of sight. There are still more who don't

understand and can't do multiplication and division. I hate to think what we will find about their understanding of place value.

It would be easy to make up an arithmetic test that without being too long, or unfairly tricky, or covering anything but what these kids are supposed to know, would stump all but a few of the children in fifth grade. Or any grade. The ninth graders I taught came to me with respectable school records in arithmetic, yet they knew little about division, less about fractions, and next to nothing about decimals.

It begins to look as if the test-examination-marks business is a gigantic racket, the purpose of which is to enable students, teachers, and schools to take part in a joint pretense that the students know everything they are supposed to know, when in fact they know only a small part of it—if any at all. Why do we always announce exams in advance, if not to give students a chance to cram for them? Why do teachers, even in graduate schools, always say quite specifically what the exam will be about, even telling the type of questions that will be given? Because otherwise too many students would flunk. What would happen at Harvard or Yale if a prof gave a surprise test in March on work covered in October? Everyone knows what would happen; that's why they don't do it.

March 20, 1959
Today Jane did one of those things that, for all her rebellious and annoying behavior in class, make her one of the best and most appealing people, young or old, that I have ever known. I was at the board, trying to explain to her a point on long division, when she said, in self-defense, "But Miss W. (her fourth-grade teacher) told us that we should take the first number . . ." Here she saw the smallest shadow of doubt on my face. She knew instantly that I did not approve of this rule, and without so much as a pause she continued, ". . . it wasn't Miss W., it was someone else . . ." and then went on talking about long division.

I was touched and very moved. How many adults would have seen what she saw, that what she was saying about Miss W.'s teaching was, in some slight degree, lowering my estimate of Miss W.? Even more to the point, how many adults, given this opportunity to shift the blame for their difficulties onto the absent Miss W., would instead have instantly changed their story to protect her from blame? For all our yammering about loyalty, not one adult in a thousand would have shown the loyalty that this little girl gave to her friend and former teacher. And she scarcely had to think to do it; for her, to defend one's friends from harm, blame, or even criticism was an instinct as natural as breathing.

Teachers and schools tend to mistake good behavior for good character. What they prize above all else is docility, suggestibility; the child who will do what he is told; or even better, the child who will do what is wanted without even having to be told. They value most in children what children least value in themselves. Small wonder that their effort to build character is such a failure; they don't know it when they see it. Jane is a good example. She has been a trial to everyone who has taught her. Even this fairly lenient school finds her barely tolerable; most schools long since would have kicked her out in disgrace. Of the many adults who have known her, probably very few have recognized her extraordinary qualities or appreciated their worth. Asked for an estimate of her character, most of them would probably say that it was bad. Yet, troublesome as she is, I wish that there were more children like her.

April 11, 1959
The things children talk about in class, when they are allowed to talk at all, are seldom close to their hearts. Only once in a great while do I feel, at the end of a class discussion, that I have come close to the real life of these children. One such discussion was about hiding places; another, just a few days ago, was about names.

This latter came up in Roman history. The time arrived in

Rome when the mob gained political power, so that the ability to arouse and inflame the mob was a sure key to high office. The kids wanted to know how this was done. I said it was done mostly with names. The way to arouse a mob against your political opponent was to call him names, the kind of names the mob hates most, or can be talked into hating. The mob spirit is weaker in these children than it will be in a few years, and they were skeptical; they wanted to know what kind of names would arouse a mob.

For answer, I asked them, "Well, what kind of names do you hate to be called?" We were off. Before the end of the period the board was covered with names. About half were what I expected, the usual ten-year-old insults—idiot, stupid, nuthead, fat slob, chicken, dope, scaredy-cat, etc. The rest surprised me. They were all terms of endearment.

It was quite a scene. There were all these bright-faced, lively children, eyes dancing with excitement and enthusiasm, seeing who could most strongly express their collective contempt and disgust for all the names that adults might suppose they like most. Someone would say, "Dearie—ug-g-g-g-gh!" Chorus of agreement. Someone else would say, "Honey—ic-c-c-c-ch!" More agreement. Every imaginable term of affection and endearment came in for its share. Not one was legitimate, not one was accepted. Nobody said of any term, "Well, that's not too bad." To some extent the children may have been carried away by the excitement of the game, but from the way they looked and sounded I felt sure, and do now, that they really meant what they were saying, that their dislike of these terms of endearment was genuine and deeply felt.

Why should this be? Of course, ten is a heroic age for most kids. They remind me in many ways of the Homeric Greeks. They are quarrelsome and combative; they have a strong and touchy sense of honor; they believe that every affront must be repaid, and with interest; they are fiercely loyal to their friends, even though they may change friends often; they have little sense of fair play, and greatly admire cunning and trickery; they are both highly possessive and very generous—no smallest trifle may be taken from them, but they are likely to give anything away, if they feel so disposed. Most of the time, they don't feel like little children, and they don't like being talked to as if they were little children.

But there is more to it than this. They suspect and resent these terms of endearment because they have too often heard them used by people who did not mean them. Everyone who deals with children these days has heard the dictum that children need to be loved, must be loved. But even to those who like them most, children are not always a joy and delight to be with. Often they are much like older people, and often they are exasperating and irritating. It is not surprising that there are many adults who do not like children much, if at all. But they feel that they ought to like them, have a duty to like them, and they try to discharge this duty by acting, particularly by talking, as if they liked them. Hence the continual and meaningless use of words like *honey*, *dearie*, etc. Hence, the dreadful, syrupy voice that so many adults use when they speak to children. By the time they are ten, children are fed up with this fake affection, and ready to believe that, most of the time, adults believe and mean very little of what they say.

∽ Henry Thoreau ∽
(1817-1862)

Henry Thoreau was born in Concord and educated at Harvard. He became interested in Transcendentalism, in part through his association with a Concord neighbor, Ralph Waldo Emerson. Thoreau was deeply appreciative of nature, and in his life and writings he combined the careful observation of a trained surveyor and botanist with the idealism of his Transcendentalist belief in the natural world as a manifestation of spiritual realities. Thoreau began keeping a journal in 1837, shortly after graduating from college, and maintained it until November, 1861, six months before his death. He frequently incorporated materials from his journals in his published writings, as can be seen by comparing some of the passages here (October, 1852) with the selection from Walden *included in Chapter Four.*

from *The Journals*

Oct. 10. Burdock, *Ranunculus acris*, rough hawkweed. A drizzling rain to-day. The air is full of falling leaves. The streets are strewn with elm leaves. The trees begin to look thin. The butternut is perhaps the first on the street to lose its leaves. Rain, more than wind, makes the leaves fall. Glow-worms in the evening.

Oct. 11. Monday. Most leaves are already somewhat faded and withered. Their tints are not so bright. The chestnut leaves already rustle with a great noise as you walk through the

From Henry Thoreau: *The Journals,* eds. Bradford Torrey and Francis Allen. Reprinted by permission of Houghton Mifflin Company.

woods, as they lie light, firm, and crisp. Now the chestnuts are rattling out. The burs are gaping and showing the plump nuts. They fill the ruts in the road, and are abundant amid the fallen leaves in the midst of the wood. The jays scream, and the red squirrels scold, while you are clubbing and shaking the trees. Now it is true autumn; all things are crisp and ripe.

I observed the other day (October 8) that those insects whose ripple I could see from the Peak were water-bugs. I could detect the progress of a water-bug over the smooth surface in almost any part of the pond, for they furrow the water slightly, making a conspicuous ripple bounded by two diverging lines, but the skaters slide over it without producing a perceptible ripple. In this clear air and with this glassy surface the motion of every water-bug, ceaselessly progressing over the pond, was perceptible. Here and there amid the skaters.

Oct. 12. I am struck by the superfluity of light in the atmosphere in the autumn, as if the earth absorbed none, and out of this profusion of dazzling light came the autumnal tints. Can it be because there is less vapor? The delicacy of the stratification in the white sand by the railroad, where they have been getting out sand for the brick-yards, the delicate stratification of this great globe like the leaves of the choicest volume just shut on a lady's table. The piled-up history! I am struck by the slow and delicate process by which the globe was formed.

Paddled on Walden. A rippled surface. Scared up ducks. Saw them first far over the surface, just risen,—two smaller, white-bellied, one larger, black. They circled round as usual, and the first went off, but the black one went round and round and over the pond five or six times at a considerable height and distance, when I thought several times he had gone to the river, and at length settled down by a slanting flight of a quarter of a mile into a distant part of the pond which I had left free; but what beside safety these ducks get by sailing in the middle of Walden I don't know. That black rolling-pin with wings, circling round you half a mile off for a quarter of an hour, at that height, from which he sees the river and Fair Haven all the while, from which he sees so many things, while I see almost him alone. Their wings set so far back. They are not handsome, but wild.

What an ample share of the light of heaven each pond and lake on the surface of the globe enjoys! No woods are so dark and deep but it is light above the pond. Its window or skylight is as broad as its surface. It lies out patent to the sky. From the mountain-top you may not be able to see out because of the woods, but on the lake you are bathed in light.

I can discern no skaters nor water-bugs on the surface of the pond, which is now rippled. Do they, then, glide forth to the middle in calm days only, by short impulses, till they have completely covered it?

A new carpet of pine leaves is forming in the woods. The forest is laying down her carpet for the winter. The elms in the village, losing their leaves, reveal the birds' nests.

I dug some ground-nuts in the railroad bank with my hands this afternoon, the vine being now dead. They were nearly as large as hen's eggs, six inches or a foot beneath the surface, on the end of a root or strung along on it. I had them roasted and boiled at supper time. The skin came readily off like a potato. Roasted, they have an agreeable taste very much like a potato, though somewhat fibrous in texture. With my eyes shut, I should not know but I was eating a rather soggy potato. Boiled, they were unexpectedly quite dry, and though in this instance a little strong, had a more nutty flavor. With a little salt, a hungry man would make a very palatable meal on them. It would not be easy to find them, especially now that the vines are dead, unless you knew beforehand where they grew.

. . .

Oct. 16. Saturday. The sidewalks are covered with the impressions of leaves which fell yesterday and were pressed into the soil by the feet of the passers, leaving a myriad dark spots— like bird-tracks or hieroglyphics to a casual observer.

What are the sparrow-like birds with striped breasts and two triangular chestnut-colored spots on the breasts which I have seen some time, picking the seeds of the weeds in the garden?

. . .

Oct. 20. Canada snapdragon, tansy, white goldenrod, blue-stemmed ditto. *Aster undulatus*, autumnal dandelion, tall buttercup, yarrow, mayweed. Picking chestnuts on Pine Hill. A rather cold and windy, somewhat wintry afternoon, the heavens overcast. The clouds have lifted in the northwest, and I see the mountains in sunshine, all the more attractive from the cold I feel here, with a tinge of purple on them, a cold but memorable and glorious outline. This is an advantage of mountains in the horizon: they show you fair weather from the midst of foul. The small red Solomon's-seal berries spot the ground here and there amid the dry leaves. The witch-hazel is bare of all but flowers.

Many a man, when I tell him that I have been on to a mountain, asks if I took a glass with me. No doubt, I could have seen further with a glass, and particular objects more distinctly,—could have counted more meeting-houses; but this has nothing to do with the peculiar beauty and grandeur of the view which an elevated position affords. It was not to see a few particular objects, as if they were near at hand, as I had been accustomed to see them, that I ascended the mountain, but to see an infinite variety far and near in their relation to each other, thus reduced to a single picture. The facts of science, in comparison with poetry, are wont to be as vulgar as looking from the mountain with a telescope. It is a counting of meeting-houses. At the public house, the mountain-house, they keep a glass to let, and think the journey to the mountain-top is lost, that you have got but half the view, if you have not taken a glass with you.

∼ George Orwell ∼

George Orwell was born in India, educated as a scholarship student at a private school in England, and completed his academic training at Eton in 1921. He then returned to the East as a member of the Indian Imperial Police and served in Burma until 1927. Disgusted with colonialism, he returned to England and tried to begin a career as a writer. His life during those impoverished years became the subject of his first book, Down and Out in Paris and London *(1933). All of these formative experiences gave Orwell a strong sympathy with the oppressed classes, a sympathy reflected in his later writings as a political journalist. He published a number of works of fiction and nonfiction, of which the best known are* Homage to Catalonia *(1938), an account of his participation in the Spanish Civil War,* Animal Farm *(1945), an allegorical satire on the social and political aftermath of the Russian Revolution, and* Nineteen Eighty-Four *(1949), a novel envisioning a totalitarian society of the future. Orwell's political conscience, the honesty and accuracy of his observation, and the clarity of his style characterize all his work, including his autobiographical writings. The selections that follow are from a diary that Orwell began after the outbreak of the Second World War and continued until November, 1942.*

from "A War-time Diary"

7 September
Air-raid alarms now frequent enough, and lasting long enough, for people habitually to forget whether the alarm is on at the

From *The Collected Essays, Journalism and Letters of George Orwell*, vol. II, eds. Sonia Orwell and Ian Angus. © 1968 by Sonia Brownell Orwell. Reprinted by permission of Harcourt Brace Jovanovich, Inc.

moment, or whether the All Clear has sounded. Noise of bombs and gunfire, except when very close (which probably means within two miles) now accepted as a normal background to sleep or conversation. I have still not heard a bomb go off with the sort of bang that makes you feel you are personally involved.

In Churchill's speech, number killed in air raids during August given as 1075. Even if truthful, probably a large understatement as it includes only civilian casualties. . . . The secretiveness officially practised about raids is extraordinary. Today's papers report that a bomb fell in a square "in central London". Impossible to find out which square it was, though thousands of people must know.

10 September

Can't write much of the insanities of the last few days. It is not so much that the bombing is worrying in itself as that the disorganisation of traffic, frequent difficulty of telephoning, shutting of shops whenever there is a raid on etc etc, combined with the necessity of getting on with one's ordinary work, wear one out and turn life into a constant scramble to catch up lost time. . . .

The delayed-action bombs are a great nuisance, but they appear to be successful in locating most of them and getting all the neighbouring people out until the bomb shall have exploded. All over South London, little groups of disconsolate-looking people wandering about with suitcases and bundles, either people who have been rendered homeless or, in more cases, who have been turned out by the authorities because of an unexploded bomb. . . .

Most of last night in the public shelter, having been driven there by recurrent whistle and crash of bombs not very far away at intervals of about a quarter of an hour. Frightful discomfort owing to overcrowding, though the place was well-appointed, with electric light and fans. People, mostly elderly working class, grousing bitterly about the hardness of the seats and the longness of the night, but no defeatist talk. . . .

People are now to be seen every night about dusk queuing up at the doors of the Shelters with their bedding. Those who come in first grab places on the floor and probably pass a reasonably good night. Day raids apart, the raiding hours are pretty regularly 8 pm to 4.30 am i.e. dusk to just before dawn.

I should think 3 months of continuous raids at the same intensity as the last 4 nights would break down everyone's morale. But it is doubtful whether anyone could keep up the attack on such a scale for 3 months, especially when he is suffering much the same himself.

12 September

As soon as the air raids began seriously, it was noticeable that people were much readier than before to talk to strangers in the street. . . . This morning met a youth of about 20, in dirty overalls, perhaps a garage hand. Very embittered and defeatist about the war, and horrified by the destruction he had seen in South London. He said that Churchill had visited the bombed area near the Elephant and at a spot where 20 out of 22 houses had been destroyed, remarked that it was "not so bad." The youth: "I'd have wrung his bloody neck if he'd said it to me." He was pessimistic about the war, considered Hitler was sure to win and would reduce London to much the same state as Warsaw. He spoke bitterly about the people rendered homeless in South London and eagerly took up my point when I said the empty houses in the West End should be requisitioned for them. He considered that all wars were fought for the profit of the rich, but agreed with me that this one would probably end in revolution. With all this, he was not unpatriotic. Part of his grouch was that he had tried to join the Air Force 4 times in the last 6 months, and always been put off.

Tonight and last night they have been trying the new device of keeping up a continuous AA barage, apparently firing blind or merely by sound, though I suppose there is some kind of sound-detector which estimates the height at which they must make the shells burst. . . . The noise is tremendous and almost continuous, but I don't mind it, feeling it to be on my side. Spent last night at Stephen Spender's place with a battery firing in the square at short intervals throughout the night. Slept through it easily enough, no bombs being audible in that place.

The havoc in the East End and South London is terrible, by all accounts. . . . Churchill's speech last night referred very seriously to danger of imminent invasion. If invasion is actually attempted and this is not a feint, the idea is presumably either to knock out our air bases along the South Coast, after which the ground defences can be well bombed, at the same time causing all possible confusion in London and its southward communications, *or* to draw as much as possible of our defensive forces south before delivering the attack on Scotland or possibly Ireland.

Meanwhile our platoon of Home Guards, after 3½ months, have about 1 rifle for 6 men, no other weapons except incendiary bombs, and perhaps 1 uniform for 4 men. After all, they have stood out against letting the rifles be taken home by individual men. They are all parked in one place, where a bomb may destroy the whole lot of them any night.

14 September
On the first night of the barrage, which was the heaviest, they are said to have fired 500,000 shells, i.e. at an average cost of £5 per shell, £2½ millions worth. But well worth it, for the effect on morale.

15 September
This morning, for the first time, saw an aeroplane shot down. It fell slowly out of the clouds, nose foremost, just like a snipe that has been shot high overhead. Terrific jubilation among the people watching, punctuated every now and then by the question, "Are you sure it's a German?" So puzzling are the directions given, and so many the types of aeroplane, that no one even knows which are German planes and which are our

own. My only test is that if a bomber is seen over London it must be a German, whereas a fighter is likelier to be ours.

17 September
Heavy bombing in this area last night till about 11 pm. . . . I was talking in the hallway of this house to two young men and a girl who was with them. Psychological attitude of all 3 was interesting. They were quite openly and unashamedly frightened, talking about how their knees were knocking together, etc and yet at the same time excited and interested, dodging out of doors between bombs to see what was happening and pick up shrapnel splinters. Afterwards in Mrs C's little reinforced room downstairs, with Mrs C and her daughter, the maid, and three young girls who are also lodgers here. All the women, except the maid, screaming in unison, clasping each other and hiding their faces, every time a bomb went past, but betweenwhiles quite happy and normal, with animated conversation proceeding. The dog subdued and obviously frightened, knowing something to be wrong. Marx is also like this during raids, i.e. subdued and uneasy. Some dogs, however, go wild and savage during a raid and have had to be shot. They allege here, and E says the same thing about Greenwich, that all the dogs in the park now bolt for home when they hear the siren.

Yesterday, when having my hair cut in the City, asked the barber if he carried on during raids. He said he did. And even if he was shaving someone? I said. Oh, yes, he carried on just the same. And one day a bomb will drop near enough to make him jump, and he will slice half somebody's face off.

Later, accosted by a man, I should think some kind of commercial traveller, with a bad type of face, while I was waiting for a bus. He began a rambling talk about how he was getting himself and his wife out of London, how his nerves were giving way and he suffered from stomach trouble, etc etc. I don't know how much of this kind of thing there is. . . . There has of course been a big exodus from the East End, and every night what amount to mass migrations to places where there is sufficient shelter accommodation. The practice of taking a 2d ticket and spending the night in one of the deep Tube stations, e.g. Piccadilly, is growing. . . . Everyone I have talked to agrees that the empty furnished houses in the West End should be used for the homeless; but I suppose the rich swine still have enough pull to prevent this from happening. The other day 50 people from the East End, headed by some of the Borough Councillors, marched into the Savoy and demanded to use the air-raid shelter. The management didn't succeed in ejecting them till the raid was over, when they went voluntarily. When you see how the wealthy are *still* behaving, in what is manifestly developing into a revolutionary war, you think of St Petersburg in 1916.

(Evening). Almost impossible to write in this infernal racket. (Electric lights have just gone off. Luckily I have some candles.) So many streets in (lights on again) the quarter roped off because of unexploded bombs, that to get home from Baker Street, say 300 yards, is like trying to find your way to the heart of a maze.

21 September

Have been unable for some days to buy another volume to continue this diary because, of the three or four stationers' shops in the immediate neighbourhood, all but one are cordoned off because of unexploded bombs.

Regular features of the time: neatly swept-up piles of glass, litter of stone and splinters of flint, smell of escaping gas, knots of sightseers waiting at the cordons.

Yesterday, at the entry to a street near here, a little crowd waiting with an ARP man in a black tin hat among them. A devastating roar, with a huge cloud of dust, etc. The man with the black hat comes running towards the ARP headquarters, where another with a white hat is emerging munching at a mouthful of bread and butter.

The man with the black hat: "Dorset Square, sir."

The man with the white hat: "OK." (Makes a tick in his notebook.)

Nondescript people wandering about, having been evacuated from their houses because of delayed-action bombs. Yesterday two girls stopping me in the street, very elegant in appearance except that their faces were filthily dirty: "Please, sir, can you tell us where we are?"

Withal, huge areas of London almost normal, and everyone quite happy in the daytime, never seeming to think about the coming night, like animals which are unable to foresee the future so long as they have a bit of food and a place in the sun.

24 September

Oxford Street yesterday, from Oxford Circus up to the Marble Arch, completely empty of traffic, and only a few pedestrians, with the late afternoon sun shining straight down the empty roadway and glittering on innumerable fragments of broken glass. Outside John Lewis's, a pile of plaster dress models, very pink and realistic, looking so like a pile of corpses that one could have mistaken them for that at a little distance. Just the same sight in Barcelona, only there it was plaster saints from desecrated churches.

Much discussion as to whether you would hear a bomb (i.e. its whistle) which was coming straight at you. All turns upon whether the bomb travels faster than sound. . . . One thing I have worked out, I think satisfactorily, is that the further away from you a bomb falls, the longer the whistle you will hear. The short whizz is therefore the sound that should make you dive for cover. I think this is really the principle one goes on in dodging a shell, but there one seems to know by a kind of instinct.

Possibilities for Writing

1. Try different kinds of relatively uncontrolled writing: free writing in which you keep going without any interruptions for a specific period of time; a more controlled version in which you occasionally pause briefly to see what new thought you might follow, but where you never take any lengthy break; a final version in which you concentrate on some particular memory of your past and try to write down everything you associate with that past experience, writing without regard to structure or complete statements, but keeping your attention on a single topic. Each of these exercises should be tried several times in different circumstances and should continue for ten to thirty minutes. Then compare how comfortable and productive each of these starting methods was for you and continue using the method of your choice regularly during the semester.

2. Try for a period of a week or two to maintain two journals. One would be a journal of experience, emphasizing your thoughts, feelings, fantasies, and those experiences which gave you a sense of the uniqueness of your own life. The other would be a journal of observation, in which you would record what you perceived in your environment, trying to capture through precise detail anything in the world that struck you as interesting and distinctive. Then compare the two journals to see what strengths as a writer you have revealed in each.

3. Keep a writer's diary of the course. Such a diary could be a

60

record of how you felt about your own writing, what subjects you chose to write about and why, what decisions you made as you were in the process of writing, and what surprised or interested or excited you when you were reviewing your own writing.

Part Three – Letters

Introduction: Addressing a Reader

The most important difference between journal writing and letter writing is that letters are written with the expectation that someone else will read them. As we saw in the last section, the special freedom of the journal is based on its privacy; writers express only what they want to express and are accountable only to their own standards. But the "Dear ————" that begins a letter is a reminder from the start that we are addressing someone else and should take our reader into account. Although a reader places limits on a writer, that is not necessarily a bad thing. Sometimes we feel our own powers of invention stimulated by the thought that we are communicating with someone who cares for us and wants to know what concerns us or with someone who differs from us and will require our best efforts to get them to understand our way of thinking.

This description of letter writing assumes we are writing to another person with whom we have or want to establish some personal relationship. Of course, much correspondence is highly impersonal, addressed to institutions and concerned with such matters as job applications or complaints about overcharges and faulty products. But such business letters usually have set forms that the writer follows, filling in specific information in the appropriate places. Personal correspondence, on the other hand, gives a special prominence to the reader; even if we have never met him, we can still infer enough about him to create a character in our heads and we shape what we have to say in order to meet this character's needs as well as our own. For example we might want to write a letter to the editor of our local paper, giving our views about a recent editorial. Even though we do not know the individual and have to address our letter to "The Editor," we will still write differently than if we were to consider the same subject in our journal. For one thing, we would be careful to begin our letter by establishing our subject and our purpose in ways that would be unnecessary if we were reflecting in our journal: "Your recent editorial against capital punishment failed to mention two arguments I have always thought were especially important." That very ordinary sentence is acknowledging the reader in a variety of ways. It makes clear immediately the subject that prompts us to make contact with him; it establishes our way of seeing the subject in relation to his way of seeing it, and it makes the social gesture of expressing some kind of kinship with the reader. Every writer must organize and present what he wants to say in ways that reduce as far as possible the reader's difficulties—an important point to remember for any public piece of writing.

Letter writing teaches these lessons while remaining, in many instances, an activity that bridges the private and public uses of writing. After all, letters are written not just to Sears Roebuck or to newspaper editors, but more frequently to relatives and close personal friends. Even though the telephone has greatly reduced the amount of letter writing we do (costing us a lot in our training as writers), most of us have had our earliest experiences as writers communicating with people we know well: writing thank-you notes, or postcards, or letters to our parents and friends when we are away from them. Such familiar readers may allow us to be much more casual in introducing ourselves and alluding to our experiences. Consider a letter from school that begins:

Dear Mom:
  Thanks for the pep talk last weekend. It had some results. Yesterday I met a girl named Yvonne in my Bio class; we worked

on a lab experiment together. She turned out to be very nice and knows a lot about science. Coincidence—she comes from Philadelphia and her father won't talk to Tom Beggins either. We're going to the movies with Eddie and Joyce on Saturday.

Here the writer can take things for granted because he knows his reader so well; for example, he can expect his mother to remember what they talked about on the weekend and to know what makes Tom Beggins a person to avoid, things that would have to be explained if an outsider were to understand fully what the letter means. At the same time, this writer would be likely to make other changes for a different familiar reader; to a friend his own age he might boast about Yvonne's good looks and say something about the movies and TV shows she liked to watch, rather than focusing on what she did as a student. All public writing, then, involves making some adjustments in what we say and how we say it, depending on whom we are writing for. Almost no one, sitting down to write to three different people, would copy the same letter three times; if he did, we would conclude he had very little interest in those three individuals.

Letter writing, even constant letter writing, does not guarantee good writing, as the example above, a letter only a mother could love, suggests. Letters, like journals, can lull us into simply filling in with commonplaces. But writing to someone we know can also spur us into a special effort to articulate our thoughts, feelings, and observations. When E. B. White writes to his brother describing Belgrade Lakes, a place in Maine where the White family had vacationed during the brothers' childhood, he doesn't merely announce that nothing has changed there. The care and fullness of his description show his concern to communicate something deeply felt, just as in a later letter he conveys good spirits and affection through some easy humor. The letter from Maine may at first not seem to include the brother at all, since it barely acknowledges him, asks no questions about his affairs, and alludes to no common friends or social experiences. But we do know that both White's parents had died shortly before he wrote this letter; in writing as he does, he may be trying to express his own feelings about his parents by fixing his impressions of one of their favorite places, and he may have been offering reassurances to his brother (or to himself) that life continues despite such losses. The question of whether White is writing to memorialize the Maine landscape for himself or to record the parts of that impression he feels his brother will particularly value need not be answered. Good writing always involves some element of self-clarification as well as the effort to make what we say understandable and significant to our reader.

Letter writing, then, as person-to-person communication, invariably makes us aware of our reader, thereby giving us a way of re-viewing our prose by imagining how our words look to another. With truly personal correspondence we scarcely have to press our imaginations at all, since in writing to somebody we feel close to we almost automatically express ourselves as we would if the person were present. But letter writing prepares us for the inevitable presence of some kind of reader, and reminds us that the less intimately we know him the more carefully we must consider how to address him.

ᴄ E. B. White ᴄ

(1899-   )

*E. B. White was born in Mt. Vernon, New York, and became
a newspaper reporter after graduating from Cornell. In 1927
he became a contributing editor to* The New Yorker, *beginning
a lifelong association with the magazine. There he established
his reputation as one of America's finest essayists and a master
of an exact and idiomatic American prose style.* Letters of E. B.
White, *which includes the following three letters to White's
brother Stanley, was published in 1976.*

[LETTERS TO HIS BROTHER]

[New York]
Saturday night, May 16 [1936]

Dear Bun:

Mother got steadily weaker, and Wednesday I went to
Washington in order to see her for the last time. I got there in
the middle of a thunder storm, the air very hot and oppressive, and found her hanging on to life regretfully, aware of the
noise and afraid of the lightning. It seemed as though her suffering was more than anybody could bear. But the next day—
a clear, cool morning with a fine sparkle—I went in and found
her in a curiously exalted state; her pains seemed to be gone,
and she talked with a sort of feverish excitement about the experience of death, which she was anxious to make us believe
(while she still had strength enough to speak) was beautiful.
She was very toxic, and focussed her eyes only with great effort, but she managed to convince us that she had achieved a

Three letters to Stanley Hart White from *Letters of E. B. White,* collected and
edited by Dorothy Lobrano Guth. Copyright © 1976 by E. B. White. Reprinted
by permission of Harper & Row, Publishers, Inc.

67

peaceful conclusion. How much of it was chicanery and how much a merciful truth, I will never know, but she appeared to be enjoying a sort of spiritual intoxication. I said: "Isn't it beautiful, Mother?" (meaning the weather), and she replied, with astonishing fervor, "Oh, my, oh, my—it's perfectly beautiful" (meaning death). Clara took her hand and said: "Mother, you're perfectly comfortable, aren't you?" And she replied: "Perfectly comfortable." "And you're perfectly happy?" "Perfectly happy." It was an enormous relief after what we had been going through. From the parochial school across the way, Mother could hear the voices of the children singing, and she spoke of that and of how much it had meant to her. Apparently she thoroughly enjoyed the Catholic symbols, and took great comfort in them—liked the big crucifix at the foot of her bed. Occasionally a shudder of pain would make her twitch, and she would murmur, "Oh, oh oh, oh" quickly adding, for our benefit: "That means nothing at all, that means absolutely nothing at all." Her whole mind seemed to be bent on convincing us that all was well with her. She died that night, around ten o'clock; Clara was with her at the time.

Today she received Burr Davis's extreme unction, with the electric organ, the stale lilies, the old colored servants sitting silent and attentive in the little chapel, together with the neighbors from across the street, the doctor who didn't know she had cancer of the liver, and the minister who was sure her soul would go to heaven. Afterwards we drove wearily out to Ferncliff, stopping for the red lights, listening to anecdotes by the interminable Mr. Scholz.[1] I walked down and found Father's stone, which I think is good. We must get another one like it.

This is a very sketchy account of what has been going on these last few days, but I thought you might like to know at least the bare facts. It seems hardly credible that in the course of a single year, Sam and Jessie have gone from this good life.

Yrs as ever,
Andy

1. Charles Scholz, executor of the wills of both White's parents.

68

Thursday
Bert Mosher's,
Belgrade Lakes, Maine
[1936?]

Dear Stan:

I returned to Belgrade. Things haven't changed much. There's a train called the Bar Harbor Express, and Portland is foggy early in the morning, and the Pullman blankets are brown and thin and cold. But when you look out of the window in the diner, steam is rising from pastures and the sun is out, and pretty soon the train is skirting a blue lake called Messalonski. Things don't change much. Even the names, you still hear them: names like Caswell, Bartlett, names like Bickford, Walter Gleason, Damren. Gram lives alone in the chowder house, down by the lake, brooding on days before the farm burnt, hanging draperies the Count sends her from abroad. The lake hangs clear and still at dawn, and the sound of a cowbell comes softly from a faraway woodlot. In the shallows along shore the pebbles and driftwood show clear and smooth on bottom, and black water bugs dart, spreading a wake and a shadow. A fish rises quickly in the lily pads with a little plop, and a broad ring widens to eternity. The water in the basin is icy before breakfast, and cuts sharply into your nose and ears and makes your face blue as you wash. But the boards of the dock are already hot in the sun, and there are doughnuts for breakfast and the smell is there, the faintly rancid smell that hangs around Maine kitchens. Sometimes there is little wind all day, and on still hot afternoons the sound of a motorboat comes drifting five miles from the other shore, and the droning lake becomes articulate, like a hot field. A crow calls, fearfully and far. If a night breeze springs up, you are aware of a restless noise along the shore, and for a few minutes before you fall asleep you hear the intimate talk between fresh-water waves and rocks that lie below bending birches. The insides of your camp are hung with pictures cut from magazines, and the camp smells of lumber and damp. Things don't change much. Meadow stream has a beginning

69

in the pickerel weeds. If you push along quietly, a blue heron will rise with a heavy squawk and a flap. The ends of logs that jut out are covered with the dung of little animals that come there to eat fresh mussels and wash their paws at the stream-side. Over at the Mills there's a frog box, sunk half in the water. People come there in boats and buy bait. You buy a drink of Birch Beer at Bean's tackle store. Big bass swim lazily in the deep water at the end of the wharf, well fed. Long lean guide boats kick white water in the stern till they suck under. There are still one cylinder engines that don't go. Maybe it's the needle valve. At twilight, cows come hesitantly down the little woods roads behind the camps to steal a drink in the cove. They belong to a man named Withers. Withers' cows. Pasture bars are cedar, stripped of bark, weathered grey. On rainy days swallows come and dip water, and the camps are cold. When the wind swings into the north, the blow comes. It comes suddenly, and you know a change has come over things, instinctively. Next day you will see a little maple, flaming red, all alone in a bog. It's cold and fearsome by the lake. The wind still holds strong into the second morning, and white caps are as thick as whiskers. When you get back on the road, away from the lake, the road lies warm and yellow, and you hear the wind fussing in the treetops behind you and you don't care. The rocks in the stream behind the Salmon Lake House are colored red and colored green, where the boats have scraped them under water. The clothesline behind Walter Gleason's house is flapping with white wash. . . . There's a house on a hill where a lady lived that used to keep cats. Along the road the apples are little and yellow and sweet. Puddles dry in the sun, and the mud cakes, and yellow butterflies diddle in the new mud. Cow trails lead up slopes through juniper beds and thistles and grey rocks, and below you the lake hangs blue and clear, and you see the islands plain. Sometimes a farm dog barks. Yes, sir, I returned to Belgrade, and things don't change much. I thought somebody ought to know.

En

25 West 43
[January 1947]
Friday

Dear Bun:

I'm glad to report that even now, at this late day, a blank sheet of paper holds the greatest excitement there is for me— more promising than a silver cloud, prettier than a little red wagon. It holds all the hope there is, all fears. I can remember, really quite distinctly, looking a sheet of paper square in the eyes when I was seven or eight years old and thinking "This is where I belong, this is it." Having dirtied up probably a quarter of a million of them and sent them down drains and through presses, I am exhausted but not done, faithful in my fashion, and fearful only that I will die before one comes out right—as though I had deflowered a quarter of a million virgins and was still expecting the perfect child. What *is* this terrible infatuation, anyway? Some mild nervous disorder, probably, that compels a man to leave a fiery tail in his wake, like a ten-cent comet, or smell up a pissing post so that the next dog will know who's been along. I have moments when I wish that I could either take a sheet of paper or leave it alone, and sometimes, in despair and vengeance, I just fold them into airplanes and sail them out of high windows, hoping to get rid of them that way, only to have an updraft (or a change of temper) bring them back in again. As for your gift of so many sheets of white bond, with rag content, I accept them in the spirit with which they were sent and shall write you a book. It will be the Greatest Book that has Ever Been Written. They all are, in the early wonderful stage before the first word gets slid into place.

Happy New Year
En

∽ Nicola Sacco ∽

(1891-1927)

Nicola Sacco was an Italian immigrant who worked in a Massachusetts shoe factory. He and a friend, Bartolomeo Vanzetti, were arrested and tried for murder in 1921 for the deaths of a guard and paymaster in a factory robbery. Because both men were ardent socialists and because both insisted on their innocence, their case attracted worldwide attention and became linked to political judgments favoring or condemning radicalism. Sacco and Vanzetti were convicted and were eventually executed in 1927. The following letter from Sacco to his son Dante was written only a few days before his death.

[A LETTER TO HIS SON]

Charlestown State Prison, August 18, 1927

My dear Son and Companion:

Since the day I saw you last I had always the idea to write you this letter, but the length of my hunger strike and the thought I might not be able to explain myself, made me put it off all this time.

The other day, I ended my hunger strike and just as soon as I did that I thought of you to write to you, but I find that I did not have enough strength and I cannot finish it at one time. However, I want to get it down in any way before they take us again to the death house, because it is my conviction that just as soon as the court refuses a new trial they will take

From *The Letters of Sacco and Vanzetti*, edited by Marion Denman Frankfurter and Gardner Jackson. Copyright © 1928, copyright © 1956 by the Viking Press, Inc. Reprinted by permission of Viking Penguin Inc.

us there. And between Friday and Monday, if nothing happens, they will electrocute us right after midnight, on August 22nd. Therefore, here I am, right with you with love and with open heart as ever I was yesterday. . . .

I never thought that our inseparable life could be separated, but the thought of seven dolorous years makes it seem it did come, but then it has not changed really the unrest and the heartbeat of affection. That has remained as it was, More. I say that our ineffable affection reciprocal, is today more than any other time, of course. That is not only a great deal but it is grand because you can see the real brotherly love, not only in joy but also and more in the struggle of suffering. Remember this, Dante. We have demonstrated this, and modesty apart we are proud of it.

Much we have suffered during this long Calvary. We protest today as we protested yesterday. We protest always for our freedom.

If I stopped hunger strike the other day, it was because there was no more sign of life in me. Because I protested with my hunger strike yesterday as today I protest for life and not for death.

I sacrificed because I wanted to come back to the embrace of your dear little sister Ines and your mother and all the beloved friends and comrades of life and not death. So Son, today life begins to revive slow and calm, but yet without horizon and always with sadness and visions of death.

Well, my dear boy, after your mother had talked to me so much and I had dreamed of you day and night, how joyful it was to see you at last. To have talked with you like we used to in the old days—in those days. Much I told you on that visit and more I wanted to say, but I saw that you will remain the same affectionate boy, faithful to your mother who loves you so much, and I did not want to hurt your sensibilities any longer, because I am sure that you will continue to be the same boy and remember what I have told you. I know that and what here I am going to tell you will touch your sensibilities, but don't cry Dante, because many years have been wasted, as your mother's have been wasted for seven years, and never did any good. So, son, instead of crying, be strong, so as to be able to comfort your mother, and when you want to distract your mother from the discouraging sadness, I will tell you what I used to do. To take her for a long walk in the quiet country, gathering wild flowers here and there, resting under the shade of trees, between the harmony of the vivid stream and the gentle tranquility of the mother-nature, and I am sure that she will enjoy this very much, as you surely would be happy for it. But remember always, Dante, in the play of happiness, don't use all for yourself only, but down yourself just one step, at your side and help the weak ones that cry for help, help the persecuted and the victim, because they are your better friends; they are the comrades that fight and fall and your father and Bartolo fought and fell yesterday for the conquest of the joy of freedom for all and the poor workers. In this struggle of life you will find more love and you will be loved.

I am sure that from what your mother has told me about what you said during these last terrible days when I was lying in the iniquitous death-house—that description gave me happiness because it showed you will be the beloved boy I had always dreamed.

Therefore whatever should happen tomorrow, nobody knows, but if they should kill us, you must not forget to look at your friends and comrades with the smiling gaze of gratitude as you look at your beloved ones, because they love you as they love every one of the fallen persecuted comrades. I tell you, your father that is all the life to you, your father that loved you and saw them, and knows their noble faith (that is mine) their supreme sacrifice that they are still doing for our freedom, for I have fought with them, and they are the ones that still hold the last of our hope that today they can still save us from electrocution, it is the struggle and fight between the rich and the poor for safety and freedom, Son, which you will understand in the future of your years to come, of this unrest and struggle of life's death.

Much I thought of you when I was lying in the death-house—the singing, the kind tender voices of the children from the playground, when there was all the life and the joy of liberty—just one step from the wall which contains the buried agony of three buried souls. It would remind me so often of you and your sister Ines, and I wish I could see you every moment. But I feel better that you did not come to the death-house so that you could not see the horrible picture of three lying in agony to be electrocuted, because I do not know what effect it would have on your young age. But then, in another way if you were not so sensitive it would be very useful to you tomorrow when you could use this horrible memory to hold up to the world the shame of the country in this cruel persecution and unjust death. Yes, Dante, they can crucify our bodies today as they are doing, but they cannot destroy our ideas, that will remain for the youth of the future to come.

Dante, when I said three human lives buried, I meant to say that with us there is another a young man by the name of Celestino Maderios that is to be electrocuted at the same time with us. He has been twice before in that horrible death-house, that should be destroyed with the hammers of real progress—that horrible house that will shame forever the future of the citizens of Massachusetts. They should destroy that house and put up a factory or school, to teach many of the hundreds of the poor orphan boys of the world.

Dante, I say once more to love and be nearest your mother and the beloved ones in these sad days, and I am sure that with your brave heart and kind goodness they will feel less discomfort. And you will also not forget to love me a little for I do—O Sonny! thinking so much and so often of you.

Best fraternal greetings to the beloved ones, love and kisses to your little Ines and mother. Most hearty affectionate embrace.

Your Father and Companion

∽ Margaret Mead ∽

(1901-1978)

Margaret Mead was one of the most distinguished social scientists of her time. Born in Philadelphia, she attended Barnard College, where she came under the tutelage of Franz Boas and Ruth Benedict and decided to become an anthropologist. She did her doctoral work on the culture of Polynesia, and her early field trips to Samoa and the Admiralty Islands led to the publication of two celebrated and influential books, Coming of Age in Samoa *(1928) and* Growing Up in New Guinea *(1930). Her many books include studies of contemporary American culture as well as of the native tribes of the Pacific.*

This selection is from Letters from the Field, 1925-1975 *(1977). Mead is writing to her parents from Samoa, during her first anthropological field trip in 1925. One unusual aspect of these letters is that Mead's parents distributed copies of them to friends; Mead knew about this practice and so was aware that she was addressing a semi-public audience.*

[LETTERS FROM SAMOA]

Nov. 14, 1925

My room is half of the back porch of the dispensary quarters building. There is a loosely woven bamboo screen which divides my room from the porch outside the dispensary and here the Samoan children gather to peek through the holes

Abridged from pages 37-38, 45-46 in *Letters from the Field, 1925-1975* by Margaret Mead. Volume 52 in the World Perspectives series, planned and edited by Ruth Nanda Anshen. Copyright © 1977 by Margaret Mead. Reprinted by permission of Harper & Row, Publishers, Inc.

and display their few English words or chatter endlessly in Samoan about Makelita's various belongings. It is really an excellent arrangement. At night I push back the curtain which divides my room off at the other end, put away the chairs, push back the tables and there is plenty of room for a small *sivasiva*—dance. The young people bring their guitars and ukeleles and dance for me. A few new ones come every night and it gives me an excellent opportunity gradually to learn their names. . . . The boys paint beards and mustaches of blue or red on their faces, tie ti leaves around their wrists, put an *ula*—necklace—or two on their oiled naked chests and dance endlessly. They never seem to tire of it and it is practically their only amusement. Out in Vaitogi they would hold a big *siva* in the chief's house, where a huge chest served as a sort of property box from which tapas and *siva* skirts were produced for visitors of rank, a bottle of coconut oil was kept handy and a whole assortment of *ulas* hung over a line in the center of the house. The performer retired outside to readjust his lavalava, and rub on some oil and returned to select a necklace. Although the dance itself is often an attractive and finished performance, usually heavily spiced with burlesque and uncouth cries, the beginning and end are strangely unfinished as the performer becomes overcome with embarrassment and retires suddenly with a scanty bow and a half-concealed agonized smirk.

Solomona, pastor and political boss of Faleasao, has presented me with one of his "good Christian girls" to be my girl. She appears on the scene every morning promptly at eight. As she speaks no English she is very good for me; at present I am extracting family histories and relationships of every household in Faleasao. She stays until about 11, when I sink exhausted on my couch and work is over until about 3:30. It's much hotter here than in Tutuila and it is practically out of the question to do anything in the middle of the day. We have lunch at 12 (the food by the way is excellent) and then a dead silence prevails for a couple of hours. Supper is at 5 and then very often I work ahead until midnight. A curious working schedule, but the only possible one. As you see, it leaves very little time for reading or writing letters. All those nice little extra hours go into a sort of drunken sleep.

This is Sunday so the schedule is varied a little. I was wakened at 6 by two maidens who insisted that it was time for church, which really starts at 7.30. After church, late breakfast, and it is now 12.30, zero hour for heat. At 1.30 my "good Christian girl," Felofiaina, will arrive to escort me to the afternoon service in Faleasao, an abominably hot walk, and Solomona warned me to start early because we would be so wet when we got there!

I am writing on the front porch. A whole procession of girls with wet lavalavas tied as sarongs under their armpits and pails of water slung on poles over their shoulders are returning from bathing in the sea. The costume problem is blessedly simplified here. I wear only a combination, a slip and a dress and Keds when I go out and walk barefoot in the house. Two little girls have just come in and two more, I see, are coming. Letter writing is over for now and conversation is in order.

. . .

Tau, Manu'a
January 16, 1926

My stay in Samoa is more than half over.

These last two weeks, since the hurricane of blessed memory, have been devoted to the ethnology of activity. The whole village is busy building itself new houses or weaving itself new walls and floors, according to the sex of the workers. Informants are not to be had for love or money, so I wander about, sometimes engaging in useful activity and sometimes merely sitting on the floor and looking on, taking notes on where the woman puts her foot when she weaves a fan, and so on. Also I help sweep the village up. Doesn't that sound well, like sweeping cobwebs out of the sky? You take a marvelous broom (the *papalagis* call them "witches' brooms" and they are worthy of the name) with a handle five feet long of bamboo and a bristly end of the spiky ribs of coconut leaves. Each prong of the broom is a different length and it works like a charm. You sweep the floor of a house, composed of small coral stones, or the half-grassy, half-stony yard and all the rubbish comes away and never a stone or blade of grass.

Last Wednesday I went fishing on the reef by torchlight. It would be worth looking at if nothing happened at all. The edge of the reef, a white line far away, the whole curving shore dotted by torches, the reef itself an amazing world of strange shapes and different densities of darkness. And in addition there are crabs to be had for the grasping and little fish to be cut in two with a swift stroke of a knife and great puckering things like pincushions—all to be jumbled in a basket. I carried the basket. Dotting the reef were the *vannas*, giant spiky black balls, sometimes with a band of white near the ends of the spikes. And flat rubbery creatures lying everywhere and brown pudgy worms plastered to the stones. The fishing is all very inefficient and festive. Some have knives and some have not, so when a fish is seen there is much hallooing and the fish, tiny creatures about four inches long, are usually half a mile away before the boy-with-a-knife arrives. It is likewise with the basket. Crabs must be dashed about to silence their struggling and fish have their heads bitten off with great dispatch. Then there is the boy-with-the-torches. These are pieces of dried bark about three feet long, a bunch of which are used together. The boy-with-the-torches is very stingy with them; he holds his bunch tight and you have to pull hard. The sparks from your torch fall on the water with a gentle hiss. You have quite forgotten which way is towards the land, but the roar of the reef warns you back towards the shore if you wander too far. . . .

Possibilities for Writing

1. Choose one recent day that remains in your memory because it provided you with a wide variety of experiences. Write three letters, each at least a page in length, describing that day and your reactions to what happened. First, write to one of your close friends; then, to an older relative (a parent, grandparent, uncle, or aunt); finally, write an open letter to the other members of your class. Compare the three letters and describe the differences you find.

2. Review Margaret Mead's letters from Samoa and then write a letter describing your school life to someone in Samoa. Remember that much of what you ordinarily take for granted will have to be described or explained.

3. Write a letter to any one of the three letter writers included in this section of the book. You can choose any subject, but what you say and your manner of saying it should reflect your awareness of the particular person you are addressing. Alternatively, write a reply to any letter in this section, assuming the role of the brother of E. B. White, the son of Nicola Sacco, or one of Margaret Mead's parents.

CHAPTER TWO

BEGINNINGS

Introduction: Engaging an Audience

This chapter turns us from the kinds of informal self-expression represented in Chapter One to the more formal task of putting oneself into words for an unknown audience whom we can reach only through the medium of our writing. Each selection has been limited to the first few paragraphs of a published autobiography, to show how each writer chooses to introduce himself to his readers. The variety among the selections demonstrates that there is no set way to manage this introduction. An inexperienced writer might suppose that a proper autobiography begins at the beginning, with some necessary facts about date and place of birth, parents' names and ages, and so forth. If he has such expectations, he is probably remembering situations in which he has been autobiographical while filling out forms, not really telling someone about himself but merely classifying himself in convenient categories: male, single, employed. In social situations, however, where we are really introducing ourselves to someone else—someone we would like to know and to be known by—we avoid engulfing the other person with all sorts of quantifiable data about ourselves. Instead we try to present ourselves as interesting and worth knowing. We offer some interesting anecdote, make some humorous remarks or some comments on whatever may be going on around us, hoping that we will awaken some lively response in the stranger. Our primary intention is not to furnish specific information; in fact, it is usually much later, when two people are better acquainted, that they begin to take an interest in factual details about each other's lives. Instead, an introductory social meeting is a time for presenting some facet of ourselves that is particularly engaging or impressive.

The same condition holds true with written autobiography, with one important difference. Writing is a monologue rather than a dialogue, at least to the extent that no actual person is present before the writer moment by moment, to cue him or urge him on by facial expression or verbal response. Because of this difference, some attributes of the talker are lost to the writer. For example, one way to make people we meet like us is to be sympathetic, interested in their experiences and judgments, and thus to impress them by the warmth and the intelligent attention we bestow on them. But the autobiographical writer has to, in effect, keep talking, compelling his audience's attention exclusively through what he says. To do this he must imagine an audience and respond to its questions and needs, so that ultimately his writing is not really a monologue but a special kind of dialogue with the other party located in the writer's own head. This other party must be intrigued by what the writer has to say; his anticipated questions have to be dealt with, and his intelligence and goodwill must be assumed and never imposed on.

One final connection should be made between meeting someone interesting in actual life and writing or reading interesting autobiographies. The word "interesting" is exasperatingly imprecise, but at least we know that saying "I met someone interesting today" is different from saying "I met someone important today." We should keep this distinction in mind when writing autobiography; it is not necessary to start off by recounting some grand and exceptional accomplishment or to worry if nothing in our lives strikes us as being very exceptional. Important people, after all, are often called self-important, meaning that they are so absorbed in their own accomplishments that they forget their responsibilities to their audience—including, if they are writers, that imaginary audience mentioned earlier. In writing autobiography we have to be interesting rather than important, for interest is clearly something created by the writer's attitude toward himself, his subject, and his audience. It may help clarify the point to review some of the beginnings reprinted here. Both George Kennan and Margaret Bourke-White were distinguished public figures, one a notable American diplomat, the other a famous photographer, yet both ignore their public careers as they begin their autobiographies. Instead, Bourke-White recalls her parents and the humorous circumstances of her birth, while Kennan involves the reader in the general problem of how one remembers the past.

Although the beginning of any piece of writing is obviously important, the selections presented here are not intended to suggest that writers should get under way by laboring endlessly over their opening paragraphs. Such an assumption would create an impossible burden; it would cut the writer off from the gratification of producing a satisfying amount of material and remove the stimulus of being able to discover new directions to pursue within the pages of a first draft. In fact, writers frequently discover their true beginnings far along in the pages of their initial draft. An opening page can always be redone when the final focus of the essay emerges.

As writers soon discover, beginnings can incorporate any kind of material in a wide variety of forms, including narration, description, or reflection—in fact, all of the forms of writing taken up by this book. In the selections that follow, Claude Brown begins his story abruptly in the middle of an event; Kate Simon describes a place that was important to her childhood; Margaret Bourke-White introduces us to an influential person in her past; George Kennan generalizes about the difficulties he experienced attempting to recall his early life.

The chapters of this anthology emphasize separate elements in the activity of writing so that students can give them special attention, not because they will always be called for in the sequence in which the chapters present them. While "general-ization" becomes a subject in Chapter Five, it should be clear that a writer generalizes in every piece of writing, just as he expresses a point of view, uses details, and appeals to a reader. The individual chapters of this anthology simply give one or another of these constant attributes sustained consideration.

This varied series of beginnings should also make clear that effective writing is whatever is capable of engaging the read-er's attention. The selections here are assembled to prove that broad and liberating definition. By their variety they should encourage us to try things out ourselves. In one selection we can see how Claude Brown chooses to thrust the reader sud-denly into the midst of a highly dramatic moment, full of violence and danger, while in another Annie Dillard evokes the intimacy of her inner mood as she awakens to a new day. Each writer has a different purpose, and each has found an appropriate way to catch our ear and our eye. Thus Brown begins with such stunning abruptness because that method underscores the sudden violence that he feels has been so much a part of his ghetto existence as a young black in Har-lem. Dillard wants her prose to suggest the wonder of living close to natural things and so she stresses lyrical and meta-phorical language. The last selection, by Raymond Mungo, is an appropriate conclusion, for Mungo dramatizes himself as a dropout from conventional society by making fun of many of the ways conventional autobiographies might begin, turn-ing all of our usual expectations into jokes.

∽ Claude Brown ∽

(1937-   )

Claude Brown was born and raised in Harlem where he lived the violent life of an adolescent gang member in the ghetto. He spent time in the Wiltwyck School for disturbed boys and in reform school. He left Harlem for Greenwich Village, completed high school, and graduated from Howard University in 1965. Manchild in the Promised Land *(1965) is his account of his early life and his self-rehabilitation.*

[I'M SHOT]

"Run!"

Where?

Oh, hell! Let's get out of here!

"Turk! Turk! I'm shot!"

I could hear Turk's voice calling from a far distance, telling me not to go into the fish-and-chips joint. I heard, but I didn't understand. The only thing I knew was that I was going to die.

I ran. There was a bullet in me trying to take my life, all thirteen years of it.

I climbed up on the bar yelling, "Walsh, I'm shot. I'm shot." I could feel the blood running down my leg. Walsh, the fellow who operated the fish-and-chips joint, pushed me off the bar and onto the floor. I couldn't move now, but I was still completely conscious.

Walsh was saying, "Git outta here, kid. I ain't got no time to play."

A woman was screaming, mumbling something about the Lord, and saying, "Somebody done shot that poor child."

Mama ran in. She jumped up and down, screaming like a crazy woman. I began to think about dying. The worst part of dying was thinking about the things and the people that I'd never see again. As I lay there trying to imagine what being dead was like, the policeman who had been trying to control Mama gave up and bent over me. He asked who had shot me. Before I could answer, he was asking me if I could hear him. I told him that I didn't know who had shot me and would he please tell Mama to stop jumping up and down. Every time Mama came down on that shabby floor, the bullet lodged in my stomach felt like a hot poker.

Another policeman had come in and was struggling to keep the crowd outside. I could see Turk in the front of the crowd. Before the cops came, he asked me if I was going to tell them that he was with me. I never answered. I looked at him and wondered if he saw who shot me. Then his question began to ring in my head: "Sonny, you gonna tell 'em I was with you?" I was bleeding on a dirty floor in a fish-and-chips joint, and Turk was standing there in the doorway hoping that I would die before I could tell the cops that he was with me. Not once did Turk ask me how I felt.

Hell, yeah, I thought, I'm gonna tell 'em.

It seemed like hours had passed before the ambulance finally arrived. Mama wanted to go to the hospital with me, but the ambulance attendant said she was too excited. On the way to Harlem Hospital, the cop who was riding with us asked Dad what he had to say. His answer was typical: "I told him about hanging out with those bad-ass boys." The cop was a little surprised. This must be a rookie, I thought.

The next day, Mama was at my bedside telling me that she had prayed and the Lord had told her that I was going to live. Mama said that many of my friends wanted to donate some blood for me, but the hospital would not accept it from narcotics users.

This was one of the worst situations I had ever been in. There was a tube in my nose that went all the way to the pit of my stomach. I was being fed intravenously, and there was a drain in my side. Everybody came to visit me, mainly out of curiosity. The girls were all anxious to know where I had gotten shot. They had heard all kinds of tales about where the bullet struck. The bolder ones wouldn't even bother to ask: they just snatched the cover off me and looked for themselves. In a few days, the word got around that I was in one piece.

∾ Kate Simon ∾

Kate Simon is best known as a travel writer; she has written books about England, Italy, and Mexico. She has also published a guidebook to New York and a social history of its most famous street, Fifth Avenue. Bronx Primitive *(1982) is an account of her childhood as the daughter of Polish immigrants who settled in New York early in this century.*

LAFONTAINE NEAR TREMONT

We lived at 2029 Lafontaine, the last house on the west side of the street from 178th to 179th, a row of five-story tenements that ended at a hat factory. To the north and solidly, interminably, along the block to 180th there stretched a bitter ugliness of high walls of big stones that held a terminal point and service barns of El trains. (It may be that my recoil from early Renaissance palaces, their pugnacious blocks of stone and fortress grimness, stems from these inimical El walls.) Across from the factory were a garage and the Italian frame houses that lined that side of the street down to 178th Street. At the corner of 178th Street, on our Jewish-German-Polish-Hungarian-Rumanian side, was Mrs. Katz's candy store. The only other store I knew at first was the grocery run by a plodding elderly couple at the corner of 179th Street and Arthur Avenue, the street to the east. In spite of their lack of English and my frail Yiddish, I eagerly ran errands there to watch their feet slide and pat in their brown felt slippers and to admire the precision with which the old man cut once, twice, into a tub of butter to dig out exactly a quarter pound. And on their side of 179th Street, about midway between Arthur and Lafontaine, there was a big tree, the only street tree in the neighborhood, which showered me, and only me, with a million white blossoms. It was my tree and I watched and touched it as carefully as the Italian grandfathers watched and touched the tomato plants in their backyards.

Our station of the El was Tremont, which was numerically 177th Street, and Main Street. Between dark Third Avenue and its changing grids and slashes of light and Lafontaine, there was Monterey Avenue, on its west side a row of tenements and on its east, running from 178th to 179th, a resplendent, high empty lot, as full of possibilities as a park. It had patches of daisies and buttercups, plumy and scratchy bushes; on its eastern edge and below our fire escapes, seductive glittering objects thrown from Lafontaine windows—a shining knife handle, red glass and blue glass, bits of etched cut glass. Once my brother and I found a seltzer bottle nozzle and once a Chinese record, a wonderment we played over and over again on the Victrola, until our parents, impatient with the repetition of high thin notes with startling starts and stops, caused it to disappear. There were two ways of getting onto the lot: 178th Street was an easy, gradual slope; 179th Street was jutting rock for a height of two stories. The few girls who managed it were never quite the same again, a little more defiant, a little more impudent.

∽ Annie Dillard ∽

(1945-   )

Annie Dillard was born in Pittsburgh, but since 1965 she has lived in rural Virginia. Her major interest as a writer has been her relation to the natural world around her. She has published poetry as well as books of reflection about nature; she has also been involved in a variety of public projects to improve the quality of our environment. This passage is the beginning of her book Pilgrim at Tinker Creek *(1974);* Tinker Creek *is the site of her farm in Virginia.*

[MORNING MATTERS]

I used to have a cat, an old fighting tom, who would jump through the open window by my bed in the middle of the night and land on my chest. I'd half-awaken. He'd stick his skull under my nose and purr, stinking of urine and blood. Some nights he kneaded my bare chest with his front paws, powerfully, arching his back, as if sharpening his claws, or pummeling a mother for milk. And some mornings I'd wake in daylight to find my body covered with paw prints in blood; I looked as though I'd been painted with roses.

It was hot, so hot the mirror felt warm. I washed before the mirror in a daze, my twisted summer sleep still hung about me like sea kelp. What blood was this, and what roses? It could have been the rose of union, the blood of murder, or the rose of beauty bare and the blood of some unspeakable sacrifice or birth. The sign on my body could have been an emblem or a stain, the keys to the kingdom or the mark of Cain. I never knew. I never knew as I washed, and the blood streaked, faded, and finally disappeared, whether I'd purified myself or ruined the blood sign of the passover. We wake, if we ever wake at all, to mystery, rumors of death, beauty, violence. . . . "Seem like we're just set down here," a woman said to me recently, "and don't nobody know why."

These are morning matters, pictures you dream as the final wave heaves you up on the sand to the bright light and drying air. You remember pressure, and a curved sleep you rested against, soft, like a scallop in its shell. But the air hardens your skin; you stand; you leave the lighted shore to explore some dim headland, and soon you're lost in the leafy interior, intent, remembering nothing.

I still think of that old tomcat, mornings, when I wake. Things are tamer now; I sleep with the window shut. The cat and our rites are gone and my life is changed, but the memory remains of something powerful playing over me. I wake expectant, hoping to see a new thing. If I'm lucky I might be jogged awake by a strange birdcall. I dress in a hurry, imagining the yard flapping with auks, or flamingos. This morning it was a wood duck, down at the creek. It flew away.

～ Margaret Bourke-White ～

(1906-1971)

Margaret Bourke-White was an exceptional photographer and journalist. She created award-winning photographic essays for many national magazines during a professional career of more than thirty years. Her autobiography, Portrait of Myself *(1963), recalls many of her assignments as a photographic correspondent, as well as her struggle against the effects of Parkinson's disease later in her life.*

MY INVITATION INTO THE WORLD

"Margaret, you can always be proud that you were invited into the world," my mother told me.

I don't know where she got this fine philosophy that children should come because they were wanted and should not be the result of accidents. She came from a poor family with a multitude of children, and she had little chance to get an education, although she made up for this after marriage by going to college at intervals until she was over sixty. When each of her own three children was on the way, Mother would say to those closest to her, "I don't know whether this will be a boy or girl and I don't care. But this child was invited into the world and *it* will be a wonderful child."

She was explicit about the invitation and believed the child should be the welcomed result of a known and definite act of love between man and wife (which Mahatma Gandhi believed—I was to learn much later—although Mother never would have gone along with the Mahatma on his ideas of celibacy between invitations. Mother believed in warmth and ardor between married partners).

Mother's plan of voluntary parenthood was so outstandingly successful in my case that not only did I come along as requested, but I arrived on the specific date that had been decided upon.

This fine flourish to my orderly entry into upper Manhattan was as much the doctor's doing as my mother's. In the early evening of June 13 my arrival was imminent, and the doctor had directed my mother to walk the floor to ease and speed the process. He noticed that my father was placing some packages wrapped as gifts on the dining room table, and inquired about it.

"Tomorrow is our wedding anniversary," said my father.

"Put that woman to bed," ordered the doctor, and devoting himself to postponing my arrival, he held me off till two o'clock the next morning.

This was a good birthday in any case for a little American girl, as on June 14 the whole nation hangs out the Stars and Stripes to commemorate the day when Betsy Ross hung the first American flag. But my friends who know my bad habits, and hear the story of my delayed arrival, are apt to complain that I have never been on time for an appointment since.

⌁ George Kennan ⌁

(1904-   )

George Kennan was born in Wisconsin and educated at Princeton. He has had a distinguished career as a diplomat, serving primarily in Germany, Russia, and Eastern Europe. Since the early 1950s, he has pursued scholarly interests as a historian associated with the Institute for Advanced Studies at Princeton and has published a series of studies of Soviet-American relations in the twentieth century. The opening pages of his Memoirs: 1925–1950 *are reprinted below.*

A PERSONAL NOTE

There are, of course, great variations in people's capacity to remember consciously their early youth. My own, I fear, falls at the weaker end of the spectrum. Beyond this, I wonder whether, in this rapidly moving age, every older man does not stand at a greater distance from his own childhood and adolescence than was the case when the pace of change was less precipitate—whether the immediacy of remembered experience is not impaired by the ruthless destruction of setting which the explosions of population and technological change have so often worked. I, in any case, see only dimly and uncertainly—too uncertainly to permit of confident judgments—the thin, tense, introverted Princeton student whose physical frame and reflexes I know myself to have inherited. More dimly do I perceive, behind him, the grubby military school

From George Kennan: *Memoirs: 1925-1950.* Copyright © 1967 by George F. Kennan. Reprinted by permission of Little, Brown and Co., in association with the Atlantic Monthly Press.

cadet. Wholly untrustworthy and inadequate are the glimpses of the grade school boy, clad in the knickerbockers of the period, traveling back and forth between school and home on the new "pay-as-you-enter" streetcars of the Milwaukee street railways system (which thrilled him inordinately), retiring into sullen rages and sit-down strikes when required to attend Bournique's dancing school on Saturday afternoons, dreaming daydreams so intense and satisfying that hours could pass in oblivion of immediate surroundings. And when one moves still further into the past and arrives at the small child, the resources of memory fail altogether. I have found myself tempted to relate that this child was deeply affected, and in a certain sense scarred for life, by the loss of his mother shortly after his birth. This is, perhaps, a rational deduction, supported by a certain amount of circumstantial evidence from later years. But it is not really anything drawn from memory.

The fact is that one moves through life like someone moving with a lantern in a dark woods. A bit of the path ahead is illuminated, and a bit of the path behind. But the darkness follows hard on one's footsteps, and envelopes our trail as one proceeds. Were one to be able, as one never is, to retrace the steps by daylight, one would find that the terrain traversed bears, in reality, little relationship to what imagination and memory had pictured. We are, toward the end of our lives, such different people, so far removed from the childhood figures with whom our identity links us, that the bond to those figures, like that of nations to their obscure prehistoric origins, is almost irrelevant.

There is another difficulty that confronts me when I try to describe the early self. In my own youthful consciousness, more, perhaps, than in the case of many others, the borderline between external and internal reality was unfirm. I lived, particularly in childhood but with lessening intensity right on to middle age, in a world that was peculiarly and intimately my own, scarcely to be shared with others or even made plausible to them. I habitually read special meanings into things, scenes,

and places—qualities of wonder, beauty, promise, or horror—
for which there was no external evidence visible, or plausible, to
others. My world was peopled with mysteries, seductive hints,
vague menaces, "intimations of immortality." For example, at
the foot of the street we lived on in Milwaukee there was a particular entryway in a particular brick building—a dark, cavernous aperture, lurking behind a heavy romanesque archway
of grimy brick, flush with the street—that held for me a sinis-
ter significance all its own. Behind it, I never doubted, lay a
house of horror—horror unnamed, unmentionable, not to be
imagined. It was plain, on the other hand, that the trunks of
the trees in Juneau Park were populated by fairies. My cousin
Catherine had told my older sister Frances that this was the
case, and long, respectful contemplation of the park on my
part convinced me that the hypothesis was probably correct.

How, then, if I am to consider my youth today in terms that
could have meaning to other people, am I to weave my way effectively between what others could accept as reality and what
they could not? How do I know what was real and what was
not? To the extent that memory can carry me back at all into
those dim recesses, it can do no more than to confront me with
these uncertainties. Perhaps the house at the end of our street
had indeed been the scene of some horrible unmentionable
tragedy; perhaps it was affected by this, as houses sometimes
are; and perhaps the fine antennae of the child picked up something of the ensuing desolation. Can I even be sure, for that
matter, that there were not really fairies in Juneau Park?
Things scarcely less strange have been known to happen. That
it would be difficult to find the fairies there today I have no
doubt. The automobiles have probably done them in, as they
have done in so many other things in that now blighted region
of central Milwaukee. But who can be sure what was there in
1910? Things are as we see them. It took two of us—the park
and myself—to make possible a given view, a given apprehension, if you will, of the place. Fairies were a part of this view.
To what extent they had their existence in the park and to what

98

extent in me we shall never know. Perhaps a long and inten-
sive self-analysis, along Freudian lines, would clarify such
things. Were I a great artist, a great criminal, the subject of
some highly complex and unusual experience, or one of exceptional personal failings and virtues, there might be reason for
it. I am none of these things.

❦ Raymond Mungo ❦

(1946-)

Raymond Mungo attended Boston University and edited the school newspaper there. He was involved in revolutionary politics during the late 1960s and helped to found the Liberation News Service, an underground press syndicate. His autobiography, Famous Long Ago *(1970), tells of his political activities and of the changes in his outlook that prompted him to take up life on a communal farm in Vermont.*

MY LIFE AND HARD TIMES

I was born in a howling blizzard in February, 1946, in one of those awful mill towns in eastern Massachusetts, and lived to tell about it. My parents were and are hard-working, ordinary people lacking the "benefits" of higher education and the overwhelming *angst* and cynicism which come with it. I was thus not raised in what most of you would call a middle-class environment, lucky for me. Were I true to my roots I'd now be a laborer in a paper or textile mill, married and the father of two children, a veteran of action in Vietnam, and a reasonably brainwashed communicant in a Roman Catholic, predominantly Irish parish. Instead, I am a lazy good-for-nothing dropout, probably a Communist dupe, and live on a communal farm way, way into the backwoods of Vermont. What went wrong?

At the age of one, I can clearly recall, I was rocked on my mother's lap in the middle of some dark New England winter night, the light from our kitchen lamp shone on the ceiling, and the rocking motion gave it a moving, undulating shape which formed beautiful patterns in my infant mind—obviously the forerunner of the psychedelic experience for me.

At the age of four, I read books—Dick and Jane readers, Bobbsey Twins, Tom Swift, and my parents' encyclopedia of human anatomy, which featured dirty pictures.

At four and one half years, I went to kindergarten, but the girl who sat next to me (her name was Patty) had clammy wet hands and since I was always made to hold her hand during ring-around-the-rosy, I dropped out.

At five and one half, I entered Sister Joseph Anthony's first grade classroom and, being physically puny, elected to become the smartest kid in school to compensate. And did.

In the second grade, I was primed for my First Holy Communion. My parents had spent money we couldn't afford on a beautiful white suit in which I was to receive Jesus for the first time. The night before this holy event, I could not sleep, and rose from my bed—over which the picture of Jesus was broadly smiling upon me—to investigate the pantry. There, I ate a whole box of peanuts reserved for First Holy Communion festivities the next day; then noticed that it was 3:30 A.M., and realized I had *broken the fast*. (In those days, Catholics were required to fast from midnight on the day they received Communion. To receive the host without having fasted was a mortal sin; that means you go to hell if you suddenly die under the wheels of a runaway car, a tableau which had often been presented to me in Sisters' school.) My alternatives were to refuse Holy Communion, thus obeying the sacred law of Rome and disappointing my parents and all my relatives, or else to receive Holy Communion, thus insulting Jesus and Mary but pleasing the family. The picture of Jesus was now crying over my bed. Next morning, I said nothing of the peanuts, just took the First Holy Communion, and nobody was the wiser. Except me, I had nightmares of runaway cars and eternal damnation for a year, until I got up the courage to confess the mortal sin to Father Gallivan.

In the eighth grade, puberty came between me and the

Church, and I went through a harrowing Stephen Dedalus thing for about three years; you know all about stuff like that so I won't bore you with the details.

For four years, I hitchhiked thirty miles twice a day to attend an R.C. prep school where everybody except me was rich and my tuition was paid by a full scholarship, for I was seen as a promising lad and a likely candidate for the priesthood. I knew the only way out of the mills was through college, so I kept my Stephen Dedalus secrets from everybody until I was safely out of that school with a bundle of college scholarships.

Life began at seventeen. I left home, which was a good and simply virtuous place, and my parents, with whom I have never had a really bad scene, and moved to Boston to get hip about the big big world out there. During my freshman year, I was a violent Marxist, friend of the working class and all that, and relished my background among the oppressed. I was also the victim of a burning need for and involvement with the theatre, having graduated from all the usual precocious-adolescent trips with Romantic poets, Italian composers, Surrealist painters, and dirty novelists. I wrote plays for Theater of the Absurd, which was a big thing back in 1963.

During my sophomore year at college, somebody (God bless him) turned me on to dope. I grew very fond of it, all kinds of it. Dope didn't really become an all-American college preoccupation until 1966 or 1967, so I was a few years ahead in that department. I was then a pacifist and in the process of getting educated about the war in Vietnam, which in 1964 most of my classmates didn't even know was going on. From Vietnam I learned to despise my countrymen, my government, and the entire English-speaking world, with its history of genocide and international conquest. I was a normal kid.

By my junior year, I had lost my virginity and that changed everything. I was living in a wretched Boston slum and working my way through school. I traveled around the country participating in demonstrations against the war in Vietnam, and lived from day to day, smoked a lot of dope and fornicated every night. It was glorious.

In my senior year, I edited the college newspaper and put a lot of stuff about draft resistance, the war, abortions, dope, black people, and academic revolutions in it. Which, even though it was 1966, people seemed to think was pretty far-out stuff indeed. I walked with Mr. LSD and met God, who taught me to flow with it and always seek to be kind. "I am striving to understand."

Toward the very end of my college daze, I had a fat fellowship to Harvard University for graduate school and for lack of anything more exciting to do, intended to use it. But a madman named Marshall Bloom flew into Boston from London one cold April day and put the question to me, did I want to join him in overthrowing the state down in Washington, D.C.? Overthrowing the state seemed to me an excellent idea, it desperately needed to get done, and since if you want something done right you must do it yourself, I said OK why not? Fare thee well simple hometown and good parents, good riddance Catholicism, so long Boston it was nice while it lasted, goodbye school and teachers and warm fat books, I'm off to make my fortune in Washington, D.C., the nation's capital. I'm out to show the emperor without his clothes and tear down the walls of the rotten imperial city and have fun doing it. Fair New England, we'll meet again in the New Age and not before.

That's me on the Merritt Parkway, hauling my cat, her kittens, my friend Steve who turned me on, and all my worldly belongings. There's me on the New Jersey Turnpike puffing on a lighthearted cigarette and leaving behind my debts, hangups, and unborn child. On to Washington to fulfill my years of dreaming of Revolution in my time! Got my manuscripts, my one oil painting, two or three dollars in change, a few records, and my friend. This is the way a young man starts his career.

Now, dear friend, you know as much about me as you need to know. What follows is a story, by no means complete, of what happened to me during the few years after I started. Please don't try to learn anything from it, for there is no message. Try to enjoy it, as I have (at least much of the time) enjoyed putting it down for you. Take it slow, don't try to read it in one sitting, by all means get distracted from time to time. Read it stoned, read it straight, give up and never finish it, it's all the same between friends. Take care of your health and get plenty of rest.

Possibilities for Writing

1. Write a beginning for your own autobiography, then make an exchange with someone else in the class and write a brief response to his beginning. In your response, comment on what you found interesting and suggest possible directions in which the autobiography could continue.

2. Experiment by writing two or three different beginnings for your own autobiography, perhaps starting one with your earliest memories, one with a formal sketch of your family background, and one with a vivid account of an important moment in your life. The selections reprinted in this section might give you some other ideas about ways of beginning your own story.

3. Choose three of the autobiographical beginnings in this section and write at least a one-page continuation for each, maintaining the style and attitude that you feel the author has tried to establish.

CHAPTER THREE

EVENTS

Introduction: Narration and Point of View

When we say that autobiography is the writer's own story, we are reminding ourselves not only that autobiography is a form of personal expression, but also that it is a story, an account of what happened to the writer. What happened can mean what he did or felt or thought, for the events of his story can just as easily emphasize the inner, private life or the outer, public one. But wherever and however the writer chooses to begin, he is sure to find himself caught up in the creative process of telling a story.

It is important to remember that creative storytelling begins when we first choose an event in our lives as an autobiographical subject. When writing about a memorable day we would not simply follow the clock ("At 7:30 I got up; at 7:45 I had breakfast") any more than we would answer a friend's casual "What've you been doing?" by taking out our appointment calendar. These examples sound absurd because such lists of what happened by clock or calendar are highly impersonal—like records of police calls and fire alarms. No individual really experiences life as an unvarying succession of equally important moments and so naturally no one remembers the past in that way either. Any writer's explanation of what happened is from the beginning a creative shaping of past experience based on what his own memory establishes as vivid and meaningful. Once the writer recognizes that memory is the storehouse of the memorable, he can call upon his memory as a creative resource.

The memory of a day on a college campus would certainly take different forms for a freshman student, a visitor from a foreign country, and a city building inspector because the things each found worth remembering would vary so widely. But even if we chose two freshmen who were close friends and compared their memories of a single hour in the same class, we could still expect to find significant differences in the kinds of selection and emphasis that govern what they remember. Obviously their accounts would overlap, but they would never be identical; we all see the world with different eyes and from the vantage point of different lives. The uniqueness of our individual perspective is something we rarely celebrate or even think about, since it is universal and inescapable, but because of it, when we begin to remember an autobiographical event, we are already regarding that event in a distinctive way.

Although our memory does a good deal of shaping and selecting, giving our experience an initial form, something more is necessary to realize that form effectively in our writing. First, and perhaps most important, we need to exploit our greatest resource, memory, to the fullest, coaxing and prodding it to yield to us more and more of the usable past. Sometimes, of course, memories can overwhelm us with extraordinary power, evoking a past whose vividness virtually displaces the present moment, and our writing seems to share this rush of energy, proceeding fluently, almost without a pause, to say everything we wish to say. But we are much more likely to remember only the outline of an event, our general feelings, and a few stray details. The writer who settles for such fragments has impoverished himself unnecessarily by not making a greater effort to have more of his past accessible for his purposes. There are many ways to make such an exploratory effort. A writer can become his own interviewer, following the methods illustrated in the first chapter, pursuing himself like a trained journalist; he can follow a process of association, linking images and ideas in ways that may eventually reveal a pattern or form; he can concentrate on producing a mental picture of the event, painstakingly visualizing detail after detail. He may simply drift in reverie, giving in to memory rather than trying to control it. Whatever method or combination of methods a writer uses in order to produce a more intense or a more expansive sense of some event in his past life, his immediate goal is to activate clusters of recollection, not necessarily connected with one another or coherently assembled, but piled high like backstage scenery. The value of such clusters is that they give the writer confidence to proceed, and they give him options about how to proceed. The more material he has at hand and the more fertile he comes to believe his own inventive powers are, the more confidently he will approach any later tasks of reorganizing his material. If he is pinched or strained for things to say, he will resist revising or cutting anything he already has on paper because he cannot be sure he will be able to produce anything in its place. Possibly the most valuable kind of confidence for a writer is his feeling that his subject (whether autobiographical or not) is richly and variously his, so that he could write about it in many different ways.

After exploring his memory and keeping as many notes and jottings as possible about what he remembers, the writer may feel that what he sees in front of him is not a record of an autobiographical event, but merely a crazy jumble of disorganized data. All writing of any imaginative power, however, exists as jumble at some stage, either at an early phase of mental groping, at a later point with successive reroutings of our trains of thought, or at a still later point when the process of translation into words written on a page begins. While most writers experience all of these stages in varying intensity, they are of course particularly aware of the last stage because the jumble is written out before their eyes. We may feel vaguely embarrassed and inferior when we see our own jumble on the page, but that is because we are so accustomed to reading written language in its published form, clear, controlled, and convincing. We assume that the sprawl and mess is leading us away n effective writing rather than toward it, but this is not the case. Instead, we need to see jumble differently, as a necessary precondition to most good writing, for jumble is part of the process by which creativity discovers itself.

At this point, the writer is ready to test out possibilities in a written draft. Creating the first draft leads him from the first crucial stage of the writing process to the second. On the one hand, the first draft should try to sustain the kind of imaginative freedom and flexibility that the process of exploration encouraged in the prewriting stage. On the other hand, the first draft also introduces in a very broad way elements of conscious choice, for the writer has to decide which memories he will use and emphasize and how he will connect one memory with another. Conscious choice, already important as the first draft gets underway, becomes crucial when the draft is completed. As he looks over his first draft, the writer must decide whether he is satisfied with what he has accomplished and whether he now approves the preliminary choices he has already made. It is possible that the first draft may also be the last draft, if he finds that his intuitions and his preliminary choices have resulted in a satisfying narrative. More often, however, as the writer reviews where he chose to begin and end, what kinds of consistency he has established within his story, and what sort of order he has used to present events, he finds something, major or minor, that he wishes to alter. When he decides to do so, he enters fully into what can be called the editing process, the conscious search for the style and the structure most appropriate to a particular subject. It is the editing process that this text will discuss, here and in subsequent chapters, by suggesting what some of a writer's most frequent decisions are likely to be and by providing some examples of the choices made by other writers in similar situations.

The episode from Maya Angelou's autobiography shows how one published writer shapes a subject already mentioned in the discussion of the exploratory stage in writing—the experience of a school graduation. It is important to remember that

Angelou must have gone through the exploratory stage and the editing stage herself, but that what we see and can discuss is the result of that process, with no indication of how short or how long, how simple or how complex the process proved to be for her. What we can be sure of is her persistent and intense exploration of memory, for her account is vividly detailed and convincing. What seems to have struck Angelou as one important part of her experience is the gap between the kind of expectations she had for her graduation and the actual feelings that came over her during the ceremony. In order to make her readers feel this contrast, she has to give prominence to those memories that have some bearing on this special subject. She takes particular care to describe at length the preparations for the great event, the days and weeks of anticipation, the pleasure and pride she felt in her own success. In the same way she dramatizes in detail how the ceremony illustrates the painful injustices of a segregated society and turns her sense of triumph into humiliation. Finally she shows how the singing of James Weldon Johnson's anthem by the graduating class alters her feelings once more, giving her a new sense of pride in the courage and determination of black people. This pattern of changing feelings is created by Angelou as she makes three choices in the editorial process: what to include or exclude, where to begin and end, and whether to emphasize something or treat it casually. None of these choices are simple either/or decisions, but they are basic choices that give to day-to-day experience the meaningful shape and proportion of narrative.

To say that selection and emphasis always play a part in good writing does not mean that all good writing narrows down to a single focus of interest. The Angelou selection includes many details that have no direct bearing on the graduation but that help to evoke the conditions of life in a small Arkansas town and to characterize her relations with members of her family—to give us, in short, the sense of the texture of her life, regardless of any particular dramatic event. Nevertheless, another writer might want to go much further than Angelou in creating the impression that he is telling us everything about his life by including far more random detail, justifying the more chaotic organization by pointing to the way he came closer to capturing the immediacy and variety of experience. Similarly, another writer might not stay within the time scheme of a single sequence of events, as Angelou does. Instead, he might want his writing to reflect a freer range of recollection, linking one event to another by a loose association of thought and feeling. In such cases, the writer is not abandoning the editing process, but is using it to stretch out the narrative sequence and to bring out complexities in the story he is telling.

A writer may also simply move out of the narrative sequence altogether, in order to explain or argue, interpret or justify, for the purpose of giving his readers an explicit commentary on the importance and meaning of the narrative. Angelou's final paragraph

> If we were a people much given to revealing secrets, we might raise monuments and sacrifice to the memories of our poets, but slavery cured us of that weakness. It may be enough, however, to have it said that we survive in exact relationship to the dedication of our poets (include preachers, musicians and blues singers).

is an example of how she can detach herself from the graduation event to give us her views on one aspect of its meaning. The selection by George Orwell, for example, makes us even more aware of a narrator for whom events are memories from a different kind of world. Orwell exemplifies the most flexible approach to autobiographical narrative, just as Piri Thomas shows how effective straightforward narrative with no shifts or deviations can be. The other selections in this chapter can be compared with both Orwell and Thomas, since they occupy different places on a spectrum bounded by narratives that comment extensively on experience and narratives that present experience directly.

The passage from Maya Angelou quoted above also suggests one final issue connected with autobiographical narrative—the question of point of view. Any writer of autobiography is telling us about himself as he was at some time in the past, but he is also writing about that past from the perspective of the present, with whatever advantages hindsight provides. The comment by Angelou about black poets and the survival of a black heritage illustrates this perspective, for it is not a comment that the ten-year-old Angelou would have been capable of making at the time of her graduation. Obviously, no writer is going to erase entirely the passage of time and re-create exactly the thoughts and feelings of the younger person he once was, but the writer must decide to what extent he wants to create some form of dramatic illusion and to reproduce the point of view of a much younger self. The writer who persistently reflects and interprets, like Orwell, is keeping the reader constantly aware of his mature self; the writer who dramatizes, like Thomas, projects the reader more forcefully into the time and conditions of his earlier life. Angelou expresses a more customary balance between thoughts and attitudes of the present interwoven with the continuing drama of past experience. These various arrangements simply show that some relationship between a past and a present self must be in any writer's mind as he attempts to recover the past and interpret it.

The awareness of how one views one's own past is part of the general issue of how the writer sees what he writes about—the issue of point of view. Progression and dramatic momentum in autobiography are created by the writer's selection of events and the emphasis he gives them, but the way that a narrative holds together depends on the writer's ability to create a point of view toward the events. Temporal sequence (how events are related to one another in time) is central to our understanding of narrative; point of view (the vantage point from which these events are seen and presented) is central to our understanding of the narrator.

We can understand the function of point of view more clearly if we look at a selection in which the writer is participating in an event and yet seeing it from an unusual or unfamiliar perspective. George Plimpton describes playing in a preseason football scrimmage as a member of a professional team. What makes Plimton's experience unusual is that he is a writer and magazine editor who has never before played tackle football, let alone competed at this level of skill. As a result, Plimpton sees things from the point of view of an anxious outsider. He stresses his own uncertainty and sense of imminent disaster, and he describes what happens in the language of someone whose frame of reference is quite different from that of a veteran football player. When Plimpton tells of a player lifting his head in the offensive huddle and looking across at the defense, "the egg-smooth surface of the helmet, its cage pointed at me, adding to the sense of that impersonal scrutiny, like a robot monster's," he clearly records the impressions of someone who sees the conventional uniforms of players as strange and inhuman. As a result, we look to Plimpton to give those of us who do not follow football a sense of what we might see and feel if we were suddenly thrust into such a game. Plimpton's point of view might also appeal to the dedicated football fan, by offering him a fresh way of looking at this sport, one which avoids the specialized language of a knowledgeable sports reporter.

Plimpton is a special case, for he has gone out of his way to locate himself in an unfamiliar situation, and therefore he is very conscious that he is presenting a distinctive point of view. For most of us, point of view, like selection and emphasis, is an aspect of the writer's craft that begins to emerge without conscious effort as soon as we put some words on a page. The basic features of our point of view depend on the images and language that come most readily to our minds, not on some highly deliberate system of choice. But the great majority of writers benefit from stepping back and considering their own vantage point as they relate a story. When the writer maintains a coherent point of view (or one whose changes in perspective are clearly marked and carefully managed), readers gain confidence in the writer's ability to see the world steadily and truly.

∿ Frank Conroy ∿

(1936-   )

Frank Conroy was born in New York and educated at Haver-
ford College. He is now a writer and an occasional piano player
in New York jazz clubs. Stop-Time *(1965), his first book, is an*
account of his boyhood in Florida and New York.

THE COLDNESS OF PUBLIC PLACES

Three boys were on the bench. I sat down with them and
watched the floor for a moment, not, as a naïve observer might
have thought, to dramatize penitence, but simply to maintain
my privacy in an important moment. Drawn close by their delinquency, the other boys whispered and passed notes, holding
off fear with artificial camaraderie. I kept quiet, acclimating
slowly to the electric air, knowing that where there was danger
there might also be salvation.

I never rehearsed a defense. I must have thought the Dean
preferred a boy who walked in and took his medicine to one
who groveled, however cleverly. And of course when the moment of recognition came, when the barriers fell and we stood
revealed, I didn't want to be in the midst of an elaborate lie. To
hasten the emergence of love I could only be completely honest. Lies might make it difficult for him to reach me, and vice-
versa.

I wanted to be won over by him, but not cheaply. If he won

me cheaply he might betray me. The sense in which I knew this is hard to explain. It wasn't a principle I'd deduced from experience, it was knowledge without thought. Had someone asked me at the time what it meant to be betrayed by another person I couldn't have answered. Without being able to conceive betrayal I none the less protected myself against it, unconsciously, in my expectation of a commitment from the other person equal to my own. A perfectly valid stance between individuals but a tragic absurdity between a child and authority.

A side door I'd never noticed before opened and a student came out smiling. I caught a glimpse of a man at a desk, and for no reason at all I became convinced he was a policeman.

"Fischberg," the Dean's secretary called without looking up. The boy next to me left the bench and went through the side door. I heard the man inside tell him to close it.

The smiling student picked up a pass from the secretary and started out. As he passed I touched his arm. "Who's that in there?"

"I don't know. Some jerk asking if I had a happy home life."

"No talking there!"

A soft buzz sounded on the secretary's intercom. "Next," she said.

There was a momentary paralysis on the bench.

"Well, what are you waiting for?" She shuffled some papers on her desk. "Conroy? Is one of you Conroy?"

I walked to the Dean's door and went in.

"All right Conroy; step over here."

I crossed the carpet and stood in front of his desk. He took off his glasses, rubbed the bridge of his nose, and put them on again. After a moment he pushed against the edge of the desk and swiveled away to face the wall, leaning back with a sigh and then letting his chin come down slowly like a man dozing off.

"Why were you late?" he asked the wall.

"There was no reason, I guess."

"No reason?"

"I mean I don't have an excuse."

"You didn't miss your bus? You didn't forget your transit pass? The subways didn't break down?"

"No sir."

"I suppose not, since you've been late three times this week. You can't possibly have an excuse so you don't give one. Isn't that right?" He stared at the wall.

I didn't answer.

"Isn't that right?" he asked again in exactly the same flat tone.

"If you say so, sir."

He turned his head to look at me for a moment, his face expressionless, and then went back to watching the wall. "I don't have time for trouble-makers, Conroy. I get rid of them."

"I don't know why I'm late so often. I try to get here on time but somehow it just happens."

"Don't make a mystery out of it, Conroy. You're late because you're lazy and inattentive."

I could feel myself beginning to close down inside, as if my soul were one of those elaborate suitcases street peddlers use to display their wares, the kind that fold up from all directions at the approach of the law.

He lifted some papers from his desk. "You're nothing but trouble. Constantly late if you get here at all, inattentive in class, disrespectful to your teachers, twice reprimanded for gambling . . ."

"It was just pitching pennies, sir."

"I know what it was. Don't interrupt."

"Yes sir."

"At this moment you are failing three subjects."

"We haven't had any tests yet. I'm sure I'll pass the tests."

He looked up, his eyes narrowing in irritation. "You're failing three subjects. That leaves the decision up to me. You stay here or you get transferred to another school. You're in that category now."

I turned away, instinctively hiding the fear that might be on my face. Getting kicked out of Stuyvesant would be a catastrophe surpassing anything in my experience, perhaps because it seemed to eliminate the possibility of turning over a new leaf. I disbelieved in self-betterment. By turning a new leaf I meant no more than avoiding the more obvious forms of trouble.

Secretly, I did hope that things would get better. That I didn't know *how* they'd get better was balanced by my inability to understand why they were bad in the first place. It was a delicate world in which one had to move carefully, dealing with elements one understood vaguely if at all, knowing only that some elements seemed to sustain life and some to threaten it. Getting thrown out of school would disrupt things profoundly. I would no longer be able to experiment with those balanced elements, probing them gingerly here and there, adding some, taking away some, trying, in the least dangerous way, to find out what they were. In a trade school, my bridges burned behind me, I imagined myself in total isolation and darkness, unable to reorganize, unable to make the slightest adjustments in the course of my life, finally and irrevocably in the hands of a disinterested fate.

"What do you think I should do?" he asked.

"I want to stay. I can make it."

"What the hell is the matter with you, Conroy?"

I looked down at the edge of the desk. Something strange was happening. I seemed to be at two removes from reality, crouching behind my own body like a man manipulating a puppet through a curtain. "I don't know." My arms were reaching in through my back to make me talk. "That's the truth."

"If you don't," he said slowly, "you had better find out."

I climbed back into myself and nodded.

He opened the drawer of his desk and took out a small notebook. "Early report for two weeks. Get here fifteen minutes before the first bell and sign in with the hall monitor." He uncapped his pen and made a notation. "Leave plenty of time. Miss once and you're out. Understand?"

"Yes sir."

"That's all." He didn't look up.

I had my hand on the doorknob when he spoke again. "And see the man in the other room before you go back to class."

The bench had refilled and the boys turned as if to read their fates in my expression. I walked past and went up to the secretary. "He says I should see the man in there."

"Go on in, then. There's nobody with him."

I tapped the door lightly and entered.

"Come in. Sit down." He was standing over a desk. "You are . . . ah . . ." He looked down at his papers.

"Conroy."

"Oh yes, Conroy." He smiled nervously, poking one of the papers across the surface of the desk with his fingers. Hunched over, he coughed into his fist as he quickly read it. "Well now, Frank," he began. (It was a slight shock to be so addressed. My official name was Conroy, and neither teachers nor students called me anything else.) "I want to ask you some questions. Understand that I have nothing to do with the school or the Dean. I'm here simply as an observer, and to help if I can. You can answer freely without fear of . . ." he hesitated, searching for the right word.

"Repercussions?"

"Yes. That's right." He sat down. "Now let's see. You're fourteen years old. Any brothers or sisters?"

"An older sister," I said. "And oh yes, the baby. Jessica. She's only a few months old."

"I see. She would be your half-sister, I imagine, since I see here your father passed away some time ago."

"Yes." I began to pick at some lint on my trousers, feeling slightly uncomfortable.

"Do you get along with them all right?"

"What do you mean?" I understood him, but the question irritated me.

"Well, there are always little fights now and then. We all lose our tempers occasionally, I wondered if outside of that you got along with them all right."

"Of course I do."

"Okay." He paused, watching me indirectly. There was no more lint to pick from my leg so I began to brush out the cuff with a finger. "Do you have a job in the morning?"

"Yes. I work in a library."

"How do you like that?"

"It's okay."

"What do you do when you get home from school at night? Do you have any hobbies? Stamp collecting, that sort of thing?"

"No hobbies."

"Well, how do you pass the time?"

"I read a lot. Sometimes I play the piano."

"What kind of books?"

I hesitated, not sure how to answer. "All kinds, I guess."

"I suppose you don't like school very much."

"I don't think about it very much."

The bell rang, all over the building, and was followed instantly by the sound of thousands of students moving through the halls. I listened abstractedly, luxuriating in the knowledge that for the moment I'd escaped the routine. How can I explain the special pleasure of listening to the machine operating all around me while I myself was removed from it? I'd cut class and climb the stairs past the top floor to the deserted landing above. I'd sit with my back against the door to the roof listening to the bells, to the boys shouting on the stairs below, and to the long silences after the halls had emptied. The mood was quietly Olympian.

I hadn't realized how much the Dean had shaken me up, but now, as the bell I didn't have to answer rang again, I felt a tremor of release play over my body. Muscles everywhere began to relax and I threw back my head in an enormous involuntary yawn.

"What does your stepfather do for a living, Frank?"

Instantly I was alert. I knew the man was harmless, but my deepest rule, a rule so deep I maintained it without the slightest conscious effort, was never to reveal anything important about life at home. "He's a cab driver," I said slowly.

"Does your mother work too?"

I stared at the floor. "Sometimes." It occurred to me that my initial relief at getting away from the Dean might have made me careless with the man I now faced. He obviously had some image of me in his mind, some psychological cliché, and by answering carelessly I might unknowingly have supported it. I moved to the edge of my chair and sat up straight.

"Is there trouble at home?" he asked quietly.

My face flushed. A stupid question. An insulting question, as if I were a case to be dealt with by the book, as if he suspected some hidden deprivation or abnormality. "No, of course not. Nothing like that." I knew what he had in his mind. He held images of drunken fathers who beat their kids, slut mothers who roamed the house in old nightgowns, and long, screaming fights with crockery flying through the air. We weren't like that. I knew we were much better than that. I stood up. "Is that all?"

He fiddled with his papers for a moment, looking off into space. "Yes, I guess so," he said reluctantly. "If and when I come back to Stuyvesant I'd like to talk to you again."

I hiked my books high under my arm and went out the door. Standing motionless in the small room, I looked at the secretary and the four boys on the bench. The bell rang.

1. What initial sense of Conroy do you get from the first three paragraphs of the selection? What kind of expectations does he have before he goes in to see the Dean? Do those expectations seem to you realistic? What do they suggest about Conroy's character?

2. Conroy uses a great deal of dialogue in presenting this scene. What are the most significant features of the conversations he presents? What relation do they have to Conroy's expectations while waiting in the outer office?

3. *Do you see the Dean and the second interviewer as quite different or quite similar figures? What details in the way they are described or in their conversation seem to you most important in conveying their characters? Do you think Conroy's decision to tell us very little about the second interviewer adds to the effectiveness of the scene?*

4. *Conroy's own role here is generally passive—he answers a few questions, nothing more. How does he still keep himself at the center of the scene? What sense of Conroy's own character emerges during the scene?*

5. *Do you expect some kind of vivid climax as you are reading this selection? What does happen at the end? Is it an effective ending? What sense of schools and of the problems of students does Conroy's narrative create?*

∽ Maya Angelou ∽

(1929-   )

*Maya Angelou grew up living with her maternal grandmother
in Stamps, Arkansas, and her childhood experiences form the
basis of her autobiography,* I Know Why the Caged Bird Sings
*(1969). As an adult she has been a dancer, a nightclub singer,
and an actress. Her involvement as a black woman with social
issues led to her work for the Southern Christian Leadership
Conference in the early 1960s. Her books include several volumes of poetry and two more volumes of autobiography,* Gather
Together in My Name *(1974) and* Singin' and Swingin' and
Gettin' Merry Like Christmas *(1976).*

[GRADUATION DAY]

The weeks until graduation were filled with heady activities.
A group of small children were to be presented in a play about
buttercups and daisies and bunny rabbits. They could be heard
throughout the building practicing their hops and their little
songs that sounded like silver bells. The older girls (nongradu-
ates, of course) were assigned the task of making refreshments
for the night's festivities. A tangy scent of ginger, cinnamon,
nutmeg and chocolate wafted around the home economics
building as the budding cooks made samples for themselves
and their teachers.

In every corner of the workshop, axes and saws split fresh
timber as the woodshop boys made sets and stage scenery. Only

the graduates were left out of the general bustle. We were free to sit in the library at the back of the building or look in quite detachedly, naturally, on the measures being taken for our event.

Even the minister preached on graduation the Sunday before. His subject was, "Let your light so shine that men will see your good works and praise your Father, Who is in Heaven." Although the sermon was purported to be addressed to us, he used the occasion to speak to backsliders, gamblers and general ne'er-do-wells. But since he had called our names at the beginning of the service we were mollified.

Among Negroes the tradition was to give presents to children going only from one grade to another. How much more important this was when the person was graduating at the top of the class. Uncle Willie and Momma had sent away for a Mickey Mouse watch like Bailey's. Louise gave me four embroidered handkerchiefs. (I gave her three crocheted doilies.) Mrs. Sneed, the minister's wife, made me an underskirt to wear for graduation, and nearly every customer gave me a nickel or maybe even a dime with the instruction "Keep on moving to higher ground," or some such encouragement.

Amazingly the great day finally dawned and I was out of bed before I knew it. I threw open the back door to see it more clearly, but Momma said, "Sister, come away from that door and put your robe on."

I hoped the memory of that morning would never leave me. Sunlight was itself still young, and the day had none of the insistence maturity would bring it in a few hours. In my robe and barefoot in the backyard, under cover of going to see about my new beans, I gave myself up to the gentle warmth and thanked God that no matter what evil I had done in my life He had allowed me to live to see this day. Somewhere in my fatalism I had expected to die, accidentally, and never have the chance to walk up the stairs in the auditorium and gracefully receive my hard-earned diploma. Out of God's merciful bosom I had won reprieve.

Bailey came out in his robe and gave me a box wrapped in Christmas paper. He said he had saved his money for months to pay for it. It felt like a box of chocolates, but I knew Bailey wouldn't save money to buy candy when we had all we could want under our noses.

He was as proud of the gift as I. It was a soft-leatherbound copy of a collection of poems by Edgar Allan Poe, or, as Bailey and I called him, "Eap." I turned to "Annabel Lee" and we walked up and down the garden rows, the cool dirt between our toes, reciting the beautifully sad lines.

Momma made a Sunday breakfast although it was only Friday. After we finished the blessing, I opened my eyes to find the watch on my plate. It was a dream of a day. Everything went smoothly and to my credit. I didn't have to be reminded or scolded for anything. Near evening I was too jittery to attend to chores, so Bailey volunteered to do all before his bath.

Days before, we had made a sign for the Store, and as we turned out the lights Momma hung the cardboard over the doorknob. It read clearly: CLOSED. GRADUATION.

My dress fitted perfectly and everyone said that I looked like a sunbeam in it. On the hill, going toward the school, Bailey walked behind with Uncle Willie, who muttered, "Go on, Ju." He wanted him to walk ahead with us because it embarrassed him to have to walk so slowly. Bailey said he'd let the ladies walk together, and the men would bring up the rear. We all laughed, nicely.

Little children dashed by out of the dark like fireflies. Their crepe-paper dresses and butterfly wings were not made for running and we heard more than one rip, dryly, and the regretful "uh uh" that followed.

The school blazed without gaiety. The windows seemed cold and unfriendly from the lower hill. A sense of ill-fated timing crept over me, and if Momma hadn't reached for my hand I would have drifted back to Bailey and Uncle Willie, and possibly beyond. She made a few slow jokes about my feet getting cold, and tugged me along to the now-strange building.

Around the front steps, assurance came back. There were my fellow "greats," the graduating class. Hair brushed back, legs oiled, new dresses and pressed pleats, fresh pocket handkerchiefs and little handbags, all homesewn. Oh, we were up to snuff, all right. I joined my comrades and didn't even see my family go in to find seats in the crowded auditorium.

The school band struck up a march and all classes filed in as had been rehearsed. We stood in front of our seats, as assigned, and on a signal from the choir director, we sat. No sooner had this been accomplished than the band started to play the national anthem. We rose again and sang the song, after which we recited the pledge of allegiance. We remained standing for a brief minute before the choir director and the principal signaled to us, rather desperately I thought, to take our seats. The command was so unusual that our carefully rehearsed and smooth-running machine was thrown off. For a full minute we fumbled for our chairs and bumped into each other awkwardly. Habits change or solidify under pressure, so in our states of nervous tension we had been ready to follow our usual assembly pattern: the American national anthem, then the pledge of allegiance, then the song every Black person I knew called the Negro National Anthem. All done in the same key, with the same passion and most often standing on the same foot.

Finding my seat at last, I was overcome with a presentiment of worse things to come. Something unrehearsed, unplanned, was going to happen, and we were going to be made to look bad. I distinctly remember being explicit in the choice of pronoun. It was "we," the graduating class, the unit, that concerned me then.

The principal welcomed "parents and friends" and asked the Baptist minister to lead us in prayer. His invocation was brief and punchy, and for a second I thought we were getting back on the high road to right action. When the principal came back to the dais, however, his voice had changed. Sounds always affected me profoundly and the principal's voice was one of my favorites. During assembly it melted and lowed weakly into the audience. It had not been in my plan to listen to him, but my curiosity was piqued and I straightened up to give him my attention.

He was talking about Booker T. Washington, our "late great leader," who said we can be as close as the fingers on the hand, etc. . . . Then he said a few vague things about friendship and the friendship of kindly people to those less fortunate than themselves. With that his voice nearly faded, thin, away. Like a river diminishing to a stream and then to a trickle. But he cleared his throat and said, "Our speaker tonight, who is also our friend, came from Texarkana to deliver the commencement address, but due to the irregularity of the train schedule, he's going to, as they say, 'speak and run.' " He said that we understood and wanted the man to know that we were most grateful for the time he was able to give us and then something about how we were willing always to adjust to another's program, and without more ado—"I give you Mr. Edward Donleavy."

Not one but two white men came through the door offstage. The shorter one walked to the speaker's platform, and the tall one moved over to the center seat and sat down. But that was our principal's seat, and already occupied. The dislodged gentleman bounced around for a long breath or two before the Baptist minister gave him his chair, then with more dignity than the situation deserved, the minister walked off the stage.

Donleavy looked at the audience once (on reflection, I'm sure that he wanted only to reassure himself that we were really there), adjusted his glasses and began to read from a sheaf of papers.

He was glad "to be here and to see the work going on just as it was in the other schools."

At the first "Amen" from the audience I willed the offender to immediate death by choking on the word. But Amens and Yes, sir's began to fall around the room like rain through a ragged umbrella.

He told us of the wonderful changes we children in Stamps had in store. The Central School (naturally, the white school was Central) had already been granted improvements that would be in use in the fall. A well-known artist was coming from Little Rock to teach art to them. They were going to have the newest microscopes and chemistry equipment for their laboratory. Mr. Donleavy didn't leave us long in the dark over who made these improvements available to Central High. Nor were we to be ignored in the general betterment scheme he had in mind.

He said that he had pointed out to people at a very high level that one of the first-line football tacklers at Arkansas Agricultural and Mechanical College had graduated from good old Lafayette County Training School. Here fewer Amen's were heard. Those few that did break through lay dully in the air with the heaviness of habit.

He went on to praise us. He went on to say how he had bragged that "one of the best basketball players at Fisk sank his first ball right here at Lafayette County Training School."

The white kids were going to have a chance to become Galileos and Madame Curies and Edisons and Gauguins, and our boys (the girls weren't even in on it) would try to be Jesse Owenses and Joe Louises.

Owens and the Brown Bomber were great heroes in our world, but what school official in the white-goddom of Little Rock had the right to decide that those two men must be our only heroes? Who decided that for Henry Reed to become a scientist he had to work like George Washington Carver, as a bootblack, to buy a lousy microscope? Bailey was obviously always going to be too small to be an athlete, so which concrete angel glued to what country seat had decided that if my brother wanted to become a lawyer he had to first pay penance for his skin by picking cotton and hoeing corn and studying correspondence books at night for twenty years?

The man's dead words fell like bricks around the auditorium and too many settled in my belly. Constrained by hard-learned manners I couldn't look behind me, but to my left and right the proud graduating class of 1940 had dropped their heads. Every girl in my row had found something new to do with her handkerchief. Some folded the tiny squares into love knots, some into triangles, but most were wadding them, then pressing them flat on their yellow laps.

On the dais, the ancient tragedy was being replayed. Professor Parsons sat, a sculptor's reject, rigid. His large, heavy body seemed devoid of will or willingness, and his eyes said he was no longer with us. The other teachers examined the flag (which was draped stage right) or their notes, or the windows which opened on our now-famous playing diamond.

Graduation, the hush-hush magic time of frills and gifts and congratulations and diplomas, was finished for me before my name was called. The accomplishment was nothing. The meticulous maps, drawn in three colors of ink, learning and spelling decasyllabic words, memorizing the whole of *The Rape of Lucrece*—it was for nothing. Donleavy had exposed us.

We were maids and farmers, handymen and washerwomen, and anything higher that we aspired to was farcical and presumptuous.

Then I wished that Gabriel Prosser and Nat Turner had killed all whitefolks in their beds and that Abraham Lincoln had been assassinated before the signing of the Emancipation Proclamation, and that Harriet Tubman had been killed by that blow on her head and Christopher Columbus had drowned in the *Santa María*.

It was awful to be Negro and have no control over my life. It was brutal to be young and already trained to sit quietly and listen to charges brought against my color with no chance of defense. We should all be dead. I thought I should like to see us all dead, one on top of the other. A pyramid of flesh with the whitefolks on the bottom, as the broad base, then the Indians with their silly tomahawks and teepees and wigwams and treaties, the Negroes with their mops and recipes and cotton sacks and spirituals sticking out of their mouths. The

Dutch children should all stumble in their wooden shoes and break their necks. The French should choke to death on the Louisiana Purchase (1803) while silkworms ate all the Chinese with their stupid pigtails. As a species, we were an abomination. All of us.

Donleavy was running for election, and assured our parents that if he won we could count on having the only colored paved playing field in that part of Arkansas. Also—he never looked up to acknowledge the grunts of acceptance—also, we were bound to get some new equipment for the home economics building and the workshop.

He finished, and since there was no need to give any more than the most perfunctory thank-you's, he nodded to the men on the stage, and the tall white man who was never introduced joined him at the door. They left with the attitude that now they were off to something really important. (The graduation ceremonies at Lafayette County Training School had been a mere preliminary.)

The ugliness they left was palpable. An uninvited guest who wouldn't leave. The choir was summoned and sang a modern arrangement of "Onward, Christian Soldiers," with new words pertaining to graduates seeking their place in the world. But it didn't work. Elouise, the daughter of the Baptist minister, recited "Invictus," and I could have cried at the impertinence of "I am the master of my fate, I am the captain of my soul."

My name had lost its ring of familiarity and I had to be nudged to go and receive my diploma. All my preparations had fled. I neither marched up to the stage like a conquering Amazon, nor did I look in the audience for Bailey's nod of approval. Marguerite Johnson, I heard the name again, my honors were read, there were noises in the audience of appreciation, and I took my place on the stage as rehearsed.

I thought about colors I hated: ecru, puce, lavender, beige and black.

There was shuffling and rustling around me, then Henry Reed was giving his valedictory address, "To Be or Not to Be."

Hadn't he heard the whitefolks? We couldn't *be*, so the question was a waste of time. Henry's voice came out clear and strong. I feared to look at him. Hadn't he got the message? There was no "nobler in the mind" for Negroes because the world didn't think we had minds, and they let us know it. "Outrageous fortune"? Now, that was a joke. When the ceremony was over I had to tell Henry Reed some things. That is, if I still cared. Not "rub," Henry, "erase." "Ah, there's the erase." Us.

Henry had been a good student in elocution. His voice rose on tides of promise and fell on waves of warnings. The English teacher had helped him to create a sermon winging through Hamlet's soliloquy. To be a man, a doer, a builder, a leader, or to be a tool, an unfunny joke, a crusher of funky toadstools. I marveled that Henry could go through with the speech as if we had a choice.

I had been listening and silently rebutting each sentence with my eyes closed; then there was a hush, which in an audience warns that something unplanned is happening. I looked up and saw Henry Reed, the conservative, the proper, the A student, turn his back to the audience and turn to us (the proud graduating class of 1940) and sing, nearly speaking,

> "Lift ev'ry voice and sing
> Till earth and heaven ring
> Ring with the harmonies of Liberty . . ."

It was the poem written by James Weldon Johnson. It was the music composed by J. Rosamond Johnson. It was the Negro national anthem. Out of habit we were singing it.

Our mothers and fathers stood in the dark hall and joined the hymn of encouragement. A kindergarten teacher led the small children onto the stage and the buttercups and daisies and bunny rabbits marked time and tried to follow:

> "Stony the road we trod
> Bitter the chastening rod

EVENTS

Felt in the days when hope, unborn, had died.
Yet with a steady beat
Have not our weary feet
Come to the place for which our fathers sighed?"

Every child I knew had learned that song with his ABC's
and along with "Jesus Loves Me This I Know." But I personally had never heard it before. Never heard the words, despite
the thousands of times I had sung them. Never thought they
had anything to do with me.

On the other hand, the words of Patrick Henry had made
such an impression on me that I had been able to stretch myself tall and trembling and say, "I know not what course others
may take, but as for me, give me liberty or give me death."

And now I heard, really for the first time:

"We have come over a way that with tears
    has been watered,
We have come, treading our path through
    the blood of the slaughtered."

While echoes of the song shivered in the air, Henry Reed
bowed his head, said "Thank you," and returned to his place
in the line. The tears that slipped down many faces were not
wiped away in shame.

We were on top again. As always, again. We survived. The
depths had been icy and dark, but now a bright sun spoke to
our souls. I was no longer simply a member of the proud graduating class of 1940; I was a proud member of the wonderful,
beautiful Negro race.

Oh, Black known and unknown poets, how often have your
auctioned pains sustained us? Who will compute the lonely
nights made less lonely by your songs, or the empty pots made
less tragic by your tales?

If we were a people much given to revealing secrets, we
might raise monuments and sacrifice to the memories of our

poets, but slavery cured us of that weakness. It may be enough, however, to have it said that we survive in exact relationship to the dedication of our poets (include preachers, musicians and blues singers).

1. How would you describe the mood Angelou creates when she writes about the morning of graduation day? What details help to establish that mood?

2. How do her feelings change as the day progresses? What causes the change in her feelings? How are her feelings related to her situation as a black student in a segregated school?

3. What perspective on the relations between black people and white people do you think Angelou is trying to give the reader? Does she dramatize these relations through one major incident or through many minor details?

4. To what extent does Angelou narrate the story of the graduation as she would have experienced it as a child? To what extent does she make you aware of herself as a mature woman seeing her past through more experienced eyes?

5. Do you think the end of the episode (the singing of the Negro national anthem) is an effective one? Does it change your sense of the situation and of the mood of the students? How would you explain what Angelou is doing in the last three paragraphs, since she no longer seems to be referring directly or exclusively to her graduation from grade school?

∽ George Plimpton ∽

(1927-   )

*George Plimpton is a member of a wealthy New York family
and was educated at Exeter and Harvard. He became a founder
and the editor-in-chief of the literary magazine* The Paris Review *in 1953, and combined his editorial work with writing
and teaching during the 1950s. Since that time, he has written
several books based on his experiences as an eager but not very
talented amateur athlete trying to play competitively in professional sports.* Paper Lion *(1964) is an account of Plimpton's
participation in the 1963 preseason training camp of the De-
troit Lions, a professional football team. Plimpton endured all
the hardships of an ordinary rookie trying out for the team,
and the selection printed here reports his brief appearance in a
practice scrimmage.*

[GETTING A CHANCE TO PLAY]

In the defensive huddle they did not seem surprised when I
trotted in and joined them. A few helmets turned. Past the helmet bars the eyes looked tired, staring from faces slick
with sweat. We leaned toward Schmidt. "The coverage is
red, George," he said to me. "That means you stick with the
flanker—one on one, you just stay with him. I'll have your ass
if you don't."

The huddle broke and I trotted back to the cornerman position. I looked over at Night Train, close by, fifteen yards or so
away, standing on the sidelines. He offered up an encouraging
smile, a shine of teeth in his dark face.

"It's red," I hissed at him.

"Stick with the flanker," he called back, cupping his hands to his mouth. "Scramble back when he come, and don' give up."

A knot of spectators had collected around him, looking out. All of them, in Bermuda shorts, seemed to have soft-drink bottles in their hands. I avoided their stares. I felt the heat build up inside my helmet. I jogged in place, working the stiffness out, and watched the offensive huddle break finally with a crack of hands in unison and move up to their positions. Jake Greer was the flanker and he came loping out along the line of scrimmage, split ten yards or so from his nearest lineman. I moved along opposite, watching him.

Plum began to call the signals. At the hike of the ball, Greer started toward me with his high, bouncy steps, slow at first, like the slow-motion advance of a klipspringer, coming head on. Then his speed picked up.

"Fetch him!" I heard Night Train yell. "Scrabble aroun'!"

I began to back-pedal, trying to keep my eye on Greer's belt buckle. He sailed up to me, and then cut to my left for the sidelines, with a little grunt, and I could hear the *shu-shu* of his football trousers as he went by, and the creak of his shoulder pads. I was leaning left to the outside when he cut, just chancing he would move for the sidelines on a down-and-out pattern, and when I reached after him I was not too far behind. He pulled up after two or three strides, and I almost cracked into him. The play was over—a pass to the other side had been knocked down by a lineman rearing up. Greer started trotting back to his huddle. I doubted he noticed that I was opposing him at cornerback. I had not seen the pass thrown—the action there as distant as if it had taken place on another practice field. I had no sense of identification with the play. Greer and I had been alone in my zone. My confrontation with him could have been an inadvertent bumbling into the track of a high hurdler out practicing in the evening.

Night Train came hurrying up to his précis. The whole action hadn't taken more than four or five seconds. I was left with a sense of anticlimax.

"I didn't feel part of that play," I said.

"Not too much to quibble," he said. "You scare the man so much they throw to the other side." He grinned. "Now," he said, "you mus' keep the angle so you see the quarterback. Look," he said. He showed me how I should have controlled Greer, a fast crablike scuttle that allowed him to keep facing downfield to watch the play, both the flanker and the quarterback in his field of vision.

I began to see what he meant by the angle of the receiver.

"Get on up there," he said. The defensive huddle was forming. I trotted up in time to hear Joe Schmidt call out a red coverage—man-to-man again.

Back in my position, Night Train called to me from the sidelines: "Jawge, this time, recall to shout out there . . . talk it up."

The spectators, their soft-drink bottles poised, leaned in behind Train, listening.

It was awkward, their being there, but I called to Train nonetheless: "What . . . what sort of thing do I say?"

"Dis*close* what your man doing," he called out. "If they float your zone with people, disclose that. Disclose the defense what is goin' on."

The offense was alternating flankers, so Terry Barr appeared opposite me on the next play. Staring downfield, being sure not to give away a move by a flick of the eyes, he stood upright, with hands on hips, his right leg slightly bent to push off. At the hike signal, he was immediately in high gear, quite unlike Greer's klipspringer bounce; with his sprinter's run, his head steady as he came, he was nearly up to me before I had a chance to plan what to do. "Barr! Barr! Barr!" I called out as he came—an identification being all I could think of to divulge. Having to announce his maneuvers nearly rooted me to the ground. It was difficult to react physically and keep up a shouted commentary at the same time, particularly as I was unsure of the appropriate vocabulary. So Barr went by me very fast, straight downfield, as I stood announcing his name, calling those loonlike wails, "Barr! Barr! Barr!" before I turned and lit out after him, with one arm outstretched in the classic pose of hopeless pursuit.

Once again, the play itself was to be to the opposite sideline, but as Barr came by on his way back he looked at me, perhaps puzzled to have heard the demonic repetition of his name, and he said, "Well, now, look who's here."

"For God's sake, keep it to yourself," I said, breathing hard from the run.

I could see him grinning behind the cage of his helmet, before he turned and began trotting back to his team. Train was at my elbow as I stared after him.

"I think he's got something to disclose," I said. "Things may get a little warmer."

"It's possible. Interception time," Train said hopefully. "You got to scatter them feet around some, and *move*. Yo' look a little stiff las' time."

As I walked in toward Schmidt I watched the offense's huddle form, keeping a nervous eye out for helmets turned in my direction. Most were turned toward Scooter McLean, just on the periphery of the huddle, still criticizing the last play; Aldo Forte was with him, talking to his offensive linemen. A play would run, and the coaches talk about it for five minutes, the players shifting their weight from foot to foot, getting their assignments straight.

Finally, the coaches backed away. "O.K., the last play of the day," George Wilson called out. Schmidt had given the same coverage, and I was back at my position. I saw the helmets duck down in the huddle, then one of them, Plum's, I supposed, rise and face in my direction, just briefly, the egg-smooth surface of the helmet, its cage pointed at me, adding to the sense of that impersonal scrutiny, like a robot monster's, and I thought, "I'm for it. Barr's told Plum."

"Train, I'm a goner," I called out.

"Get yo' angle right," Night Train replied through cupped hands. He offered a last odd flurry of instructions: "Scrabble 'roun'! Don' regard the jukin'! Recovah! Disclose! In*form!*"

The huddle broke. The flanker coming out opposite me was Barr again—being rewarded, the thought crossed my mind, for suggesting that there was a flaw, a serious one, in the defense. His face was no longer expressionless. I suspected a big grin behind the helmet bar.

The strength was lined up to his side. Bent over his center, Plum began the signals, his the only helmet turning as he surveyed the defense in that cataleptic instant, around him the whole frieze of his teammates' helmets motionless, and then he unleashed them as the ball slapped back into his palm, yielding them to the quick imperative of action.

Since in the two preceding plays the concentration of the play had been elsewhere, I had felt alone with the flanker. Now, the whole heave of the play was toward me, flooding the zone not only with confused motion but noise—the quick stomp of feet, the creak of football gear, the strained grunts of effort, the faint *ah-ah-ah*, of piston-stroke regularity, and the stiff calls of instruction, like exhalations. "Inside, inside! Take him inside!" Someone shouted, tearing by me, his cleats thumping in the grass. A call—a parrot squawk—may have erupted from me. My feet splayed in hopeless confusion as Barr came directly toward me, feinting in one direction, and then stopping suddenly, drawing me toward him for the possibility of a buttonhook pass, and as I leaned almost off balance toward him, he turned and came on again, downfield, moving past me at high speed, leaving me poised on one leg, reaching for him, trying to grab at him despite the illegality, anything to keep him from getting by. But he was gone, and by the time I had turned to set out after him, he had ten yards on me, drawing away fast with his sprinter's run, his legs pinwheeling, the row of cleats flicking up a faint wake of dust behind.

"Ball! Ball! Ball!" I could hear Night Train yelling.

I looked up as I ran, and straight above, against the sky, I could see the football heading downfield, as high as a punt it seemed—the bomb!—and I put up a hand instinctively though the ball must have been twenty feet over my head. It was astonishingly distinct—I suppose because my eyes were concentrated on it with such longing—the white laces turning, a faint wobble to its nose, even the literature on it discernable, the trade name "Duke" turning, DUKE, DUKE, DUKE. It sailed downfield, then seemed to drift down, and there was Barr running under it, barely having to reach up for it as he collected it to him. He kept on sprinting with the football, across the goal line, never looking back, finally slowing to a trot as he headed for the gym.

1. *However much you know about football, choose at least two passages where you feel Plimpton gives you a sense of the game you were never conscious of before. Then examine the passages in order to decide what aspects of the game Plimpton has emphasized and how as a writer he has made them vivid and interesting to you.*
2. *Plimpton obviously needs to characterize himself as someone who is an amateur, not a true insider in the world of professional football. Choose at least two passages where you feel that the football world is being described by someone who comes from another background and explain how this different perspective changes the way in which football is seen.*
3. *Contrast the way Plimpton writes about a seasoned professional, Night Train Lane, and the way he writes about himself. What differences do you find in the portraits?*
4. *How does Plimpton manage to keep you interested in the episode? Do you find that he creates some suspense? If so, how?*
5. *Who do you think Plimpton has in mind as an audience when he writes: dedicated football fans or people who know very little about football? Or do you think he is appealing to both in different ways? Explain your choice.*

～ Mary Mebane ～

(1933-   )

Mary Mebane grew up in the back country of North Carolina. She attended a black college in the state and went on to earn her doctorate at the University of North Carolina in Chapel Hill. She now teaches at the University of Wisconsin. Her autobiography, Mary *(1981), portrays her struggle to overcome the limitations of her early life as a poor black woman in the rural South. This selection presents her account of her first job, when, as a teenager, she was hired to process green tobacco at a cigarette factory.*

[SUMMER JOB]

It was summer 1949, and I needed a job. Everybody tried to "get on" at the tobacco factory during "green season," when lots of extra workers were hired to "work up" new tobacco—that is, process it for cigarettes. Some people made their chief money of the year during the ten-to-twelve-week green season. The factory paid more money than days work, so lots of women gladly left their housekeeping jobs and went to the factories. In Durham there were two major factories and several smaller ones. The major factories worked up tobacco, but they also made cigarettes and had a shipping department and research laboratories. The smaller factories mainly worked up tobacco for the larger ones, in Durham and in other cities. Of the two major factories in Durham, Liggett and Myers did relatively little hiring in green season; it had a stable year-round force and gave preference to its former workers during the season. My mother worked there. The American Tobacco Company, the other factory, hired a great many temporary workers.

I was told that my best bet was the American. I wasn't eighteen, but I was tall and stocky and could pass for older, and besides, they never asked to see your birth certificate; so, a few months short of my sixteenth birthday, I went to get work at the American, makers of Lucky Strike cigarettes and other brands. From the start, I knew that I wouldn't get a job on the "cigarette side." That was easy work, and I was told that mostly whites worked over there. I would get a chance on the belt on the "tobacco side." Several women in the neighborhood who had worked at the American during the green season instructed me about how to get on. I was told to get there early and stand on the sidewalk in front of the employment office and just as close as possible to it, so that when they came out to select workers I would be easily seen. Also I was told to say, if they asked me, that I had worked there before. Nobody ever checked the records. So, on the morning that hiring began for green season, I went to Durham.

I accompanied neighbors who had received postcards informing them they could come to work. They left me outside while they went in. I was dismayed, for the whole street in front of the employment office was filled with black women. They crowded around the brick porch leading to the employment office; they were on the sidewalk; they overflowed the street and covered the sidewalk behind. They were directly in front of the office, spreading out fanwise in both directions from it. Nobody was allowed on the porch except those who already had cards.

A pudgy white man with a cigar in his mouth came and stood on the porch and said, "All those who have cards, come forward." Those who had cards held them up over their heads and started pushing through the crowd. Sometimes they had to remonstrate with some stubborn woman who refused to give way: "Let me pass, please! Move out of my way!" Slowly the one blocking her path would grudgingly give ground. Others quickly surged forward, trying to fill the space that was left, taking advantage of the confusion to try to push even nearer the office. When the favored ones got in, there began the long wait for the man to come back and start selecting more "hands" from the crowd of women left standing there. The crowd continued to grow bigger by the minute as new arrivals came.

You could tell the veterans from the rookies by the way they were dressed. The knowledgeable ones had their heads covered by kerchiefs, so that if they were hired, tobacco dust wouldn't get in their hair; they had on clean dresses that by now were faded and shapeless, so that if they were hired they wouldn't get tobacco dust and grime on their best clothes. Those who were trying for the first time had their hair freshly done and wore attractive dresses; they wanted to make a good impression. But the dresses couldn't be seen at the distance that many were standing from the employment office, and they were soon crumpled in the crush.

Some women looked as if they had large families; they looked tired and anxious, but determined. Some looked single; they had on lipstick and eyebrow pencil, and some even wore black patent-leather pumps with stockings.

The morning passed and the sun got hotter; there was no shade on the sidewalks or in the street. The street stayed full, except when trucks edged their way in and the crowd gave way slowly.

After a while, the pudgy white man with the big cigar came to the door and stood and looked. Instantly the whole mass surged forward. The shorter ones tried to stand on tiptoe to be seen over the heads of their taller sisters. Hands shot up in the air, trying to make him notice them. Those at the front who'd gotten shoved against the brick porch shouted, "Stop pushing, stop pushing, ya'll! You're hurting me!"

Finally the pudgy man spoke, standing on the porch with

his cigar in his mouth. "Until ya'll stop pushing and shoving I'm not gonna hire none of ya'll." Then he stood for a moment to see what effect his words were having on the crowd. Sensing that they were having no discernible effect, the man went back inside, and the surge forward stopped for the time being.

The women stood and stood; the sun grew hotter. Some grew tired of waiting: "I left by baby with a neighbor. I told her that if I didn't get on I'd be back before twelve. I gotta go." Others left, saying that they were "tired of this mess." One woman said, "All ya'll might as well go home. He's got his number for today. Come back tomorrow when they'll know how many more they'll need." At that, even more women faded away. The mass shrunk, but it was still a mass.

Finally, shortly before noon, the pudgy man came quietly to the porch and pointed quickly to two women standing close by. Before the crowd knew people were getting on, the two women were on the porch and in the hall, following him. The crowd surged forward but the man was gone. "What time is it?" someone said. "Nigh noon" was the answer and everyone seemed to agree that there would be no more hiring until one or two o'clock, after lunch.

Some sat right down on the sidewalk up against the building and took out their sandwiches. Others drifted away from the crowd and down to a nearby luncheonette for cold drinks and sandwiches. I had a tomato sandwich that had become soggy in the press and the heat. I went with some other women far down the street to sit on the grass and eat my sandwich. They talked in front of me as if I were grown, so I knew that I would have no trouble if I got hired. What they said was so interesting that the crowd was re-forming in front of the employment office in the hot, boiling sun before I knew it.

Word came over the grapevine that they needed some more helpers and would hire some more today. This gave everybody courage, so the crowd grew calm. Then the pudgy man came again. He made an announcement: "Any shoving, any pushing, and there'll be no more hiring today." The women grew quiet. Those who had been impatient hadn't come back from lunch, leaving those who were determined to get on.

The man selected two more women; the crowd gave a little surge forward, but nothing like the shoving and pushing of the morning. In another hour he came back for one more, and soon the word came over the grapevine that we might as well go home. The crowd started fading away, but not the diehards. They didn't believe the grapevine and were determined to stay to see what was going to happen. I had no choice; I was staying until the people I rode with got off from work. It was now three o'clock and we all had been standing in the sun since eight o'clock in the morning. When the neighbors I was waiting for came, they said, "Don't worry. You'll get on tomorrow." Besides, they would go in earlier now that they were on.

I lay in bed that night, too tired to do anything else, and thought about the day. Hundreds of women had stood in the hot sun for seven or eight hours under really bad conditions. There was no bathroom, no drinking fountain, no place to sit down. Those who had to leave lost their place in line and, thus, their chance for a job. Why was this? Because they needed work and the factory didn't need them. The factory had more hands available than it could use. That is why they could treat the surplus as they chose, and there was nothing that the women could do about it.

The next day I was there early and standing in place by the steps before the employment office opened. I recognized some of the faces from the day before, and there were some that looked new to me. The crowd stretched out as far as it had the previous day. The sun was already hot when the pudgy man came to the platform with his cigar in his mouth. "Anyone here with a card?" he called. A few women who hadn't come in yesterday came forward. He went back inside.

I was close enough to see into the hall inside and the glass-faced side of the employment office. It was shut off from the hall by glass because it was air-conditioned. There was a man, so slim and shapely that he looked like a girl, who came to the door and watched as the pudgy man came back and stood over the crowd. He watched the crowd surge forward, and he stepped back a little as if all the energy would wash over him. It seemed to give him great satisfaction to see the sea of black women struggling forward, trying to get a job in his factory; he'd stand and watch for a while, then turn and go into the air-conditioned office. At first the women thought that he was going to do some of the hiring and they pressed close to him and looked up. But once they'd determined that he had nothing to do with the hiring, he ceased to exist for them and they paid him no more attention.

More and more women were hired; the pudgy man would point here and there, then take them off. In an hour or so, he'd come back and hire one or two more. Lunch came and the crowd scattered. I'd brought a meat sandwich, hoping that it wouldn't get crumpled and soggy like my tomato sandwich the day before. I knew enough not to leave my good place near the porch, so I ate standing in the hot sun, along with the rest of the women who had good places. I had been listening to the crowd for two days, so now I knew the words and phrases that would make me sound like a veteran, and I employed them. Evidently nothing was wrong with what I said, for no one looked at me "funny."

Around two o'clock the pudgy man came back and his eye fell on me and the woman standing beside me. He motioned us in. I was now a factory hand.

The air-conditioning in the office chilled me after the heat of the street as I gave the necessary information. I made up a birthday and nobody questioned it. Then I was taken to a "line" on the first floor.

It was a cavernous room, long and tall. The man who led me there called to the boss, who came over to tell me what to do, but the machinery was so loud that I couldn't hear him and I was so startled by my new surroundings that I didn't really concentrate on what he said. I was afraid to take a deep breath, for the room was so cloudy with tobacco dust that brown particles hung in the air. I held my breath as long as I could and then took a deep breath. I started to cough and my eyes watered. I saw lots of women and some men, each doing a task seemingly unrelated to the others', but I knew that there must be a plan.

My job had something to do with a conveyor belt. It was shaped like a child's sliding board, only it had a deep trough and it moved. Shredded tobacco was on this belt—I think that it came from upstairs—and my job was to sit by the belt and pick out the pieces whose stems were too large. I tried to determine what kind of stem was too large, for the belt was constantly moving, and obviously I couldn't pick out every single stem on the belt. I looked at the others, but I couldn't see what method they were using. I was in misery, for this was my first "public" job and I didn't want to do badly on it. I did the best that I could, but soon the boss came and told me he was going to put me on the belt upstairs. I was glad, for my back hurt from bending over, trying to pick out stems. Maybe I could do better upstairs.

The air was full of tobacco dust there, too, but not as much as it had been downstairs; also, it was quieter. This belt moved horizontally, from right to left; women stood parallel to it, two women facing each other on the same side of the belt, with a barrel of tied tobacco leaves in front of them. They worked in pairs, taking the tobacco from the barrel, the hogshead, and putting it on the belt. The important thing, as my partner explained to me, was to make sure that the tied ends faced me, for the belt was on its way to the cutter and the machine would cut off the hard tied end—which would not go into the making of cigarettes—while the leaves went another way.

The job seemed easy enough as I picked up bundle after bundle of tobacco and put it on the belt, careful to turn the knot end toward me so that it would be placed right to go under the cutting machine. Gradually, as we worked up our

tobacco, I had to bend more, for as we emptied the hogshead
we had to stoop over to pick up the tobacco, then straighten
up and put it on the belt just right. Then I discovered the
hard part of the job: the belt kept moving at the same speed
all the time and if the leaves were not placed on the belt at
the same tempo there would be a big gap where your bundle
should have been. So that meant that when you got down
lower, you had to bend down, get the tobacco, straighten up
fast, make sure it was placed knot end toward you, place it on
the belt, and bend down again. Soon you were bending down,
up; down, up; down, up. All along the line, heads were bobbing—down, up; down, up—until you finished the barrel.
Then you could rest until the men brought you another one.

To make sure that you kept the belt filled, there was a line
boss, a little blond man who looked scared most of the time.
He'd walk up and down behind you, saying, "Put the tobacco
on the belt, girls. Put the tobacco on the belt. Too many empty
spaces, girls. Too many empty spaces." You'd be working
away, when suddenly behind you you'd hear this voice: "Put
the tobacco on the belt, girls. Put the tobacco on the belt. No
empty spaces, girls. No empty spaces." I noticed that no one
paid him any mind. He could be standing right by the belt
talking, and it was as if he were invisible. The line kept moving, and the women kept bending and putting tobacco on the
belt.

Over him was the floor boss. He had charge of all the operations on the floor. He was the line boss's boss, and the line
boss was clearly afraid of him. Over the floor boss was the big
boss, who seldom came on the floor unless there was real trouble. Most of the women had never seen him, but same had and
said that he was mean as the devil.

I bent and straightened and bent and straightened and
thought that my back would break. Once in the afternoon
I got a ten-minute break in the "house" (toilet). I went there
and collapsed into a chair.

That evening on the way home I tried to talk cheerfully

to my neighbors about the new job. They were quite pleased that I had gotten on. That was the one thing that kept me from quitting. I didn't want to let them down by telling them that I found the work killing. So I made up my mind to stay, no matter what, for I knew it was a short season.

1. *Why does Mebane devote so much of her account to the day she is not hired? Does it prepare for her story of the following day, when she actually begins work?*

2. *What details does Mebane use to introduce the scene and portray the system of hiring? What impression of the company and its ways does she give?*

3. *How does Mebane portray the actual work she is assigned to do? What parts of her account reflect the need to describe work that would not be familiar to her readers? What parts communicate Mebane's attitude toward her job?*

4. *Does Mebane suggest that she is in any way different from the other women who are looking for work? How does her story reflect the viewpoint of someone who has never worked before? How does it reflect the viewpoint of a woman who has escaped the restrictions of the kind of life she describes?*

∽ Lincoln Steffens ∽

(1866-1936)

Lincoln Steffens became famous in the early part of the twentieth century through his work as a crusading newspaper and magazine journalist. He grew up in an affluent family in California and was a restless and unconventional student at universities in America and Europe. When he returned to the United States, he worked as a newspaper reporter and became interested in municipal reform, writing a number of exposés of political corruption. The book by Steffens most widely read today is his Autobiography (*1931*), *a lively and entertaining narrative from which this selection, a memory of a boyhood Christmas, is taken.*

A MISERABLE, MERRY CHRISTMAS

What interested me in our new neighborhood was not the school, nor the room I was to have in the house all to myself, but the stable which was built back of the house. My father let me direct the making of a stall, a little smaller than the other stalls, for my pony, and I prayed and hoped and my sister Lou believed that that meant that I would get the pony, perhaps for Christmas. I pointed out to her that there were three other stalls and no horses at all. This I said in order that she should answer it. She could not. My father, sounded, said that some day we might have horses and a cow; meanwhile a stable added to the value of a house. "Some day" is a pain to a boy who lives in and knows only "now." My good little sisters, to comfort me, remarked that Christmas was coming, but Christmas was always coming and grown-ups were always talking about it, asking you what you wanted and then giving you what they wanted you to have. Though everybody knew what I wanted, I told them all again. My mother knew that I told God, too, every night. I wanted a pony, and to make sure that they understood, I declared that I wanted nothing else.

"Nothing but a pony?" my father asked.

"Nothing," I said.

"Not even a pair of high boots?"

That was hard. I did want boots, but I stuck to the pony. "No, not even boots."

"Nor candy? There ought to be something to fill your stocking with, and Santa Claus can't put a pony into a stocking."

That was true, and he couldn't lead a pony down the chimney either. But no. "All I want is a pony," I said. "If I can't have a pony, give me nothing, nothing."

Now I had been looking myself for the pony I wanted, going to sales stables, inquiring of horsemen, and I had seen several that would do. My father let me "try" them. I tried so many ponies that I was learning fast to sit a horse. I chose several, but my father always found some fault with them. I was in despair. When Christmas was at hand I had given up all hope of a pony, and on Christmas Eve I hung up my stocking along with my sisters', of whom, by the way, I now had three. I haven't mentioned them or their coming because, you understand, they were girls, and girls, young girls, counted for nothing in my manly life. They did not mind me either; they were so happy that Christmas Eve that I caught some of their merriment. I speculated on what I'd get; I hung up the biggest stocking I had, and we all went reluctantly to bed to wait till morning. Not to sleep; not right away. We were told that we must not only sleep promptly, we must not wake up till seven-thirty the next morning—or if we did, we must not go to the fireplace for our Christmas. Impossible.

We did sleep that night, but we woke up at six A.M. We lay in our beds and debated through the open doors whether to obey till, say, half-past six. Then we bolted. I don't know who started it, but there was a rush. We all disobeyed; we raced to disobey and get first to the fireplace in the front room downstairs. And there they were, the gifts, all sorts of wonderful things, mixed-up piles of presents; only, as I disentangled the mess, I saw that my stocking was empty; it hung limp; not a thing in it; and under and around it—nothing. My sisters had knelt down, each by her pile of gifts; they were squealing with delight, till they looked up and saw me standing there in my nightgown with nothing. They left their piles to come to me and look with me at my empty place. Nothing. They felt my stocking: nothing.

I don't remember whether I cried at that moment, but my sisters did. They ran with me back to my bed, and there we all cried till I became indignant. That helped some. I got up, dressed, and driving my sisters away, I went alone out into the yard, down to the stable, and there, all by myself, I wept. My mother came out to me by and by; she found me in my pony stall, sobbing on the floor, and she tried to comfort me. But I heard my father outside; he had come part way with her, and she was having some sort of angry quarrel with him. She tried to comfort me; besought me to come to breakfast. I could not; I wanted no comfort and no breakfast. She left me and went on into the house with sharp words for my father.

I don't know what kind of a breakfast the family had. My sisters said it was "awful." They were ashamed to enjoy their own toys. They came to me, and I was rude. I ran away from them. I went around to the front of the house, sat down on the steps, and, the crying over, I ached. I was wronged, I was hurt—I can feel now what I felt then, and I am sure that if one could see the wounds upon our hearts, there would be found still upon mine a scar from that terrible Christmas morning. And my father, the practical joker, he must have been hurt, too, a little. I saw him looking out of the window. He was watching me or something for an hour or two, drawing back the curtain never so little lest I catch him, but I saw his face, and I think I can see now the anxiety upon it, the worried impatience.

After—I don't know how long—surely an hour or two—I was brought to the climax of my agony by the sight of a man riding a pony down the street, a pony and a brand-new saddle; the most beautiful saddle I ever saw, and it was a boy's saddle; the man's feet were not in the stirrups; his legs were too long. The outfit was perfect; it was the realization of all my dreams, the answer to all my prayers. A fine new bridle, with a light curb bit. And the pony! As he drew near, I saw that the pony was really a small horse, what we called an Indian pony, a bay, with black mane and tail, and one white foot and a white star on his forehead. For such a horse as that I would have given, I could have forgiven, anything.

But the man, a disheveled fellow with a blackened eye and a fresh-cut face, came along, reading the numbers on the houses, and, as my hopes—my impossible hopes—rose, he looked at our door and passed by, he and the pony, and the saddle and the bridle. Too much. I fell upon the steps, and having wept before, I broke now into such a flood of tears that I was a floating wreck when I heard a voice.

"Say, kid," it said, "do you know a boy named Lennie Steffens?"

I looked up. It was the man on the pony, back again, at our horse block.

"Yes," I spluttered through my tears. "That's me."

"Well," he said, "then this is your horse. I've been looking all over for you and your house. Why don't you put your number where it can be seen?"

"Get down," I said, running out to him.

He went on saying something about "ought to have got here at seven o'clock; told me to bring the nag here and tie him to your post and leave him for you. But, hell, I got into a drunk—and a fight—and a hospital, and—"

"Get down," I said.

He got down, and he boosted me up to the saddle. He offered

to fit the stirrups to me, but I didn't want him to. I wanted to ride.

"What's the matter with you?" he said, angrily. "What you crying for? Don't you like the horse? He's a dandy, this horse. I know him of old. He's fine at cattle; he'll drive 'em alone."

I hardly heard, I could scarcely wait, but he persisted. He adjusted the stirrups, and then, finally, off I rode, slowly, at a walk, so happy, so thrilled, that I did not know what I was doing. I did not look back at the house or the man, I rode off up the street, taking note of everything—of the reins, of the pony's long mane, of the carved leather saddle. I had never seen anything so beautiful. And mine! I was going to ride up past Miss Kay's house. But I noticed on the horn of the saddle some stains like rain-drops, so I turned and trotted home, not to the house but to the stable. There was the family, father, mother, sisters, all working for me, all happy. They had been putting in place the tools of my new business: blankets, curry-comb, brush, pitchfork—everything, and there was hay in the loft.

"What did you come back so soon for?" somebody asked. "Why didn't you go on riding?"

I pointed to the stains. "I wasn't going to get my new saddle rained on," I said. And my father laughed. "It isn't raining," he said. "Those are not rain-drops."

"They are tears," my mother gasped, and she gave my father a look which sent him off to the house. Worse still, my mother offered to wipe away the tears still running out of my eyes. I gave her such a look as she had given him, and she went off after my father, drying her own tears. My sisters remained and we all unsaddled the pony, put on his halter, led him to his stall, tied and fed him. It began really to rain; so all the rest of that memorable day we curried and combed that pony. The girls plaited his mane, forelock, and tail, while I pitchforked hay to him and curried and brushed, curried and brushed. For a change we brought him out to drink; we led him up and down, blanketed like a race-horse; we took turns at that. But the best, the most inexhaustible fun, was to clean him. When we went reluctantly to our midday Christmas dinner, we all smelt of horse, and my sisters had to wash their faces and hands. I was asked to, but I wouldn't, till my mother bade me look in the mirror. Then I washed up—quick. My face was caked with the muddy lines of tears that had coursed over my cheeks to my mouth. Having washed away that shame, I ate my dinner, and as I ate I grew hungrier and hungrier. It was my first meal that day, and as I filled up on the turkey and the stuffing, the cranberries and the pies, the fruit and the nuts—as I swelled, I could laugh. My mother said I still choked and sobbed now and then, but I laughed, too; I saw and enjoyed my sisters' presents till—I had to go out and attend to my pony, who was there, really and truly there, the promise, the beginning, of a happy double life. And—I went and looked to make sure—there was the saddle, too, and the bridle.

But that Christmas, which my father had planned so carefully, was it the best or the worst I ever knew? He often asked me that; I never could answer as a boy. I think now that it was both. It covered the whole distance from broken-hearted misery to bursting happiness—too fast. A grown-up could hardly have stood it.

1. What are the characteristics of the young "Lennie Steffens"? Does he strike you as a familiar or as an unusual type of child? Does Steffens take pains to make him attractive or not?

2. What details does Steffens use to make the boy's anguish clear to the reader? How does he show the transition to delight when the boy gets his Christmas wish?

3. What kind of description of family life does Steffens offer? How are Steffens' parents presented in this episode. Does Steffens look back critically on his younger self or not?

4. How does Steffens make the event he describes dramatic? At the end, he refers to that Christmas Day as the "best" and the "worst." Does his narrative make you believe that such extreme language is justified?

∾ Piri Thomas ∾

(1928-   )

Piri Thomas was born in Spanish Harlem. Growing up in a world of gangs, drugs, and petty crime, he became an addict while in his teens, was convicted of attempted armed robbery in 1950, and served six years of a fifteen-year sentence. Thomas has since worked for and organized drug rehabilitation programs in New York and Puerto Rico and has begun a career as a writer. Down These Mean Streets *(1967), from which this selection is taken, was his first book. This incident begins with an account of Thomas's difficulties, as a Puerto Rican schoolboy, when his family moves into a predominantly Italian block in one of the poorer sections of New York City.*

ALIEN TURF

I got through the days trying to play it cool and walk on by Rocky and his boys like they weren't there. One day I passed them and nothing was said. I started to let out my breath. I felt great; I hadn't been seen. Then someone yelled in a high, girlish voice, "Yoo-hoo . . . Hey, *paisan* . . . we see yoo . . ." And right behind that voice came a can of evaporated milk—whoosh, clatter. I walked cool for ten steps then started running like mad.

This crap kept up for a month. They tried to shake me up. Every time they threw something at me, it was just to see me jump. I decided that the next fucking time they threw something at me I was gonna play bad-o and not run. That next time came about a week later. Momma sent me off the stoop to the Italian market on 115th Street and First Avenue, deep in Italian country. Man, that was stompin' territory. But I went, walking in the style which I had copped from the colored cats I had seen, a swinging and stepping down hard at every step. Those cats were so down and cool that just walking made a way-out sound.

Ten minutes later I was on my way back with Momma's stuff. I got to the corner of First Avenue and 114th Street and crushed myself right into Rocky and his fellas.

"Well-l, fellas," Rocky said. "Lookee who's here."

I didn't like the sounds coming out of Rocky's fat mouth. And I didn't like the sameness of the shitty grins spreading all over the boys' faces. But I thought, *No more! No more! I ain't gonna run no more.* Even so, I looked around, like for some kind of Jesus miracle to happen. I was always looking for miracles to happen.

"Say, *paisan*," one guy said, "you even buying from us *paisans*, eh? Man, you must wantta be Italian."

Before I could bite that dopey tongue of mine, I said, "I wouldn't be a guinea on a motherfucking bet."

"Wha-at?" said Rocky, really surprised. I didn't blame him; I was surprised myself. His finger began digging a hole in his ear, like he hadn't heard me right. "Wha-at? Say that again?"

I could feel a thin hot wetness cutting itself down my leg. I had been so ashamed of being so damned scared that I had peed on myself. And then I wasn't scared any more; I felt a fuck-it-all attitude. I looked real bad at Rocky and said, "Ya heard me. I wouldn't be a guinea on a bet."

"Ya little sonavabitch, we'll kick the shit outta ya," said one guy, Tony, who had made a habit of asking me if I had any sen-your-ritas for sisters.

"Kick the shit outta me yourself if you got any heart, you motherfuckin' fucker," I screamed at him. I felt kind of happy, the kind of feeling that you get only when you got heart.

Big-mouth Tony just swung out, and I swung back and heard all of Momma's stuff plopping all over the street. My fist hit Tony smack dead in the mouth. He was so mad he threw a fist at me from about three feet away. I faked and jabbed and did fancy dance steps. Big-mouth put a stop to all that with a punch in my mouth. I heard the home cheers of "Yea, yea, bust that spic wide open!" Then I bloodied Tony's nose. He blinked and sniffed without putting his hands to his nose, and I remembered Poppa telling me, "Son, if you're ever fighting somebody an' you punch him in the nose, and he just blinks an' sniffs without holding his nose, you can do one of two things: fight like hell or run like hell—'cause that cat's a fighter."

Big-mouth came at me and we grabbed each other and pushed and pulled and shoved. *Poppa*, I thought, *I ain't gonna cop out. I'm a fighter, too.* I pulled away from Tony and blew my fist into his belly. He puffed and butted my nose with his head. I sniffed back. *Poppa, I didn't put my hands to my nose.* I hit Tony again in that same weak spot. He bent over in the middle and went down to his knees.

Big-mouth got up as fast as he could, and I was thinking how much heart he had. But I ran toward him like my life depended on it; I wanted to cool him. Too late, I saw his hand grab a fistful of ground asphalt which had been piled nearby to fix a pothole in the street. I tried to duck; I should have closed my eyes instead. The shitty-gritty stuff hit my face, and I felt the scrappy pain make itself a part of my eyes. I screamed and grabbed for two eyes with one hand, while the other I beat some kind of helpless tune on air that just couldn't be hurt. I heard Rocky's voice shouting, "Ya scum bag, ya didn't have to fight the spic dirty; you could've fucked him up fair and square!" I couldn't see. I heard a fist hit a face, then Big-mouth's voice: "Whatta ya hittin' me for?" and then Rocky's voice: *"Putana!* I ought ta knock all your fuckin' teeth out."

I felt hands grabbing at me between my screams. I punched out. *I'm gonna get killed*, I thought. Then I heard many voices:

"Hold it, kid." "We ain't gonna hurt ya." "Je-*sus*, don't rub your eyes." "Ooooohhhh, shit, his eyes is fulla that shit."

You're fuckin' right, I thought, *and it hurts like* coño.

I heard a woman's voice now: "Take him to a hospital." And an old man asked: "How did it happen?"

"Momma, Momma," I cried.

"Comon, kid," Rocky said, taking my hand. "Lemme take ya home." I fought for the right to rub my eyes. "Grab his other hand, Vincent," Rocky said. I tried to rub my eyes with my eyelids. I could feel hurt tears cutting down my cheeks. "Come on, kid, we ain't gonna hurt ya," Rocky tried to assure me. "Swear to our mudders. We just wanna take ya home."

I made myself believe him, and trying not to make pain noises, I let myself be led home. I wondered if I was gonna be blind like Mr. Silva, who went around from door to door selling dish towels and brooms, his son leading him around.

"You okay, kid?" Rocky asked.

"Yeah," what was left of me said.

"A-huh," mumbled Big-mouth.

"He got much heart for a nigger," somebody else said.

A *spic*, I thought.

"For anybody," Rocky said. "Here we are, kid," he added. "Watch your step."

I was like carried up the steps. "What's your apartment number?" Rocky asked.

"One-B—inna back—ground floor," I said, and I was led there. Somebody knocked on Momma's door. Then I heard running feet and Rocky's voice yelling back, "Don't rat, huh, kid?" And I was alone.

I heard the door open and Momma say, "*Bueno*, Piri, come in." I didn't move. I couldn't. There was a long pause; I could hear Momma's fright. "My God," she said finally. "What's happened?" Then she took a closer look. "Ai-eeee," she screamed. *Dios mío!*

"I was playing with some kids, Momma," I said, "an' I got some dirt in my eyes." I tried to make my voice come out without the pain, like a man.

"*Dios eterno*—your eyes!"

"What's the matter? What's the matter?" Poppa called from the bedroom.

"*Está ciego!*" Momma screamed. "He is blind!"

I heard Poppa knocking things over as he came running. Sis began to cry. Blind, hurting tears were jumping out of my eyes. "Whattya mean, he's blind?" Poppa said as he stormed into the kitchen. "What happened?" Poppa's voice was both scared and mad.

"Playing, Poppa."

"Whatta ya mean, 'playing'?" Poppa's English sounded different when he got warm.

"Just playing, Poppa."

"Playing? Playing got all that dirt in your eyes? I bet my ass. Them damn Ee-ta-liano kids ganged up on you again." Poppa squeezed my head between the fingers of one hand. "That settles it—we're moving outta this damn section, outta this damn block, outta this damn shit."

Shit, I thought, *Poppa's sure cursin' up a storm.* I could hear him slapping the side of his leg, like he always did when he got real mad.

"Son," he said, "you're gonna point them out to me."

"Point who out, Poppa? I was playin' an'—"

"Stop talkin' to him and take him to the hospital!" Momma screamed.

"*Pobrecito*, poor Piri," cooed my little sister.

"You sure, son?" Poppa asked. "You was only playing?"

"Shit, Poppa, I said I was."

Smack—Poppa was so scared and mad, he let it out in a slap to the side of my face.

"*Bestia!* Ani-*mul!*" Momma cried. "He's blind, and you hit him!"

"I'm sorry, son, I'm sorry," Poppa said in a voice like almost-crying. I heard him running back into the bedroom, yelling, "Where's my pants?"

Momma grabbed away fingers that were trying to wipe away the hurt in my eyes. "*Caramba*, no rub, no rub," she said, kissing me. She told Sis to get a rag and wet it with cold water.

Poppa came running back into the kitchen. "Let's go, son, let's go. Jesus! I didn't mean to smack ya, I really didn't," he said, his big hand rubbing and grabbing my hair gently.

"Here's the rag, Momma," said Sis.

"What's that for?" asked Poppa.

"To put on his eyes," Momma said.

I heard the smack of a wet rag, *blapt*, against the kitchen wall. "We can't put nothing on his eyes. It might make them worse. Come on, son," Poppa said nervously, lifting me up in his big arms. I felt like a little baby, like I didn't hurt so bad. I wanted to stay there, but I said, "Let me down, Poppa, I ain't no kid."

"Shut up," Poppa said softly. "I know you ain't, but it's faster this way."

"Which hospeetal are you taking him to?" Momma asked.

"Nearest one," Poppa answered as we went out the door. He carried me through the hall and out into the street, where the bright sunlight made a red hurting color through the crap in my eyes. I heard voices on the stoop and on the sidewalk: "Is that the boy?"

"A-huh. He's probably blinded."

"We'll get a cab, son," Poppa said. His voice loved me. I heard Rocky yelling from across the street, "We're pulling for ya, kid. Remember what we . . ." The rest was lost to Poppa's long legs running down to the corner of Third Avenue. He hailed a taxi and we zoomed off toward Harlem Hospital. I felt the cab make all kinds of sudden stops and turns.

"How do you feel, *hijo?*" Poppa asked.

"It burns like hell."

"You'll be okay," he said, and as an afterthought added, "Don't curse, son."

I heard cars honking and the Third Avenue el roaring above us. I knew we were in Puerto Rican turf, 'cause I could hear our language.

"Son."

"Yeah, Poppa."

"Don't rub your eyes, fer Christ sake." He held my skinny wrists in his one hand, and everything got quiet between us.

The cab got to Harlem Hospital. I heard change being handled and the door opening and Poppa thanking the cabbie for getting here fast. "Hope the kid'll be okay," the driver said.

I will be, I thought. *I ain't gonna be like Mr. Silva.*

Poppa took me in his arms again and started running. "Where's emergency, mister?" he asked someone.

"To your left and straight away," said a voice.

"Thanks a lot," Poppa said, and we were running again. "Emergency?" Poppa said when we stopped.

"Yes, sir," said a girl's voice. "What's the matter?"

"My boy's got his eyes full of ground-up tar an'—"

"What's the matter?" said a man's voice.

"Youngster with ground tar in his eyes, doctor."

"We'll take him, mister. You just put him down here and go with the nurse. She'll take down the information. Uh, you the father?"

"That's right, doctor."

"Okay, just put him down here."

"Poppa, don't leave me," I cried.

"Sh, son, I ain't leaving you. I'm just going to fill out some papers, an' I'll be right back."

I nodded my head up and down and was wheeled away. When the rolling stretcher stopped, somebody stuck a needle in me and I got sleepy and started thinking about Rocky and his boys, and Poppa's slap, and how great Poppa was, and how my eyes didn't hurt no more . . .

I woke up in a room blind with darkness. The only lights were the ones inside my head. I put my fingers to my eyes and felt bandages. "Let them be, sonny," said a woman's voice.

I wanted to ask the voice if they had taken my eyes out, but I didn't. I was afraid the voice would say yes.

"Let them be, sonny," the nurse said, pulling my hand away

from the bandages. "You're all right. The doctor put the bandages on to keep the light out. They'll be off real soon. Don't you worry none, sonny."

I wished she would stop calling me sonny. "Where's Poppa?" I asked cool-like.

"He's outside, sonny. Would you like me to send him in?"

I nodded, "Yeah." I heard walking-away shoes, a door opening, a whisper, and shoes walking back toward me. "How do you feel, *hijo?*" Poppa asked.

"It hurts like shit, Poppa."

"It's just for awhile, son, and then off come the bandages. Everything's gonna be all right."

I thought, *Poppa didn't tell me to stop cursing.*

"And son, I thought I told you to stop cursing," he added.

I smiled. Poppa hadn't forgotten. Suddenly I realized that all I had on was a hospital gown. "Poppa, where's my clothes?" I asked.

"I got them. I'm taking them home an'—"

"Whatta ya mean, Poppa?" I said, like scared. "You ain't leavin' me here? I'll be damned if I stay." I was already sitting up and feeling my way outta bed. Poppa grabbed me and pushed me back. His voice wasn't mad or scared any more. It was happy and soft, like Momma's.

"Hey," he said, "get your ass back in bed or they'll have to put a bandage there too."

"Poppa," I pleaded. "I don't care, wallop me as much as you want, just take me home."

"Hey, I thought you said you wasn't no kid. Hell, you ain't scared of being alone?"

Inside my head there was a running of *Yeah, yeah, yeah,* but I answered, "Naw, Poppa, it's just that Momma's gonna worry and she'll get sick an' everything, and—"

"Won't work, son," Poppa broke in with a laugh.

I kept quiet.

"It's only for a couple days. We'll come and see you an' everybody'll bring you things."

I got interested but played it smooth. "What kinda things, Poppa?"

Poppa shrugged his shoulders and spread his big arms apart and answered me like he was surprised that I should ask. "Uh . . . fruits and . . . candy and ice cream. And Momma will probably bring you chicken soup."

I shook my head sadly. "Poppa, you know I don't like chicken soup."

"So we won't bring chicken soup. We'll bring what you like. Goddammit, whatta ya like?"

"I'd like the first things you talked about, Poppa," I said softly. "But instead of soup I'd like"—I held my breath back, then shot it out—"some roller skates!"

Poppa let out a whistle. Roller skates were about $1.50, and that was rice and beans for more than a few days. Then he said, "All right, son, soon as you get home, you got 'em."

But he had agreed too quickly. I shook my head from side to side. Shit, I was gonna push all the way for the roller skates. It wasn't every day you'd get hurt bad enough to ask for something so little like a pair of roller skates. I wanted them right away.

"Fer Christ sakes," Poppa protested, "you can't use 'em in here. Why, some kid will probably steal 'em on you." But Poppa's voice died out slowly in a "you win" tone as I just kept shaking my head from side to side. "Bring 'em tomorrow," he finally mumbled, "but that's it."

"Thanks, Poppa."

"Don't ask for no more."

My eyes were starting to hurt like mad again. The fun was starting to go outta the game between Poppa and me. I made a face.

"Does it hurt, son?"

"Naw, Poppa. I can take it." I thought how I was like a cat in a movie about Indians, taking it like a champ, tied to a stake and getting like burned toast.

Poppa sounded relieved. "Yeah, it's only at first it hurts."

His hand touched my foot. "Well, I'll be going now . . ." Poppa rubbed my foot gently and then slapped me the same gentle way on the side of my leg. "Be good, son," he said and walked away. I heard the door open and the nurse telling him about how they were gonna move me to the ward 'cause I was out of danger. "Son," Poppa called back, "you're *un hombre.*"

I felt proud as hell.

"Poppa."

"Yeah, son?"

"You won't forget to bring the roller skates, huh?"

Poppa laughed. "Yeah, son."

I heard the door close.

1. *Thomas uses a great deal of dialogue in presenting this event. What do you think a writer gains when he depends primarily on dialogue? What elements of this story are most memorable?*

2. *The two most important characters in the scene are Thomas and his father: show how Thomas is able to convey the strength of their relationship without ever stating how important his father is to him.*

3. *Thomas is portraying life in the "mean streets" of a ghetto in New York City. What conditions of life do you become aware of in this episode and how does Thomas communicate them? What kind of positive values does Thomas find as he recalls a harsh moment in his childhood?*

4. *Examine any page of the selection and analyze how the details of people's speeches and gestures help to characterize them and the situation.*

5. *Part of the effect of this selection depends on Thomas's ear for language as it is actually spoken in his world. Choose two or three passages and discuss how they demonstrate the writer's skill in using colloquial or profane language in expressive ways.*

∾ George Orwell ∾

(1903-1950)

See the biographical note on page 53. "Shooting An Elephant" was written in 1936, but it recalls an incident during Orwell's service with the Indian Imperial Police in Moulmien, Burma (1926–27). Orwell went home to England on leave in August, 1927 and never returned.

SHOOTING AN ELEPHANT

In Moulmein, in Lower Burma, I was hated by large numbers of people—the only time in my life that I have been important enough for this to happen to me. I was sub-divisional police officer of the town, and in an aimless, petty kind of way anti-European feeling was very bitter. No one had the guts to raise a riot, but if a European woman went through the bazaars alone somebody would probably spit betel juice over her dress. As a police officer I was an obvious target and was baited whenever it seemed safe to do so. When a nimble Burman tripped me up on the football field and the referee (another Burman) looked the other way, the crowd yelled with hideous laughter. This happened more than once. In the end the sneering yellow faces of young men that met me everywhere, the insults hooted after me when I was at a safe distance, got badly on my nerves. The young Buddhist priests were the worst of all. There were several thousands of them in the town and none of them seemed to have anything to do except stand on street corners and jeer at Europeans.

All this was perplexing and upsetting. For at that time I had already made up my mind that imperialism was an evil thing and the sooner I chucked up my job and got out of it the better. Theoretically—and secretly, of course—I was all for the Burmese and all against their oppressors, the British. As for the job I was doing I hated it more bitterly than I can perhaps make clear. In a job like that you see the dirty work of Empire at close quarters. The wretched prisoners huddling in the stinking cages of the lock-ups, the grey, cowed faces of the long-term convicts, the scarred buttocks of the men who had been flogged with bamboos—all these oppressed me with an intolerable sense of guilt. But I could get nothing into perspective. I was young and ill-educated and I had had to think out my problems in the utter silence that is imposed on every Englishman in the East. I did not even know that the British Empire is dying, still less did I know that it is a great deal better than the younger empires that are going to supplant it. All I knew was that I was stuck between my hatred of the empire I served and my rage against the evil-spirited little beasts who tried to make my job impossible. With one part of my mind I thought of the British Raj as an unbreakable tyranny, as something clamped down, in *sæcula sæculorum*, upon the will of prostrate peoples; with another part I thought that the greatest joy in the world would be to drive a bayonet into a Buddhist priest's guts. Feelings like these are the normal by-products of imperialism; ask any Anglo-Indian official, if you can catch him off duty.

One day something happened which in a roundabout way was enlightening. It was a tiny incident in itself, but it gave me a better glimpse than I had had before of the real nature of imperialism—the real motives for which despotic governments act. Early one morning the sub-inspector at a police station the other end of the town rang me up on the 'phone and said that an elephant was ravaging the bazaar. Would I please come and do something about it? I did not know what I could do, but I wanted to see what was happening and I got on to a pony and started out. I took my rifle, an old .44 Winchester and much too small to kill an elephant, but I thought the noise might be useful *in terrorem*. Various Burmans stopped me on the way and told me about the elephant's doings. It was not, of course, a wild elephant, but a tame one which had gone "must." It had been chained up, as tame elephants always are when their attack of "must" is due, but on the previous night it had broken its chain and escaped. Its mahout, the only person who could manage it when it was in that state, had set out in pursuit, but had taken the wrong direction and was now twelve hours' journey away, and in the morning the elephant had suddenly reappeared in the town. The Burmese population had no weapons and were quite helpless against it. It had already destroyed somebody's bamboo hut, killed a cow and raided some fruit-stalls and devoured the stock; also it had met the municipal rubbish van, and, when the driver jumped out and took to his heels, had turned the van over and inflicted violences upon it.

The Burmese sub-inspector and some Indian constables were waiting for me in the quarter where the elephant had been seen. It was a very poor quarter, a labyrinth of squalid bamboo huts, thatched with palm-leaf, winding all over a steep hillside. I remember that it was a cloudy, stuffy morning at the beginning of the rains. We began questioning the people as to where the elephant had gone, and, as usual, failed to get any definite information. That is invariably the case in the East; a story always sounds clear enough at a distance, but the nearer you get to the scene of events the vaguer it becomes. Some of the people said that the elephant had gone in one direction, some said that he had gone in another, some professed not even to have heard of any elephant. I had almost made up my mind that the whole story was a pack of lies, when we heard yells a little distance away. There was a loud, scandalized cry of "Go away, child! Go away this instant!" and an old woman with a switch in her hand came round the corner of a hut, violently shooing away a crowd of naked children. Some more women followed, clicking their tongues and exclaiming; evidently there was something that the children ought not to have seen. I rounded the hut and saw a man's dead body sprawling in the mud. He was an Indian, a black Dravidian coolie, almost naked, and he could not have been dead many minutes. The people said that the elephant had come suddenly upon him round the corner of the hut, caught him with its trunk, put its foot on his back and ground him into the earth. This was the rainy season and the ground was soft, and his face had scored a trench a foot deep and a couple of yards long. He was lying on his belly with arms crucified and head sharply twisted to one side. His face was coated with mud, the eyes wide open, the teeth bared and grinning with an expression of unendurable agony. (Never tell me, by the way, that the dead looked peaceful. Most of the corpses I have seen look devilish.) The friction of the great beast's foot had stripped the skin from his back as neatly as one skins a rabbit. As soon as I saw the dead man I sent an orderly to a friend's house nearby to borrow an elephant rifle. I had already sent back the pony, not wanting it to go mad with fright and throw me if it smelt the elephant.

The orderly came back in a few minutes with a rifle and five cartridges, and meanwhile some Burmans had arrived and told us that the elephant was in the paddy fields below, only a few hundred yards away. As I started forward practically the whole population of the quarter flocked out of the houses and followed me. They had seen the rifle and were all shouting excitedly that I was going to shoot the elephant. They had not shown much interest in the elephant when he was merely ravaging their homes, but it was different now that he was going to be shot. It was a bit of fun to them, as it would be to an English crowd; besides they wanted the meat. It made me vaguely uneasy. I had no intention of shooting the elephant—I had merely sent for the rifle to defend myself if necessary—and it is always unnerving to have a crowd following you. I marched down the hill, looking and feeling a fool, with the rifle over my shoulder and an ever-growing army of people jostling at my heels. At the bottom, when you got away from the huts, there was a metalled road and beyond that a miry waste of paddy fields a thousand yards across, not yet ploughed but soggy from the first rains and dotted with coarse grass. The elephant was standing eight yards from the road, his left side towards us. He took not the slightest notice of the crowd's approach. He was tearing up bunches of grass, beating them against his knees to clean them and stuffing them into his mouth.

I had halted on the road. As soon as I saw the elephant I knew with perfect certainty that I ought not to shoot him. It is a serious matter to shoot a working elephant—it is comparable to destroying a huge and costly piece of machinery—and obviously one ought not to do it if it can possibly be avoided. And at that distance, peacefully eating, the elephant looked no more dangerous than a cow. I thought then and I think now that his attack of "must" was already passing off; in which case he would merely wander harmlessly about until the mahout came back and caught him. Moreover, I did not in the least want to shoot him. I decided that I would watch him for a little while to make sure that he did not turn savage again, and then go home.

But at that moment I glanced round at the crowd that had followed me. It was an immense crowd, two thousand at the least and growing every minute. It blocked the road for a long distance on either side. I looked at the sea of yellow faces above the garish clothes—faces all happy and excited over this bit of fun, all certain that the elephant was going to be shot. They were watching me as they would watch a conjurer about to perform a trick. They did not like me, but with the magical rifle in my hands I was momentarily worth watching. And suddenly I realized that I should have to shoot the elephant after all. The people expected it of me and I had got to do it; I could feel their two thousand wills pressing me forward, irresistibly. And it was at this moment, as I stood there with the rifle in my hands, that I first grasped the hollowness, the futility of the white man's dominion in the East. Here was I, the white man with his gun, standing in front of the unarmed native crowd—seemingly the leading actor of the piece; but in reality I was only an absurd puppet pushed to and fro by the will of those yellow faces behind. I perceived in this moment that when the white man turns tyrant it is his own freedom that he destroys. He becomes a sort of hollow, posing dummy, the conventionalized figure of a sahib. For it is the condition of his rule that he shall spend his life in trying to impress the "natives," and so in every crisis he has got to do what the "natives" expect of him. He wears a mask, and his face grows to fit it. I had got to shoot the elephant. I had committed myself to doing it when I sent for the rifle. A sahib has got to act like a sahib; he has got to appear resolute, to know his own mind and do definite things. To come all that way, rifle in hand, with two thousand people marching at my heels, and then to trail feebly away, having done nothing—no, that was impossible. The crowd would laugh at me. And my whole life, every white man's life in the East, was one long struggle not to be laughed at.

But I did not want to shoot the elephant. I watched him beating his bunch of grass against his knees, with that preoccupied grandmotherly air that elephants have. It seemed to me that it would be murder to shoot him. At that age I was not squeamish about killing animals, but I had never shot an elephant and never wanted to. (Somehow it always seems worse to kill a *large* animal.) Besides, there was the beast's owner to be considered. Alive, the elephant was worth at least a hundred pounds; dead, he would only be worth the value of his tusks, five pounds, possibly. But I had got to act quickly. I turned to some experienced-looking Burmans who had been there when we arrived, and asked them how the elephant had been behaving. They all said the same thing: he took no notice of you if you left him alone, but he might charge if you went too close to him.

It was perfectly clear to me what I ought to do. I ought to walk up to within, say, twenty-five yards of the elephant and test his behaviour. If he charged I could shoot, if he took no notice of me it would be safe to leave him until the mahout came back. But also I knew that I was going to do no such thing. I was a poor shot with a rifle and the ground was soft mud into which one would sink at every step. If the elephant charged and I missed him, I should have about as much chance as a toad under a steam-roller. But even then I was not thinking particularly of my own skin, only of the watchful yellow faces behind. For at that moment, with the crowd watching me, I was not afraid in the ordinary sense, as I would have been if I had been alone. A white man mustn't be frightened in front of "natives"; and so, in general, he isn't frightened. The sole thought in my mind was that if anything went wrong those two thousand Burmans would see me pursued, caught, trampled on and reduced to a grinning corpse like that Indian up the hill. And if that happened it was quite probable that some of them would laugh. That would never do. There was only one alternative. I shoved the cartridges into the magazine and lay down on the road to get a better aim.

The crowd grew very still, and a deep, low, happy sigh, as of people who see the theatre curtain go up at last, breathed from innumerable throats. They were going to have their bit of fun after all. The rifle was a beautiful German thing with cross-hair sights. I did not then know that in shooting an elephant one would shoot to cut an imaginary bar running from ear-hole to ear-hole. I ought, therefore, as the elephant was sideways on, to have aimed straight at his ear-hole; actually I aimed several inches in front of this, thinking the brain would be farther forward.

When I pulled the trigger I did not hear the bang or feel the kick—one never does when a shot goes home—but I heard the devilish roar of glee that went up from the crowd. In that instant, in too short a time, one would have thought, even for the bullet to get there, a mysterious, terrible change had come over the elephant. He neither stirred nor fell, but every line of his body had altered. He looked suddenly stricken, shrunken, immensely old, as though the frightful impact of the bullet had paralysed him without knocking him down. At last, after what seemed a long time—it might have been five seconds, I dare say—he sagged flabbily to his knees. His mouth slobbered. An enormous senility seemed to have settled upon him. One could have imagined him thousands of years old. I fired again into the same spot. At the second shot he did not collapse but climbed with desperate slowness to his feet and stood weakly upright, with legs sagging and head drooping. I fired a third time. That was the shot that did for him. You could see the agony of it jolt his whole body and knock the last remnant of strength from his legs. But in falling he seemed for a moment to rise, for as his hind legs collapsed beneath him he seemed to tower upwards like a huge rock toppling, his trunk reaching skywards like a tree. He trumpeted, for the first and only time. And then down he came, his belly towards me, with a crash that seemed to shake the ground even where I lay.

I got up. The Burmans were already racing past me across the mud. It was obvious that the elephant would never rise again, but he was not dead. He was breathing very rhythmically with long rattling gasps, his great mound of a side painfully rising and falling. His mouth was wide open—I could see far down into caverns of pale pink throat. I waited a long time for him to die, but his breathing did not weaken. Finally I fired my two remaining shots into the spot where I thought his heart must be. The thick blood welled out of him like red velvet, but still he did not die. His body did not even jerk when the shots hit him, the tortured breathing continued without a pause. He was dying, very slowly and in great agony, but in some world remote from me where not even a bullet could damage him further. I felt that I had got to put an end to that dreadful noise. It seemed dreadful to see the great beast lying there, powerless to move and yet powerless to die, and not even be able to finish him. I sent back for my small rifle and poured shot after shot into his heart and down his throat. They seemed to make no impression. The tortured gasps continued as steadily as the ticking of a clock.

In the end I could not stand it any longer and went away. I heard later that it took him half an hour to die. Burmans were bringing dahs and baskets even before I left, and I was told they had stripped his body almost to the bones by the afternoon.

Afterwards, of course, there were endless discussions about the shooting of the elephant. The owner was furious, but he was only an Indian and could do nothing. Besides, legally I had done the right thing, for a mad elephant has to be killed, like a mad dog, if its owner fails to control it. Among the Europeans opinion was divided. The older men said I was right, the younger men said it was a damn shame to shoot an elephant for killing a coolie, because an elephant was worth more than any damn Coringhee coolie. And afterwards I was very glad that the coolie had been killed; it put me legally in the right and it gave me a sufficient pretext for shooting the elephant. I often wondered whether any of the others grasped that I had done it solely to avoid looking a fool.

1. *What kind of perspective does Orwell presently have that makes the story of shooting an elephant important to him? How much of what he tells you is what he knew then and how much is what he knows now?*

2. *Do you think Orwell is interested in having his readers see him as a representative man? Representative of what and in what way?*

3. *How does Orwell develop his account of the event up to the point where he confronts the elephant? Does he tend to emphasize the drama and potential danger involved? Why or why not? Why does he describe the death of the elephant in such detail? Comment specifically on the language Orwell uses in those paragraphs.*

4. *How does Orwell characterize himself as an officer? In what ways does the characterization influence our understanding of the climax of the episode when Orwell shoots the elephant?*

5. *What is the purpose of the final paragraph of the essay, describing the aftermath of the shooting? How does it help you to understand the colonial world in which the shooting takes place?*

Possibilities for Writing

1. Develop an autobiographical narrative that depends to some extent upon dialogue to recreate the incident. Try to make the dialogue differentiate the people in the scene and reveal something significant about the way they behave. You could compare your technique with that used by Frank Conroy or Piri Thomas.

2. Write about an autobiographical event in which you have had to face someone in authority in a situation where you were at a disadvantage. After you have finished, compare the kind of situation you have chosen and your method of presenting it with what Frank Conroy or Mary Mebane has written.

3. Narrate an event in which you played a very prominent role and then retell the same event, this time assuming that you have become an onlooker rather than a participant. Try to make each narration consistent with what you would be likely to see and feel; then examine your two versions and note the differences.

4. Choose one of the autobiographical selections in this chapter and retell the event, using the perspective of some person other than the autobiographer. For example, you could retell Maya Angelou's story from the point of view of the black principal or the white guest speaker or Lincoln Steffens' story from the point of view of his father.

CHAPTER FOUR

PLACES

Introduction: Description and the Organization of Detail

If autobiography is essentially the story of the writer's life as he has acted it, it is also the story of the world in which those actions take place. We write about what happened to us, but often the context of where it happened makes what we think, feel, and do comprehensible. As we try to evoke for the reader our world in all its concrete detail, we depend upon our descriptive powers to document direct sensory impressions with accuracy and discrimination.

Most often, writers rely on visual perceptions, since the eye, as the primary recorder of our impressions, takes in many qualities of objects in the external world, such as size, dimension, color, and design. But at times other sense impressions may dominate, as when Alfred Kazin remembers the crunch of the gravel on the local running track or the "rusty smell" of a nearby warehouse. On other occasions, a writer may feel that all his senses were engaged at some particular moment and his autobiographical description will interweave a record of the various elements which combined to create this total impression. In his account of the first night of a boyhood visit to a farm in Nebraska, Wright Morris tells of hearing the drone of the locusts, inhaling the sweetness of the night air, and seeing the darkening fields and the brightening bowl of the sky.

Obviously Morris' account of life on the farm is not effective simply because he draws upon all of his senses in remembering the event. However, a situation of unusual drama or anxiety (visiting some great natural wonder, like the Grand Canyon; thinking there is a burglar in the house) often makes our senses especially alert, and these impressions can be made to reemerge and give immediacy to our writing. A writer is particularly likely to mix sensory impressions when he wishes to convey intimacy, since visual memory alone suggests greater detachment. The smells of cooking from the family kitchen, for example, are often among the strongest of childhood memories, linked as they are with the intimacy of parents and children around the supper table. What should influence a writer is not some arbitrary rule about including varied sense impressions, but only the awareness that visual impressions usually come readily to mind and are easiest to verbalize. Therefore, the resources of other senses may be neglected in describing the world (even though they are not neglected in experiencing it), unless the writer makes some conscious effort to reflect on nonvisual sense impressions as part of autobiographical memory.

In recording our sense impressions, we may tend to think of nouns and adjectives as our primary tools, as Alfred Kazin does in his description of life as a boy in Brooklyn:

> Our life every day was fought out on the pavement and in the gutter, up against the walls of the houses and the glass fronts of the drugstore and the grocery, in and out of the fresh steaming piles of horse manure, the wheels of passing carts and automobiles, along the spikes of the stairway to the cellar, the jagged edge of the open garbage cans, the crumbly steps of the old farmhouses still left on one side of the street.

But writers have many verbal resources with which to communicate their sense of the physical world. Here, for example, is Henry Thoreau's description of waterbugs and skater insects at Walden Pond:

> You can even detect a water-bug (Gyrinus) ceaselessly progressing over the smooth surface a quarter of a mile off; for they furrow the

water slightly, making a conspicuous ripple bounded by two diverging lines, but the skaters glide over it without rippling it perceptibly. When the surface is considerably agitated there are no skaters nor water-bugs on it, but apparently, in calm days, they leave their havens and adventurously glide forth from the shore by short impulses till they completely cover it.

This passage depends as much on verbs (furrow, glide) and adverbs (ceaselessly, adventurously) as on any adjective to register the impression made by the insects. Thoreau's passage, as distinguished from Kazin's, reminds us that description can often be more than a record of the static qualities in our surroundings. We can describe a scene by rendering such qualities precisely (Kazin's "jagged edge of the garbage cans"), but we can also describe a scene by capturing the activities and the interrelationships of things in it, as Thoreau does with his insects "adventurously gliding" and rippling the water with their movements.

Thoreau's word "adventurously" (which suggests a comparison of insects to people) shows that another way of describing our world can be to juxtapose it with another world: that is, to convey our perceptions by analogy. An analogy explains our impressions by comparison, and the degree to which analogies are bound to our senses can be measured by how often such phrases as "looks like" and "sounds like" crop up in our speech. Sometimes analogies are submerged in a single word, barely noticeable, as when Thoreau uses "furrow," a word associated with the surface of the land, to describe how insects affect the surface of Walden Pond. At times, analogies are more explicit—George Orwell conveys the exotic setting of a Moroccan burial ground by noting "a huge waste of hummocky earth, like a derelict building-lot." At other times, analogies are developed more elaborately, as when Thoreau describes the surface of the pond: "It is like molten glass cooled but not congealed, and the few motes in it are pure and beautiful like the imperfection in glass."

The last two quotations from Orwell and Thoreau show in

miniature what a writer seeks to do with description. Two different processes may be involved. The writer may try to make the unfamiliar familiar, in order to bring it within his reader's range of experience, as Orwell illustrates. Conversely, he may try to create a fresh perception of anything his reader would customarily regard as trite or conventional, as Thoreau does when he makes us look again at the surface of a pond. Of course, what is familiar or unfamiliar depends upon the writer and his sense of his audience—a Moroccan writing for his countrymen about Marrakech would not proceed in the same way that Orwell does. Writers find many different ways to bring their sense of the world freshly before the reader: often by striking analogy, as in the likeness of the pond's surface to a special state of molten glass, or by unusually attentive scrutiny, as in the description of the insects on the pond's surface, or by recording a highly subjective response, as in Thoreau's "In such transparent and seemingly bottomless water, I seemed to be floating through the air as in a balloon." Whatever techniques they choose, autobiographical writers, especially, strive to communicate how the world in which they live affects them personally.

We have seen how description originates in sense impressions, and have pointed to some ways these impressions are conveyed in language. The question remains: what should the writer do with these accumulated details once he has made them the touchstones of his world? In other words, how are they organized and made to contribute to the writer's larger purposes? It should already be clear that description is not merely the accumulation of details, any more than narrative is an accumulation of events. Description is as much an arrangement in space as we found narrative to be in time. For example, Henry Thoreau and Michael Collins both focus on single places—that is, despite their great difference in size, the pond and the moon are both regarded by the writers as single objects in their vision. Thoreau lives close to Walden Pond and occasionally even sails on it or immerses himself in it, while Collins sees the moon from a great distance away through the windows of a speeding space rocket. What both writers rely on is the variety created by their own changing vantage points, as well as the changes in the object itself. As they move, they see different facets of the pond or of the moon, and their writing expresses the complexity of their vision.

Not only does the writer place himself in relation to whatever he is describing, but he also places the various elements in his description in relation to one another. Malcolm X and Alfred Kazin both describe sections of New York by gathering together an enormous number of different details, but the details do not simply accumulate at random, Malcolm X creates a marvelous panorama of the kinds of excitement in the night life of Harlem that dazzled a young black seeing it all for the first time. The music, the crowds, the clubs, the dancing tumble over one another to create the same rush of impressions that would have engulfed the young Malcolm. Kazin's memory produces a similar quantity of detail, but it emerges in a different way. He is a youngster wanting gradually to go beyond the boundaries of his familiar neighborhood, and so his details are usually organized geographically in sequences that move out from the block to the less familiar world beyond, a series of forays into new territory which the boy associates with freedom.

Whatever way the writer chooses to organize these details in space, he also needs to unify them through a consistent point of view. Malcolm X not only links the various details in his panorama of Harlem by grouping them according to the sources of excitement the city offers, but he also conveys his own sense of wonder at all of this energy, color, and life. Michael Collins surprises us by *not* being full of wonder at coming so close to the moon. He sees it as a "withered, sun-seared peach pit" and shows his lack of awe by including casual humor in his description—"Hello, moon, how's the old back side." That kind of informality, in turn, contrasts with

Alfred Kazin's highly dramatic way of describing a common-place of city life, neighborhood boys playing handball. He seeks to re-create their passion through his emotional language: "Every day we smashed a small black viciously hard regulation handball against it with fanatical cuts and drives and slams, beating and slashing at it almost in hatred for the blind strength of the wall itself."

As descriptive details are brought within the compass of the writer's attitude, they show us the kind of bargain the writer has made with the world he lives in, the way he explores it or adapts to it. Description, then, enters into all autobiographical writing; we cannot feel we know the writer's life until we know something of the external conditions of that life. At the same time, those conditions are only a part of the ongoing process of a life, and so description remains only a part, subordinate to the narrative pattern of autobiography. Although we have been discussing description as if it had some independent existence within the selections in this chapter, we have done so primarily to isolate the techniques of description and to get a clearer view of their functions. What we find when we read the selections, however, is that description is often the bass line in a complex orchestration. If we look back to the end of the last paragraph, we can see that Kazin's sentence about the handball game describes, but it also narrates action in time, and it also registers the strong emotional involvement of the writer. Clearly, in putting that experience into words, Kazin, like any good writer, is not thinking about such abstract categories as narration and description. But he is aware of the need to ground his account in the concrete record of what his senses have told him. Our consciousness of descriptive writing should be this same awareness of the look and feel of the world we live in and of the need to place the events we narrate firmly in a recognizable place and time. Description may be subordinate but it is irreplaceable, testifying to the writer's alertness and sensitivity and leading his readers to trust his accuracy in larger matters.

∽ Michael Collins ∽

(1930-   )

*Michael Collins is a graduate of the United States Military
Academy. He was commissioned by the Air Force and served
as an experimental flight test pilot. Becoming an astronaut in
1963, he piloted the Gemini X mission in 1966, and was the
pilot of the Apollo XI for the first moon landing in July, 1969.*
Carrying the Fire *(1974) is his account of his life as an astronaut, and this selection describes the spaceship's approach to
the moon.*

[APPROACHING THE MOON]

Day 4 has a decidedly different feel to it. Instead of nine hours'
sleep, I get seven—and fitful ones at that. Despite our concentrated attempt to conserve our energy on the way to the moon,
the pressure is overtaking us (or me at least), and I feel that all
of us are aware that the honeymoon is over and we are about to
lay our little pink bodies on the line. Our first shock comes as
we stop our spinning motion and swing ourselves around so as
to bring the moon into view. We have not been able to see the
moon for nearly a day now, and the change in its appearance
is dramatic, spectacular, and electrifying. The moon I have
known all my life, that two-dimensional, small yellow disk in
the sky, has gone away somewhere, to be replaced by the most
awesome sphere I have ever seen. To begin with, it is *huge*,
completely filling our window. Second, it is three-dimensional.
The belly of it bulges out toward us in such a pronounced fash-

ion that I almost feel I can reach out and touch it, while its surface obviously recedes toward the edges. It is between us and the sun, creating the most splendid lighting conditions imaginable. The sun casts a halo around it, shining on its rear surface, and the sunlight which comes cascading around its rim serves mainly to make the moon itself seem mysterious and subtle by comparison, emphasizing the size and texture of its dimly lit and pockmarked surface.

To add to the dramatic effect, we find we can see the stars again. We are in the shadow of the moon now, in darkness for the first time in three days, and the elusive stars have reappeared as if called especially for this occasion. The 360-degree disk of the moon, brilliantly illuminated around its rim by the hidden rays of the sun, divides itself into two distinct central regions. One is nearly black, while the other basks in a whitish light reflected from the surface of the earth. Earthshine, as it's called, is sunlight which has traveled from the sun to the earth and bounced off it back to the moon. Earthshine on the moon is considerably brighter than moonshine on the earth. The vague reddish-yellow of the sun's corona, the blanched white of earthshine, and the pure black of the star-studded surrounding sky all combine to cast a bluish glow over the moon. This cool, magnificent sphere hangs there ominously, a formidable presence without sound or motion, issuing us no invitation to invade its domain. Neil sums it up: "It's a view worth the price of the trip." And somewhat scary too, although no one says that.

Before we become too engrossed in the mystery of the moon, however, Houston restores some of our perspective with an earful of terrestrial chatter. We must check the flow of fluid through our secondary coolant system by bringing a second radiator onto the line. This is a test I have long opposed ("If the goddamned primary system is working O.K., why screw around with testing the secondary?"), but I have been overruled in a series of meetings. After I have successfully put the system through its paces, I guess I grump a little bit and tell

Houston, "Well at least we don't have to have any more meetings on the subject." "The flight director says 'Ouch,' " replies the CAPCOM. Have I offended Cliff Charlesworth. "No, no 'ouch' intended. I enjoyed every one of those meetings," I lie. Houston rewards us with the day's news, mostly baseball and other trivia. They do mention that Pravda has referred to Neil as the "Czar of the Ship," which title I heartily endorse for the remainder of the flight, and there is one amusing (at least to me) story about my son Michael. "What do you think," Michael is asked, "about your father going down in history," "Fine," says Michael; and after considerable pause, "What *is* history, anyway."

Houston is on to bigger things now, pumping us up with all the last-minute information we require before disappearing out of sight around the left-hand side of the moon. We have to know how to get into lunar orbit, and if trouble develops, how to get out of it—all without help from the ground. Our line-of-sight radio dictates that we can talk only to those people we can see; behind the moon, we will see no one. For the last fourteen hours we have been in the lunar sphere of influence, and our velocity has gradually picked up from a low of three thousand feet per second to its present seventy-six hundred feet per second. To be captured by the moon's gravity, we must slow down, by 2,917 feet per second to be exact, and we do this by burning our service module engine for six minutes and two seconds. Known as LOI_1, or the first lunar orbit insertion, this burn will put us in an elliptical orbit around the moon. Four hours later, we will attempt LOI_2, which should achieve a sixty-mile circular orbit.

As we ease on around the left side of the moon, I marvel again at the precision of our path. We have missed hitting the moon by a paltry three hundred nautical miles, at a distance of nearly a quarter of a million miles from earth, and don't forget that the moon is a moving target and that we are racing through the sky just ahead of its leading edge. When we launched the other day, the moon was nowhere near where it is now; it was some 40 degrees of arc, or nearly 200,000 miles behind where it is now, and yet those big computers in the basement in Houston didn't even whimper but belched out super-accurate predictions. I hope. As we pass behind the moon, finally, we have just over eight minutes to go before the burn. We are super-careful now, checking and rechecking each step several times. It is very much like the de-orbit burn of Gemini 10, when John Young and I must have checked our directions thirty times. If only one digit got slipped in our computer, the worst possible digit, we could be turned around backward and be about to blast ourselves into an orbit around the sun, instead of the moon, thereby becoming a planet the next generation might discover as the last one has discovered Pluto. No thanks.

When the moment finally arrives, the big engine instantly springs into action and reassuringly plasters us back in our seats. The acceleration is only a fraction of one G, but it feels good nonetheless. For six minutes we sit there peering intent as hawks at our instrument panel, scanning the important dials and gauges, making sure that the proper thing is being done to us. When the engine shuts down, we discuss the matter with our computer and I read out the results: "Minus one, minus one, plus one. Jesus! I take back any bad things I ever said about M.I.T." What I mean is that the accuracy of the overall system is phenomenal: out of a total of nearly three thousand feet per second, we have velocity errors in our body axis co-ordinate system of only one tenth of one foot per second in each of three directions. That is one accurate burn, and even Neil acknowledges the fact. "That was a beautiful burn," he says, and I echo, "Goddamn, I guess! . . . I don't know if we're at sixty miles or not, but at least we haven't hit that mother." Buzz queries the computer as to our orbit. "Look at that, 169.6 by 60.9," and I reply, "Beautiful, beautiful, beautiful, beautiful!" "You want to write that down or something," Buzz wants to know. Why not? "Write it down just for the hell of it; 170 by 60, like gangbusters." Buzz is precise. "We only missed by a couple of tenths of a mile." I am elated. "Hello, moon, how's the old back side?" We have arrived.

Once LOI₂ has passed, and established us in a near-circular orbit, averaging sixty miles altitude above the surface, we have a chance to examine the old back side, the front side, and parts in between. We are especially keen to study the landing site, the actual spot, just as we have been studying the photos of it for the last few months. Neil sums it up for Houston. "It looks very much like the pictures, but like the difference between watching a real football game and watching it on TV. There's no substitute for actually being here." Neil and Buzz also call out the familiar features along tomorrow's landing approach path: Mount Marilyn (named after Jim Lovell's wife), Boot Hill, Duke Island (named after Charlie Duke), Diamondback and Sidewinder (two sinuous rills etched in the Sea of Tranquility which look exactly like rattlesnakes), and so on, right up to the landing site itself. The Sea of Tranquility is just past dawn, and the sun's rays are intersecting its surface at a mere 1 degree angle. Under these lighting conditions, craters cast extremely long shadows, and to me the entire region looks distinctly forbidding, with no evidence that any part of its surface is smooth enough to park a baby buggy, never mind a lunar module. I can't resist commenting on it ("rough as a cob"), but all three of us know (we do?) that it will look a lot smoother tomorrow as the sun angle climbs toward the 10 degrees it will reach by the time of landing.

If anything, the rear side of the moon looks even rougher than the front. It doesn't have any "flat" *maria*, or seas, as the front does, but is a continuous region of "highlands," an uninterrupted jumble of tortured hills, cratered and recratered by 5 billion years of meteorite bombardment. There is no atmosphere surrounding the moon to produce clouds or smog or otherwise obscure the surface, so the details are uniformly clear. CAVU, as pilots describe a perfect day on earth: clear and visibility unlimited. The only thing that changes is the lighting, as our spacecraft passes from sunshine into earthshine, that eerie region of reflected sunlight, and then into total darkness. The feeling is more like circling in earth orbit than hanging suspended in cislunar space, as the past three days have been spent, but there are marked differences as well. First, we are traveling only one fifth as fast as we would in earth orbit, because the moon has much less mass than the earth and therefore produces a weaker gravitational pull, which, in turn, means that we require a slower orbital velocity to counterbalance this gravitational force with our own centrifugal force. However, since the moon is much smaller (2,160-mile diameter vs. the earth's 7,927), we get around it almost as fast, taking two hours for one orbit instead of ninety minutes. Also, because we are in a lower orbit (you can't orbit the earth at sixty miles because of its atmosphere), we get a noticeable sensation of speed. It's not quite as exhilarating a feeling as orbiting the earth, but it's close. In addition, it has an exotic, bizarre quality due entirely to the nature of the surface below. The earth from orbit is a delight—alive, inviting, enchanting—offering visual variety and an emotional feeling of belonging "down there." Not so with this withered, sun-seared peach pit out my window. There is no comfort to it; it is too stark and barren; its invitation is monotonous and meant for geologists only. Look at this crater, look at that one, are they the result of impacts, or volcanism, or a mixture of both?

As three amateur geologists, it doesn't take us long to get caught up with the mystery of the place and the fascination of discovering new craters on the back side. "What a spectacular view!" exclaims Neil. I agree. "Fantastic. Look back there behind us, sure looks like a gigantic crater; look at the mountains going around it. My gosh, they're monsters." Neil points out another one, even larger, and I'm even more impressed by it. "God, it's huge! It is enormous! It's so big I can't even get it in the window. That's the biggest one you have ever seen in your life. Neil, God, look at this central mountain peak. Isn't that a huge one? . . . You could spend a lifetime just geologizing that one crater alone, you know that?" Neil doesn't sound taken with *that* idea. "You could," he grunts. I hasten to add, "That's not how I'd like to spend my lifetime, but—picture that. Beautiful!" Buzz pipes up. "Yes, there's a big mother over here, too!" "Come on now, Buzz, don't refer to them as big mothers; give them some scientific name." Buzz ignores me and goes on. "It looks like a lot of them have slumped down." "A slumping big mother? Well, you see those every once in a while." Buzz decides to descend to my level. "Most of them are slumping. The bigger they are, the more they slump—that's a truism, isn't it? That is, the older they get." This conversation is taking a turn for the worse, and it will only be another few minutes until the earth pops up over the moon's rugged rim, so I drop the subject and start talking about camera and gimbal angles, as we all wait for our old friend to reappear. Still . . . the possibilities of weightlessness are there for the ingenious to exploit. No need to carry bras into space, that's for sure. Imagine a spacecraft of the future, with a crew of a thousand ladies, off for Alpha Centauri, with two thousand breasts bobbing beautifully and quivering delightfully in response to their every weightless movement . . . and I am the commander of the craft, and it is Saturday morning and time for inspection, naturally . . .

I am wrenched back to reality by the sudden appearance of the earth, a truly dramatic moment or two that we all scramble to record with our cameras. It pokes its little blue bonnet up over the craggy rim and then, not having been shot at, surges up over the horizon with a rush of unexpected color and motion. It is a welcome sight for several reasons: it is intrinsically beautiful, it contrasts sharply with the smallpox below, and it is home and voice for us. This is not at all like sunrise on earth, whose brilliance commands one's attention; it is easily missed, and therefore all the more precious to us, as we have anticipated its appearance and prepared for it. As it bursts into view, Houston starts talking, and we are back to business as usual.

1. What are some of the ways Collins's story reflects the fact that he is describing something no human has seen in this way before? How does his description of the moon help you to comprehend the unfamiliarity of the experience?

2. Can you think of an alternative description of the moon, one that Collins does not use? How does your description help you to understand the distinctive qualities of Collins's account?

3. What distinguishes Collins's way of writing about activities inside the spaceship from his descriptions of what he sees outside the spaceship?

4. What are the reactions of the astronauts as they approach the moon? Does Collins's own narration reflect the same reactions or are his responses more complex? Does the fact that he is recollecting the experience alter his sense of it?

5. Collins, like the other astronauts, is a highly trained and technologically sophisticated individual. To what extent are the details of his story those that might be provided by an untrained observer and to what extent do they reflect his special background? How is he able to integrate the two kinds of details in his account?

∽ Henry Thoreau ∽

(1817-1862)

See the biographical note on page 49. Thoreau published Walden *in 1854. It is his masterpiece, an account of the time he spent in a small cabin at the shore of Concord's Walden Pond, confronting nature and discovering her universal laws.*

THE PONDS

A lake is the landscape's most beautiful and expressive feature. It is earth's eye; looking into which the beholder measures the depth of his own nature. The fluviatile trees next the shore are the slender eyelashes which fringe it, and the wooded hills and cliffs around are its overhanging brows.

Standing on the smooth sandy beach at the east end of the pond, in a calm September afternoon, when a slight haze makes the opposite shore line indistinct, I have seen whence came the expression, "the glassy surface of a lake." When you invert your head, it looks like a thread of finest gossamer stretched across the valley, and gleaming against the distant pine woods, separating one stratum of the atmosphere from another. You would think that you could walk dry under it to the opposite hills, and that the swallows which skim over might perch on it. Indeed, they sometimes dive below the line, as it were by mistake, and are undeceived. As you look over the pond westward you are obliged to employ both your hands to

From Henry Thoreau: *Walden* (*The Variorum Walden*), ed. Walter Harding. Reprinted by permission of Twayne Publishers.

defend your eyes against the reflected as well as the true sun, for they are equally bright; and if, between the two, you survey its surface critically, it is literally as smooth as glass, except where the skater insects, at equal intervals scattered over its whole extent, by their motions in the sun produce the finest imaginable sparkle on it, or, perchance, a duck plumes itself, or, as I have said, a swallow skims so low as to touch it. It may be that in the distance a fish describes an arc of three or four feet in the air, and there is one bright flash where it emerges, and another where it strikes the water; sometimes the whole silvery arc is revealed; or here and there, perhaps, is a thistle-down floating on its surface, which the fishes dart at and so dimple it again. It is like molten glass cooled but not congealed, and the few motes in it are pure and beautiful like the imperfections in glass. You may often detect a yet smoother and darker water, separated from the rest as if by an invisible cobweb, boom of the water nymphs, resting on it. From a hill-top you can see a fish leap in almost any part; for not a pickerel or shiner picks an insect from this smooth surface but it manifestly disturbs the equilibrium of the whole lake. It is wonderful with what elaborateness this simple fact is advertised,— this piscine murder will out,—and from my distant perch I distinguish the circling undulations when they are half a dozen rods in diameter. You can even detect a water-bug (*Gyrinus*) ceaselessly progressing over the smooth surface a quarter of a mile off; for they furrow the water slightly, making a conspicuous ripple bounded by two diverging lines, but the skaters glide over it without rippling it perceptibly. When the surface is considerably agitated there are no skaters nor water-bugs on it, but apparently, in calm days, they leave their havens and adventurously glide forth from the shore by short impulses till they completely cover it. It is a soothing employment, on one of those fine days in the fall when all the warmth of the sun is fully appreciated, to sit on a stump on such a height as this, overlooking the pond, and study the dimpling circles which are incessantly inscribed on its otherwise invisible surface amid the reflected skies and trees. Over this great expanse there is no disturbance but it is thus at once gently smoothed away and assuaged, as, when a vase of water is jarred, the trembling circles seek the shore and all is smooth again. Not a fish can leap or an insect fall on the pond but it is thus reported in circling dimples, in lines of beauty, as it were the constant welling up of its fountain, the gentle pulsing of its life, the heaving of its breast. The thrills of joy and thrills of pain are undistinguishable. How peaceful the phenomena of the lake. Again the works of man shine as in the spring. Ay, every leaf and twig and stone and cobweb sparkles now at mid-afternoon as when covered with dew in a spring morning. Every motion of an oar or an insect produces a flash of light; and if an oar falls, how sweet the echo!

In such a day, in September or October, Walden is a perfect forest mirror, set round with stones as precious to my eye as if fewer or rarer. Nothing so fair, so pure, and at the same time so large, as a lake, perchance, lies on the surface of the earth. Sky water. It needs no fence. Nations come and go without defiling it. It is a mirror which no stone can crack, whose quicksilver will never wear off, whose gilding Nature continually repairs; no storms, no dust, can dim its surface ever fresh;—a mirror in which all impurity presented to it sinks, swept and dusted by the sun's hazy brush,—this the light dust-cloth,—which retains no breath that is breathed on it, but sends its own to float as clouds high above its surface, and be reflected in its bosom still.

A field of water betrays the spirit that is in the air. It is continually receiving new life and motion from above. It is intermediate in its nature between land and sky. On land only the grass and trees wave, but the water itself is rippled by the wind. I see where the breeze dashes across it by the streaks or flakes of light. It is remarkable that we can look down on its surface. We shall, perhaps, look down thus on the surface of air at length, and mark where a still subtler spirit sweeps over it.

The skaters and water-bugs finally disappear in the latter part of October, when the severe frosts have come; and then and in November, usually, in a calm day, there is absolutely nothing to ripple the surface. One November afternoon, in the calm at the end of a rain storm of several days' duration, when the sky was still completely overcast and the air was full of mist, I observed that the pond was remarkably smooth, so that it was difficult to distinguish its surface; though it no longer reflected the bright tints of October, but the sombre November colors of the surrounding hills. Though I passed over it as gently as possible, the slight undulations produced by my boat extended almost as far as I could see, and gave a ribbed appearance to the reflections. But, as I was looking over the surface, I saw here and there at a distance a faint glimmer, as if some skater insects which had escaped the frosts might be collected there, or, perchance, the surface, being so smooth, betrayed where a spring welled up from the bottom. Paddling gently to one of these places, I was surprised to find myself surrounded by myriads of small perch, about five inches long, of a rich bronze color in the green water, sporting there and constantly rising to the surface and dimpling it, sometimes leaving bubbles on it. In such transparent and seemingly bottomless water, reflecting the clouds, I seemed to be floating through the air as in a balloon, and their swimming impressed me as a kind of flight or hovering, as if they were a compact flock of birds passing just beneath my level on the right or left, their fins, like sails, set all around them. There were many such schools in the pond, apparently improving the short season before winter would draw an icy shutter over their broad skylight, sometimes giving to the surface an appearance as if a slight breeze struck it, or a few rain-drops fell there. When I approached carelessly and alarmed them, they made a sudden plash and rippling with their tails, as if one had struck the water with a brushy bough, and instantly took refuge in the depths. At length the wind rose, the mist increased, and the waves began to run, and the perch leaped much higher than before, half out of water, a hundred black points, three inches long, at once above the surface. Even as late as the fifth of December, one year, I saw some dimples on the surface, and thinking it was going to rain hard immediately, the air being full of mist, I made haste to take my place at the oars and row homeward; already the rain seemed rapidly increasing, though I felt none on my cheek, and I anticipated a thorough soaking. But suddenly the dimples ceased, for they were produced by the perch, which the noise of my oars had scared into the depths, and I saw their schools dimly disappearing; so I spent a dry afternoon after all.

An old man who used to frequent this pond nearly sixty years ago, when it was dark with surrounding forests, tells me that in those days he sometimes saw it all alive with ducks and other water fowl, and that there were many eagles about it. He came here a-fishing, and used an old log canoe which he found on the shore. It was made of two white-pine logs dug out and pinned together, and was cut off square at the ends. It was very clumsy, but lasted a great many years before it became waterlogged and perhaps sank to the bottom. He did not know whose it was; it belonged to the pond. He used to make a cable for his anchor of strips of hickory bark tied together. An old man, a potter, who lived by the pond before the Revolution, told him once that there was an iron chest at the bottom, and that he had seen it. Sometimes it would come floating up to the shore; but when you went toward it, it would go back into deep water and disappear. I was pleased to hear of the old log canoe, which took the place of an Indian one of the same material but more graceful construction, which perchance had first been a tree on the bank, and then, as it were, fell into the water, to float there for a generation, the most proper vessel for the lake. I remember that when I first looked into these depths there were many large trunks to be seen indistinctly lying on the bottom, which had either been blown over formerly, or left on the ice at the last cutting, when wood was cheaper; but now they have mostly disappeared.

When I first paddled a boat on Walden, it was completely surrounded by thick and lofty pine and oak woods, and in some of its coves grape vines had run over the trees next the water and formed bowers under which a boat could pass. The hills which form its shores are so steep, and the woods on them were then so high, that, as you looked down from the west end, it had the appearance of an amphitheatre for some kind of sylvan spectacle. I have spent many an hour, when I was younger, floating over its surface as the zephyr willed, having paddled my boat to the middle, and lying on my back across the seats, in a summer forenoon, dreaming awake, until I was aroused by the boat touching the sand, and I arose to see what shore my fates had impelled me to; days when idleness was the most attractive and productive industry. Many a forenoon have I stolen away, preferring to spend thus the most valued part of the day; for I was rich, if not in money, in sunny hours and summer days, and spent them lavishly; nor do I regret that I did not waste more of them in the workshop or the teacher's desk. But since I left those shores the woodchoppers have still further laid them waste, and now for many a year there will be no more rambling through the aisles of the wood, with occasional vistas through which you see the water. My Muse may be excused if she is silent henceforth. How can you expect the birds to sing when their groves are cut down?

Now the trunks of trees on the bottom, and the old log canoe, and the dark surrounding woods, are gone, and the villagers, who scarcely know where it lies, instead of going to the pond to bathe or drink, are thinking to bring its water, which should be as sacred as the Ganges at least, to the village in a pipe, to wash their dishes with!—to earn their Walden by the turning of a cock or drawing of a plug! That devilish Iron Horse, whose ear-rending neigh is heard throughout the town, has muddied the Boiling Spring with his foot, and he it is that has browsed off all the woods on Walden shore; that Trojan horse, with a thousand men in his belly, introduced by mercenary Greeks! Where is the country's champion, the Moore of Moore Hall, to meet him at the Deep Cut and thrust an avenging lance between the ribs of the bloated pest?

Nevertheless, of all the characters I have known, perhaps Walden wears best, and best preserves its purity. Many men have been likened to it, but few deserve that honor. Though the woodchoppers have laid bare first this shore and then that, and the Irish have built their sties by it, and the railroad has infringed on its border, and the ice-men have skimmed it once, it is itself unchanged, the same water which my youthful eyes fell on; all the change is in me. It has not acquired one permanent wrinkle after all its ripples. It is perennially young, and I may stand and see a swallow dip apparently to pick an insect from its surface as of yore. It struck me again tonight, as if I had not seen it almost daily for more than twenty years,— Why, here is Walden, the same woodland lake that I discovered so many years ago; where a forest was cut down last winter another is springing up by its shore as lustily as ever; the same thought is welling up to its surface that was then; it is the same liquid joy and happiness to itself and its Maker, ay, and it *may* be to me. It is the work of a brave man surely, in whom there was no guile! He rounded this water with his hand, deepened and clarified it in his thought, and in his will bequeathed it to Concord. I see by its face that it is visited by the same reflection; and I can almost say, Walden, is it you?

> It is no dream of mine,
> To ornament a line;
> I cannot come nearer to God and Heaven
> Than I live to Walden even.
> I am its stony shore,
> And the breeze that passes o'er;
> In the hollow of my hand
> Are its water and its sand,
> And its deepest resort
> Lies high in my thought.

The cars never pause to look at it; yet I fancy that the engineers and firemen and brakemen, and those passengers who have a season ticket and see it often, are better men for the sight. The engineer does not forget at night, or his nature does not, that he has beheld this vision of serenity and purity once at least during the day. Though seen but once, it helps to wash out State-street and the engine's soot. One proposes that it be called "God's Drop."

I have said that Walden has no visible inlet nor outlet, but it is on the one hand distantly and indirectly related to Flint's Pond, which is more elevated, by a chain of small ponds coming from that quarter, and on the other directly and manifestly to Concord River, which is lower, by a similar chain of ponds through which in some other geological period it may have flowed, and by a little digging, which God forbid, it can be made to flow thither again. If by living thus reserved and austere, like a hermit in the woods, so long, it has acquired such wonderful purity, who would not regret that the comparatively impure waters of Flint's Pond should be mingled with it, or itself should ever go to waste its sweetness in the ocean wave?

1. *How does Thoreau support his statement that "a lake is the landscape's most beautiful and expressive feature"? Does his account make you understand what he means by "expressive"?*
2. *Much of what Thoreau describes involves activities characteristic of virtually any pond—for example, in the second paragraph he writes of the surface of the pond and the insects and fish that disturb it, and in the fifth paragraph he describes fish swimming in the pond. Reread these paragraphs and explain how Thoreau can write about such commonplace incidents and make them represent his distinctive perceptions of the pond.*
3. *Thoreau was a trained surveyor and a skilled amateur botanist as well as a poet and philosopher. To what extent do you find the different facets of his background reflected in the way he describes the pond? Where is he highly detailed and factually precise? Where is he metaphorical and poetic? How are the two strains related?*

4. Try to decide how often Thoreau changes his vantage point—in time or in place—as he describes the pond. After you have identified such shifts, explain how some kind of unity or progression still remains in the description.

5. In the next to last paragraph, Thoreau says that all those who see Walden Pond while riding past on the train "are better men for the sight." Has his description of the pond given you any understanding of how he could make this statement?

∽ Alfred Kazin ∽

(1915-   )

Alfred Kazin was born, brought up, and educated in New York City. His influential study of modern American prose, On Native Grounds *(1942), published while still in his twenties, began his career as a critic, editor, and teacher. Much of his writing has been concerned with American life and with its literary and social traditions. He now teaches at the City University of New York. He has published several volumes of autobiography, including* A Walker in the City *(1951), dealing with his boyhood in the Jewish immigrant neighborhood of Brownsville in east Brooklyn, and* Starting Out in the Thirties *(1965).*

THE BLOCK AND BEYOND

The block: *my* block. It was on the Chester Street side of our house, between the grocery and the back wall of the old drugstore, that I was hammered into the shape of the streets. Everything beginning at Blake Avenue would always wear for me some delightful strangeness and mildness, simply because it was not of my block, *the* block, where the clang of your head sounded against the pavement when you fell in a fist fight, and the rows of storelights on each side were pitiless, watching you. Anything away from the block was good: even a school you never went to, two blocks away: there were vegetable gardens in the park across the street. Returning from "New York," I would take the longest routes home from the subway, get off a station ahead of our own, only for the unexpectedness of walking through Betsy Head Park and hearing the gravel crunch under my feet as I went beyond the vegetable gardens, smelling the sweaty sweet dampness from the pool in summer and the dust on the leaves as I passed under the ailanthus trees. On the block itself everything rose up only to test me.

We worked every inch of it, from the cellars and the backyards to the sickening space between the roofs. Any wall, any stoop, any curving metal edge on a billboard sign made a place against which to knock a ball; any bottom rung of a fire escape ladder a goal in basketball; any sewer cover a base; any crack in the pavement a "net" for the tense sharp tennis that we played by beating a soft ball back and forth with our hands between the squares. Betsy Head Park two blocks away would always feel slightly foreign, for it belonged to the Amboys and the Bristols and the Hopkinsons as much as it did to us. *Our* life every day was fought out on the pavement and in the gutter, up against the walls of the houses and the glass fronts of the drugstore and the grocery, in and out of the fresh steaming piles of horse manure, the wheels of passing carts and automobiles, along the iron spikes of the stairway to the cellar, the jagged edge of the open garbage cans, the crumbly steps of the old farmhouses still left on one side of the street.

As I go back to the block now, and for a moment fold my body up again in its narrow arena—there, just there, between the black of the asphalt and the old women in their kerchiefs and flowered housedresses sitting on the tawny kitchen chairs— the back wall of the drugstore still rises up to test me. Every day we smashed a small black viciously hard regulation handball against it with fanatical cuts and drives and slams, beating and slashing at it almost in hatred for the blind strength of the wall itself. I was never good enough at handball, was always practicing some trick shot that might earn me esteem, and when I was weary of trying, would often bat a ball down Chester Street just to get myself to Blake Avenue. I have this memory of playing one-o'-cat by myself in the sleepy twilight, at a moment when everyone else had left the block. The sparrows floated down from the telephone wires to peck at every fresh pile of horse manure, and there was a smell of brine from the delicatessen store, of egg crates and of the milk scum left in the great metal cans outside the grocery, of the thick white paste oozing out from behind the fresh Hecker's Flour ad on the metal signboard. I would throw the ball in the air, hit it with my bat, then with perfect satisfaction drop the bat to the ground and run to the next sewer cover. Over and over I did this, from sewer cover to sewer cover, until I had worked my way to Blake Avenue and could see the park.

With each clean triumphant ring of my bat against the gutter leading me on, I did the whole length of our block up and down, and never knew how happy I was just watching the asphalt rise and fall, the curve of the steps up to an old farmhouse. The farmhouses themselves were streaked red on one side, brown on the other, but the steps themselves were always gray. There was a tremor of pleasure at one place; I held my breath in nausea at another. As I ran after my ball with the bat heavy in my hand, the odd successiveness of things in myself almost choked me, the world was so full as I ran—past the cobblestoned yards into the old farmhouses, where stray chickens still waddled along the stones; past the little candy store where we went only if the big one on our side of the block was out of Eskimo Pies; past the three neighboring tenements where the last of the old women sat on their kitchen chairs yawning before they went up to make supper. Then came Mrs. Rosenwasser's house, the place on the block I first identified with what was farthest from home, and strangest, because it was a "private" house; then the fences around the monument works, where black cranes rose up above the yard and you could see the smooth gray slabs that would be cut and carved into tombstones, some of them already engraved with the names and dates and family virtues of the dead.

Beyond Blake Avenue was the pool parlor outside which we waited all through the tense September afternoons of the World's Series to hear the latest scores called off the ticker tape—and where as we waited, banging a ball against the bottom of the wall and drinking water out of empty coke bottles, I breathed the chalk off the cues and listened to the clocks ringing in the fire station across the street. There was an old warehouse next to the pool parlor; the oil on the barrels and the iron staves had the same rusty smell. A block away was the park, thick with the dusty gravel I liked to hear my shoes crunch in as I ran round and round the track; then a great open pavilion, the inside mysteriously dark, chill even in summer; there I would wait in the sweaty coolness before pushing on to the wading ring where they put up a shower on the hottest days.

Beyond the park the "fields" began, all those still unused lots where we could still play hard ball in perfect peace—first shooing away the goats and then tearing up goldenrod before laying our bases. The smell and touch of those "fields," with their wild compost under the billboards of weeds, goldenrod, bricks, goat droppings, rusty cans, empty beer bottles, fresh new lumber, and damp cement, lives in my mind as Brownsville's great open door, the wastes that took us through to the west. I used to go round them in summer with my cousins selling near-beer to the carpenters, but always in a daze, would stare so long at the fibrous stalks of the goldenrod as I felt their harshness in my hand that I would forget to make a sale, and usually go off sick on the beer I drank up myself. Beyond! Beyond! Only to see something new, to get away from each day's narrow battleground between the grocery and the back wall of the drugstore! Even the other end of our block, when you got to Mrs. Rosenwasser's house and the monument works, was dear to me for the contrast. On summer nights, when we played Indian trail, running away from each other on prearranged signals, the greatest moment came when I could plunge into the darkness down the block for myself and hide behind the slabs in the monument works. I remember the air whistling around me as I ran, the panicky thud of my bones in my sneakers, and then the slabs rising in the light from the street lamps as I sped past the little candy store and crept under the fence.

In the darkness you could never see where the crane began.

We liked to trap the enemy between the slabs and sometimes jumped them from great mounds of rock just in from the quarry. A boy once fell to his death that way, and they put a watchman there to keep us out. This made the slabs all the more impressive to me, and I always aimed first for that yard whenever we played follow-the-leader. Day after day the monument works became oppressively more mysterious and remote, though it was only just down the block; I stood in front of it every afternoon on my way back from school, filling it with my fears. It was not death I felt there—the slabs were usually faceless. It was the darkness itself, and the wind howling around me whenever I stood poised on the edge of a high slab waiting to jump. Then I would take in, along with the fear, some amazement of joy that I had found my way out that far.

1. Can you categorize the kinds of details that Kazin uses most often in portraying his neighborhood? How frequently does Kazin use details other than those supplied by visual memories? What do these other details contribute to your sense of his experience?

2. What sense of Kazin as a boy do you get from his account? Do you think that he is trying to emphasize his uniqueness as a child or his representativeness? Explain how you arrived at your judgment.

3. What attitude does Kazin take toward his past as he tells you about it? Does he seem detached from it or immersed in it? Nostalgic for it or relieved to be free of it? How does his attitude express itself in the details he uses and the way he presents them?

4. Since Kazin does not use any strict chronological order in writing about his experiences, what kind of order does he provide? How are his memories related to one another?

5. Kazin rarely describes incidents that happened once and once only. Why not? How does he create the impression of recurring experiences? What does that contribute to his autobiography?

∾ Malcolm X ∾

(1925-1965)

*Born Malcolm Little in Omaha, Malcolm X spent his ado-
lescence in the black communities of Roxbury, Massachusetts,
and Harlem. He soon became involved with the underworld
life of the ghetto, first as a drug seller, then as a burglar. Convicted of burglary in 1946, he was sentenced to ten years in
prison. There he was converted to the Black Muslim religion.
After his parole in 1952, he became an outspoken and controversial minister for the Muslim leader, Elijah Muhammad,
and he lectured widely in behalf of black separatism. Later,
disagreements with Elijah Muhammad led Malcolm to form
his own group, The Organization of African Unity. He was
murdered while addressing one of its meetings in Harlem in
1965. His* Autobiography *(1964) recounts his turbulent past,
his conversion, and his rise to leadership in the black nation-
alist movement.*

HARLEMITE

The cooks took me up to Harlem in a cab. White New York
passed by like a movie set, then abruptly, when we left Central
Park at the upper end, at 110th Street, the people's complexion
began to change.

Busy Seventh Avenue ran along in front of a place called
Small's Paradise. The crew had told me before we left Boston
that it was their favorite night spot in Harlem, and not to miss
it. No Negro place of business had ever impressed me so much.

From Malcolm X (with the assistance of Alex Haley): *The Autobiography of
Malcolm X*. Copyright © 1964 by Alex Haley and Malcolm X, © 1965 by Alex
Haley and Betty Shabazz. Reprinted by permission of Random House, Inc.

Around the big, luxurious-looking, circular bar were thirty or forty Negroes, mostly men, drinking and talking.

I was hit first, I think, by their conservative clothes and manners. Wherever I'd seen as many as ten Boston Negroes— let alone Lansing Negroes—drinking, there had been a big noise. But with all of these Harlemites drinking and talking, there was just a low murmur of sound. Customers came and went. The bartenders knew what most of them drank and automatically fixed it. A bottle was set on the bar before some.

Every Negro I'd ever known had made a point of flashing whatever money he had. But these Harlem Negroes quietly laid a bill on the bar. They drank. They nonchalantly nodded to the bartender to pour a drink for some friend, while the bartenders, smooth as any of the customers, kept making change from the money on the bar.

Their manners seemed natural; they were not putting on any airs. I was awed. Within the first five minutes in Small's, I had left Boston and Roxbury forever.

I didn't yet know that these weren't what you might call everyday or average Harlem Negroes. Later on, even later that night, I would find out that Harlem contained hundreds of thousands of my people who were just as loud and gaudy as Negroes anywhere else. But these were the cream of the older, more mature operators in Harlem. The day's "numbers" business was done. The night's gambling and other forms of hustling hadn't yet begun. The usual night-life crowd, who worked on regular jobs all day, were at home eating their dinners. The hustlers at this time were in the daily six o'clock congregation, their favorite bars all over Harlem largely to themselves.

From Small's, I taxied over to the Apollo Theater. (I remember so well that Jay McShann's band was playing, because his vocalist was later my close friend, Walter Brown, the one who used to sing "Hooty Hooty Blues.") From there, on the other side of 125th Street, at Seventh Avenue, I saw the big, tall, gray Theresa Hotel. It was the finest in New York

City where Negroes could then stay, years before the downtown hotels would accept the black man. (The Theresa is now best known as the place where Fidel Castro went during his U.N. visit, and achieved a psychological coup over the U.S. State Department when it confined him to Manhattan, never dreaming that he'd stay uptown in Harlem and make such an impression among the Negroes.)

The Braddock Hotel was just up 126th Street, near the Apollo's backstage entrance. I knew its bar was famous as a Negro celebrity hang-out. I walked in and saw, along that jampacked bar, such famous stars as Dizzy Gillespie, Billy Eckstine, Billie Holiday, Ella Fitzgerald, and Dinah Washington.

As Dinah Washington was leaving with some friends, I overheard someone say she was on her way to the Savoy Ballroom where Lionel Hampton was appearing that night—she was then Hamp's vocalist. The ballroom made the Roseland in Boston look small and shabby by comparison. And the lindy-hopping there matched the size and elegance of the place. Hampton's hard-driving outfit kept a red-hot pace with his greats such as Arnett Cobb, Illinois Jacquet, Dexter Gordon, Alvin Hayse, Joe Newman, and George Jenkins. I went a couple of rounds on the floor with girls from the sidelines.

Probably a third of the sideline booths were filled with white people, mostly just watching the Negroes dance; but some of them danced together, and, as in Boston, a few white women were with Negroes. The people kept shouting for Hamp's "Flyin' Home," and finally he did it. (I could believe the story I'd heard in Boston about this number—that once in the Apollo, Hamp's "Flyin' Home" had made some reefer-smoking Negro in the second balcony believe he could fly, so he tried—and jumped—and broke his leg, an event later immortalized in song when Earl Hines wrote a hit tune called "Second Balcony Jump.") I had never seen such fever-heat dancing. After a couple of slow numbers cooled the place off, they brought on Dinah Washington. When she did her "Salty Papa Blues," those people just about tore the Savoy roof off.

(Poor Dinah's funeral was held not long ago in Chicago. I read that over 20,000 people viewed her body, and I should have been there myself. Poor Dinah! We became great friends, back in those days.)

But this night of my first visit was Kitchen Mechanics' Night at the Savoy, the traditional Thursday night off for domestics. I'd say there were twice as many women as men in there, not only kitchen workers and maids, but also war wives and defense-worker women, lonely and looking. Out in the street, when I left the ballroom, I heard a prostitute cursing bitterly that the professionals couldn't do any business because of the amateurs.

Up and down along and between Lenox and Seventh and Eighth Avenues, Harelm was like some technicolor bazaar. Hundreds of Negro soldiers and sailors, gawking and young like me, passed by. Harlem by now was officially off limits to white servicemen. There had already been some muggings and robberies, and several white servicemen had even been found murdered. The police were also trying to discourage white civilians from coming uptown, but those who wanted to still did. Every man without a woman on his arm was being "worked" by the prostitutes. "Baby, wanna have some fun?" The pimps would sidle up close, stage-whispering, "All kinds of women, Jack—want a white woman?" And the hustlers were merchandising: "Hundred dollar ring, man, diamond; ninety-dollar watch, too—look at 'em. Take 'em both for twenty-five."

In another two years, I could have given them all lessons. But that night, I was mesmerized. This world was where I belonged. On that night I had started on my way to becoming a Harlemite. I was going to become one of the most depraved parasitical hustlers among New York's eight million people— four million of whom work, and the other four million of whom live off them.

I couldn't quite believe all that I'd heard and seen that night as I lugged my shoulder-strap sandwich box and that heavy five-gallon aluminum coffee pot up and down the aisles of the "Yankee Clipper" back to Boston. I wished that Ella and I had been on better terms so that I could try to describe to her how I felt. But I did talk to Shorty, urging him to at least go to see the Big Apple music world. Sophia listened to me, too. She told me that I'd never be satisfied anywhere but New York. She was so right. In one night, New York—Harlem—had just about narcotized me.

That sandwich man I'd replaced had little chance of getting his job back. I went bellowing up and down those train aisles. I sold sandwiches, coffee, candy, cake, and ice cream as fast as the railroad's commissary department could supply them. It didn't take me a week to learn that all you had to do was give white people a show and they'd buy anything you offered them. It was like popping your shoeshine rag. The dining car waiters and Pullman porters knew it too, and they faked their Uncle Tomming to get bigger tips. We were in that world of Negroes who are both servants and psychologists, aware that white people are so obsessed with their own importance that they will pay liberally, even dearly, for the impression of being catered to and entertained.

Every layover night in Harlem, I ran and explored new places. I first got a room at the Harlem YMCA, because it was less than a block from Small's Paradise. Then, I got a cheaper room at Mrs. Fisher's rooming house which was close to the YMCA. Most of the railroad men stayed at Mrs. Fisher's. I combed not only the bright-light areas, but Harlem's residential areas from best to worst, from Sugar Hill up near the Polo Grounds, where many famous celebrities lived, down to the slum blocks of old rat-trap apartment houses, just crawling with everything you could mention that was illegal and immoral. Dirt, garbage cans overflowing or kicked over; drunks, dope addicts, beggars. Sleazy bars, storefront churches with gospels being shouted inside, "bargain" stores, hockshops, undertaking parlors. Greasy "home-cooking" restaurants, beauty shops smoky inside from Negro women's hair getting fried, barbershops advertising conk experts. Cadillacs, second-hand and new, conspicuous among the cars on the streets.

All of it was Lansing's West Side or Roxbury's South End magnified a thousand times. Little basement dance halls with "For Rent" signs on them. People offering you little cards advertising "rent-raising parties." I went to one of these—thirty or forty Negroes sweating, eating, drinking, dancing, and gambling in a jammed, beat-up apartment, the record player going full blast, the fried chicken or chitlins with potato salad and collard greens for a dollar a plate, and cans of beer or shots of liquor for fifty cents. Negro and white canvassers sidled up alongside you, talking fast as they tried to get you to buy a copy of the *Daily Worker:* "This paper's trying to keep your rent controlled . . . Make that greedy landlord kill them rats in your apartment . . . This paper represents the only political party that ever ran a black man for the Vice Presidency of the United States . . . Just want you to read, won't take but a little of your time . . . Who do you think fought the hardest to help free those Scottsboro boys?" Things I overheard among Negroes when the salesmen were around let me know that the paper somehow was tied in with the Russians, but to my sterile mind in those early days, it didn't mean much; the radio broadcasts and the newspapers were then full of our-ally-Russia, a strong, muscular people, peasants, with their backs to the wall helping America to fight Hitler and Mussolini.

But New York was heaven to me. And Harlem was Seventh Heaven! I hung around in Small's and the Braddock bar so much that the bartenders began to pour a shot of bourbon, my favorite brand of it, when they saw me walk in the door. And the steady customers in both places, the hustlers in Small's and the entertainers in the Braddock, began to call me "Red," a natural enough nickname in view of my bright red conk. I now had my conk done in Boston at the shop of Abbott and Fogey; it was the best conk shop on the East Coast, according to the musical greats who had recommended it to me.

1. *How does Malcolm create the sense that Harlem is a very special and distinctive community? How does he make it reflect some of the life styles of black Americans?*

2. *Malcolm is describing Harlem as he saw it for the first time as a young and inexperienced teenager. In what ways does he suggest his youthful point of view in presenting his description of Harlem?*

3. *Malcolm is writing his autobiography at a time when he has been converted to the Muslim religion and is committed to black nationalism and to a strict code of moral conduct. Does this viewpoint of the older Malcolm find some expression in the selection?*

4. *What happens to Malcolm himself after he first arrives in Harlem? Do the descriptions of Harlem provide a setting that helps to explain the young Malcolm's actions? How does he establish himself as a "Harlemite"?*

5. *Characterize Malcolm's use of specific details in describing Harlem. Does he use many or few? Are they closely or loosely related? What effect do they have on you as a reader?*

∽ Willie Morris ∽

(1934-   )

Willie Morris was raised in Mississippi and educated at the
University of Texas and at Oxford University. His interest in
journalism began when he worked for the school newspaper at
Texas and resulted in his later becoming editor-in-chief of The
Texas Observer *and then an editor of* Harper's Magazine *in the*
1960s. He has since devoted himself to his own writing, pub-
lishing among other books the autobiographical volumes Good
Old Boy *(1971) and* North Toward Home *(1967).*

NEW YORK

The apartment I found was in the east twenties, between
Madison and Park. The other places that I had seen and liked,
airy places with parks nearby, never rented for less than $250
or $300 a month, for rents in the city were criminal. This one
rented at $125, and it occupied the third floor of a narrow gray
building next to a parking lot. The exposed side was pocked
with holes and ridges, and someone had written on it in white
enamel: "The Dukes." Looking at this unusual structure from
a block down the street, one was struck by its lean-to quality;
it seemed to have no business existing at all. It rose from the
west side of the parking lot, gaunt and improvised. Someone
walking down the street with the address almost always
walked right past it, thinking that the place might not be in-
habited. One reason may have been that there was a red canopy over the sidewalk at the front door advertising the short-

order take-home service which shared the entrance off to the left.

One walked up the three flights through several padlocked doors, often past the garbage which the landlords had neglected to remove for two or three days. Once inside our place, things were not bad at all. There was a big front room with an old floor, a little alcove for a study, and to the back a short corridor opening up into a tiny bedroom for my son and a larger bedroom in the back. The kitchen was in the back bedroom. I had not been able to find a view of an extensive body of water at popular prices, but from the back window, about forty yards out, there *was* a vista of a big tank, part of some manufacturing installation in the building under it, and the tank constantly bubbled with some unidentified greenish substance. From this window one could also see the tarred rooftops of the surrounding buildings, and off to the right a quiet stretch of God's earth, this being the parking lot next door.

From the front room the view of the street was more animated. Across the street there was a large bar which seemed to remain open twenty-four hours a day, and in front of this, on the corner, one could look down at any hour and see the little circles of people, just standing, watching the mad traffic on lower Madison. We were without sunlight, which was unable to penetrate down from the tall office building across the street; and when it rained, which was often that first year, I remembered the hard cold rainfalls in the Mississippi delta of my childhood, and how they encompassed the green earth and fields and trees in such a torrent that one seemed at the mercy of nature itself; here, from the front window, the rain merely kicked up little pools of dirt and debris on East 26th, and sent people under the canopy of the bar. One oppressive Saturday afternoon, our old Texas friends Ronnie Dugger and Larry Goodwyn sat here in our front room with us; our separate work had all brought us briefly together in New York City. We sat here talking of old times and places; then, out of a gray sky, there came a blizzard. We watched the big flakes come down for a while, a little depressed and intimidated. Suddenly Good-wyn opened the window, stuck his head out, and gazed down at the scene on East 26th. Then he put his head back in, turned around, and said, "Well, boys, they got us all up here together . . . and then they *snowed* on us." The subway was also diffi-cult to get used to. There was a station twenty yards from the building; every five minutes the building rocked and groaned at its very foundations.

I was only seven blocks from my office at *Harper's*, and in the mornings I could walk up Madison to work. On a fine day, carrying my black briefcase with poems from housewives in the Midwest, or stream-of-consciousness prose from the gradu-ate schools, I enjoyed making my way up the avenue through the bustling crowds on the sidewalks, feeling very much the cosmopolite. But on some grim foggy morning, when the steam came out of the sewers in the streets as if the earth be-neath were on fire, the city had a dreadful claustrophobic qual-ity, like death itself: closed-in, blind, and airless, compressed by the endless concrete and asphalt exteriors. The horns from the cabs, the cursing of the drivers, the harsh violence of the streetworkers dodging the already clogged traffic, caused a new arrival to feel that humanity here was always at war with its machines and with itself. In the course of a year, walking seven blocks to work and back over the same route, I saw three people killed by cars and four others badly hurt. The most likely place for this mayhem was the curious intersection of Park and 33rd. Here there was a tunnel which came suddenly out of nowhere. Cars whipped out of it at terrific speeds, catch-ing pedestrians crossing against the red light on Park. There was no sign suggesting the existence of this tunnel, which added somewhat to the spirit of adventure. At first it would be disrupting to see the white sheet covering an unfortunate pe-destrian caught by surprise by some taxicab coming out of the tunnel, the crowds milling around with that sullen big-city curiosity looking at the blood, the cop or two waiting perfunc-torily for the ambulance to arrive. After a time I grew used to the spectacle, however, and would walk gingerly past the broken body and its spectators as if it were all in the morning's walk.

Many times, walking home from work, I would see some unknowing soul venture across that intersection against the light and then freeze in horror when he saw the cars ripping out of the tunnel toward him. For a brief instant the immobile human would stand there, transfixed by the vehicle bearing down upon him, the contrast of desperate vulnerable flesh and hard chrome never failing to send a horrible tremor through an onlooker's being. Then, suddenly, the human reflex would take over, and the pedestrian would jackknife first one way, then another, arms flaying the empty air, and often the car would literally *skim* the man, brushing by him so close it would touch his coat or his tie. If another car coming behind did not nail him then, much the way a linebacker moves in for the kill after the tackle or end merely slows down a ball-carrier, the pedestrian would stand there briefly, all the blood drained from his face, oblivious to the curses from the driver of the car which had just missed him. If there was a cop on the corner he would wait while the man staggered in his shock to the sidewalk beyond, there to accost him: "Ya crazy, hah? Ya stupid? Walkin' against the light! Hah! Ya almost got killed, ya know it? Ya *know* it?" I saw this ritual several times; on one occasion, feeling sorry for the person who had brushed against the speeding car, I hurried across the intersection after him to cheer him up a little. Catching up with him down by 32nd I said, "That was good legwork, sir. Excellent moves for a big man!" but the man looked at me with an empty expression in his eyes, and then moved away mechanically and trancelike, heading for the nearest bar.

On a number of occasions on my peregrinations from 33rd to 26th there would be some bum sprawled out on the sidewalk, and the people would walk right past him, or sometimes step over him, glancing back a little nervously, usually saying to their companions, "Somebody should call a cop." The first time I saw a man lying prone on the concrete, blood trickling slightly from his nose, I bent over and asked him if he was all right, and he moaned a little, and I went into a restaurant and phoned the police to report his distress. But after a while, like the others when confronted with such a sight, I would keep going too, though always a little guiltily; wishing a cop would come by soon. Why should people in such a city be *expected* to stop and do something about their fallen wounded, not knowing them nor caring? The existence involved in moving daily to and from work in the immense and faceless crowds inevitably hardens one's senses to violence and despair. I came to feel it perfectly natural, this isolated callousness of the city-dweller. Anyone who expected valor or compassion in everyday acts in a monstrous American city in these times expected too much of human nature, and would sooner or later be disappointed. The cops became the guardians of benevolence; they were our salaried Samaritans.

Along the sidewalks in our neighborhood roamed two old walkers who made their mark on the area. One was a bent-over old man who wore pince-nez; he carried an American flag, a Bible, and a megaphone. At almost any hour of the day you could hear him, standing on some street corner nearby, delivering a feverish sermon on sin, redemption, and patriotism, or moving along the sidewalk with his dragging gait shouting vengeance on every moving object in the vicinity, animal or vegetable. He was just as content trying to convert a Chevrolet pick-up truck as he was in shouting his evangelical threats to the little Italian boys who congregated at the fruit stand on Lexington. There was a horror to this old man, to the echo of his grating voice coming down the narrow streets between the big buildings. Thin trickles of saliva would form on his mouth and drip to the pavement; his moist insane proselytizing seemed as inexorable and illogical as the city itself, as its insane flow of vehicles and people. One Christmas morning, as my son played with his toys in the front room of our apartment, I heard him from down the block, and through a drab

December mist I saw him shuffling along on 26th street, solitary and mad; suddenly I felt sorry for him, alone on this Christmas day. I picked up a couple of cans of fancy sardines and rushed down the stairs, catching up with him on the sidewalk. "Merry Christmas," I said, the first words I had ever spoken to him, and handed him the sardines. A puffed-up smile creased his face. He took the gift and said, "What is your religion, young man?" "I'm an old Mississippi Methodist," I replied. "Ah . . . Methodist," he said. "Then you don't believe in Jesus. Pity on you, young man." And he walked away, gingerly putting the sardines in his coat pocket.

The other neighborhood apparition was a woman of about sixty, a gaunt old specter who worked regularly as clockwork. She was a junkie, and every afternoon from three to five she roamed the streets shouting some demented gibberish, a considerable tumult for such a scrawny old woman. Once I saw the evangelist and the drug addict meet by chance in front of a shabby building on Lexington with a plaque explaining that Chester A. Arthur had been sworn in here as President of the USA after Garfield was assassinated, and they shouted at one another as if mortal enemies, and the old man walked away, whispering through his megaphone, *"Doomed. Doomed!"* The woman's shouts were even more disrupting than the man's, however, because they were self-inflicted, and because she worked on a schedule, coming out of God knows what place every day to exercise her private perspectives. Both were always alone and always ignored. Except when taunted by the neighborhood kids they seemed quite self-sufficient.

In our apartment my son walked and crawled around the front room, exploring the edges of his new existence. There was nowhere to take him to run. Running him down the sidewalks of Madison or Park or Lexington in early evening was like taking a nighttime trot in the Carlsbad Caverns. Once the traffic had thinned out at night, traffic lights for the taxis were as physically efficacious as a resolution of the UN General Assembly; I had never seen red lights ignored with such disdain.

Madison Park, the closest piece of earth in the vicinity, was a good place to watch the drunks and the old men sleeping under shrubs, but no likely retreat for a three-year-old child. Finally I took to playing with him in the parking lot next door, throwing a tennis ball against our apartment house and letting him retrieve it, until the man who owned the lot came by one bright fall evening and said, "Cancha see that *sign:* it says *private property.* If ya can't read, mistuh, go back to trainin' school."

We missed the easy, open life of Texas, the impromptu beer parties in our house on Bridle Path, the casual way people had of dropping by on friends, the old German beer hall and the tables under the trees in back. The only person we knew in the neighborhood was Nick, who sold newspapers at a little stand on Madison. I could leave my son with him for half an hour or so while I went off on an errand, and come back and find the child behind the counter, helping sell the *Journal-American* and the *World-Telegram.* Returning to the newsstand one night, I sidled up to the papers and saw my son selling a *Post* to a cabdriver, who gave him a nickel tip; the Harpers of Mississippi seemed far, far away.

1. *What kind of details does Morris present as characteristic of big-city life? How are they different from the kind of description of New York that Malcolm X provides?*
2. *Morris was raised in the South. How does he create an impression of the city as seen by someone familiar with another way of life? What can you infer are the characteristics of that other way of life? What are some of the qualities of city life he emphasizes that a long-time resident might ignore?*
3. *Do the details Morris uses suggest the variety of city life or do they reinforce one another to emphasize only one aspect of the city?*
4. *What is Morris's attitude when he describes the dangers to pedestrians at the intersection of Park Avenue and 33rd Street? In the fourth paragraph, why does he call it a "curious inter-*

section"? *In the next paragraph, how does he make you see the meeting of car and pedestrian? How would you explain his behavior to the pedestrian afterwards?*

5. *When Morris describes the apartment he has rented, what aspects of it does he concentrate on and what does he ignore? How does his choice of details fit his general portrait of city life?*

∾ Wright Morris ∾

(1910-   )

*Wright Morris has published more than thirty books, predom-
inantly works of fiction. He is also an essayist, a literary critic,
and a noted photographer. Many of his novels are set in
Nebraska, where Morris was born and grew up; they often
concern the contrasts between an earlier rural world and modern American life.* Will's Boy (1981) *is Morris' account of
growing up in Nebraska with his father, a wanderer who had
more success with women than with business. The selection
here concerns the summer Morris, age thirteen, was sent to
live on the family farm, owned by his father's brother.*

   Throughout Will's Boy, *Morris interpolates passages from
his novels that were based on his memories of his early life.
Those passages have not been included in this selection.*

[ON THE FARM]

When I got off the train in the late summer twilight, I had a
fiber mailing carton with a change of clothes washed and
ironed by Mrs. Mulligan. I was wearing city clothes to travel
in, my cap still stiff with the paper lining, on my feet a new
pair of green leather shoes with a dark patch of leather on the
ankles and toes. The soles were also green and resisted bending, pulling away from my heels with each step I took. They
were so new I'd only worn them up and down the aisle of the
train.

   Uncle Harry was not there to meet me when I arrived. I

Abridged from pages 67-74 in *Will's Boy: A Memoir* by Wright Morris. Copyright © 1981 by Wright Morris. Reprinted by permission of Harper & Row,
Publishers, Inc.

watched the taillights of the coach go over the horizon, and when the throbbing of the gas motor died, a noise settled around me like it was trapped in my ears. I had never heard anything like it. On both sides of the dirt road that led to the east the weeds were almost as high as my head. Fireflies rose from the dark fields to hover like a cloud of sparklers. The night air was heavy and sweet with the smell of hay. As the fields around me darkened, the bowl of the sky above me seemed to brighten. My stiff-soled shoes flicked the sand of the road to fall into the heels of my shoes. In the overall drone of the sounds around me I was able to distinguish the cadence of the locusts. It began slowly, built to a climax, then tailed off into silence. At the rim of the eastern sky I could see stars. When I stopped in the road to look around me I experienced a pleasurable apprehension. Big bugs and millers flew into my face. I sucked in small insects when I inhaled. Far down the road, in which I stood at the center, two small flickering lights came toward me. The putter of the motor rose and fell as the road tilted upward or declined. As the car approached me a cloud of insects obscured the lights. I had to move from the road to let the car pass me and proceed to a point where the driver was able to turn it around. Coming back toward me, it went ahead a few yards before it stopped. In the dusky light I saw an erect dark figure gripping with both hands the vibrating steering wheel. No feature of his face was visible.

"So you made it," he said to me, then spit into the weeds to the left of the road. What I said to him, if anything, I have forgotten. "Climb in, boy," he added, and I did as I was told.

The summer I met him, my Uncle Harry was a heavy, dour, silent man with his family, but given to deadpan joshing with his neighbors, his puckered lips sealed and stained with tobacco juice. After spitting, if his hands were free, he would pinch his pursed lips between his thumb and forefinger, then give a twist as if tightening a cap on a bottle. His wife, Clara, was a tall, lath-flat woman with a high-pitched voice, who liked to work. Her daughter, Mae, away at school that summer, planned to teach school. Her son, Will, had attended the aggie college in Lincoln and farmed the adjoining acres. His house could be seen through the stand of catalpa trees along the drive-in from the road. Just the year before, Will had married a black-haired young woman from Missouri. While I was on the farm she would bring over her baby and let it crawl around the floor while she helped Clara with the canning.

Harry and Clara's house was square, without gables, a lightning rod with a blue ball on it at the roof's peak, the windows of the upstairs bedrooms almost flush to the floor. I could lie stretched out on the floor and look out. I had Will's old room, with clothes stored in the dresser, the curtained and screened window facing the drive-in between the two houses. In the pulsing flashes of heat lightning I would see the intricate pattern of the glass curtain, the screen behind it alive with crawling, clicking, fluttering insects. The cats howled and the owls hooted. About dawn I would hear the gagging sound of the pump, and then the splash into the pail as Harry pumped up the water. As he approached the house, carrying two pails, I'd hear the occasional slurp of the water and the rub of the denim between his thighs. Up the stairwell from the kitchen would rise the smell of the kerosene spilled on the cobs. The flames would whoosh and roar in the chimney, then settle back to a steady crackle. The new day had begun, but I would pretend to sleep until Clara's shrill voice cried, "Wright, you coming?" Since I was always coming, I never really knew if she would call me twice.

. . .

Clara baked biscuits, fried eggs and cooked oatmeal for breakfast. The eggs were fried hard, in bacon fat, the oatmeal thick and chewy as taffy. After sitting all night, the separated cream had to be spooned out of the pitcher. My Uncle Harry would spread it on a hot biscuit like jam.

My daily chores were to fetch water and baskets of cobs. The cobs could be seen pressing against the windows of the first small house they had built on the farm. When I stooped to scoop them into the basket I might hear mice rustle the tassels. Sometimes I carried a mouse into the house. I would see it later, its whiskers twitching, spying on me over the rim of the basket. Clara set traps for mice in her cupboards, but if I heard them go off I knew she hadn't caught one. She had little respect for a boy as old as I was who couldn't set a trap.

Clara kept about thirty-eight Plymouth Rock chickens, and Harry milked about twenty Jersey cows. The cow pasture was at the far north end of the farm, down a lane of cottonwoods that Harry himself had planted. Nothing I had ever seen grew so close to the sky. Some nights the cows would come into the barn, and other nights I would have to go after them. There was always one cow, when she saw me coming, that would go to the farthest corner of the pasture, where the weeds were high. In the knee-high weeds near the barn I had seen both garter snakes and sand vipers. What to do? What I had learned to do was run. Once I got behind the last cow I would hoot and holler like I was crazy, and once you get an old cow riled up she likes to run with her tail up, like a whip in a stock, her udder swinging. I'd let up running and walk once I reached the tree lane, but some of the cows would still be mooing when they reached the barn. What was it they'd seen? Uncle Harry asked me. He was also puzzled why his cows, with such good pasture, were giving so little milk. In my first week on the farm the one thing I had learned was to keep my own counsel, and my mouth shut. The cows didn't much like me in the stable either, mooing and milling around when I came near them, so I would just stand around the stable door watching Harry squirt milk right from the teat at a row of cats. To make sure they didn't miss any, they would rise up and let it splash on their fronts, then lick it off.

· · ·

When I didn't have my chores to do I liked to sit in the sun, my back against the warm boards of the barn. I wanted to look like a farmboy, my face and arms tan, when I got back to Omaha. Compared to the noise at night, the day seemed to me as quiet as a church. Here and there I saw a butterfly zig-zagging, or grass stems waggle when a grasshopper jumped. Cloud shadows passed over the scarecrow in Clara's garden, the straw sticking out of one of Harry's coat sleeves. It scared the crows, but the shiny blackbirds, with eyes like hatpins, perched on his shoulders. If I listened hard I could hear Uncle Harry "gee" and "haw" his team at the end of each furrow. He plowed with horses although his son, Will, had told him there was no place for a horse on a farm. Harry had sent Will to the aggie college in Lincoln, then refused to believe anything he had learned. He scoffed at everything Will did or said. Will was not so tall, but he took after Clara, with her big adam's apple, her high-pitched voice and unblinking eyes. The way his adam's apple pumped when he swallowed made it look like he had a bend in his neck. With Will's .22 rifle I shot my first jackrabbit, but when I picked him up, his big eyes wide open, I dropped him and ran.

The Sunday before I left, the Morris and Warner families had a big reunion at their grove in Warnerville. People came from as far as Lincoln, where my father's sister May had married a Warner who sorted mail in one of the Union Pacific mail cars. May was my father's favorite sister, and the happiest grown-up person I had ever met. She laughed all the time and liked everybody. All the women at the reunion brought along whatever it was they cooked the best. We had chicken and hams, potato salad and cole slaw, with everything else in a white sauce. Clara had made berry pies the week before and stored them in the storm cave until the reunion, wiping off the mold with a cloth dampened with vinegar. It didn't work for pies with meringue toppings, but it worked for hers. All I did was chase my cousins in and out of the house until we were eaten up by mosquitoes and had to sit inside. Two of my cousins from Lincoln had run around barefoot and cut the skin between their toes on the sharp sickle grass. Not having lived on a farm, or brought in cows from the pasture, they didn't know about sickle grass or very much else.

226

When it was time for me to leave I was tanned on my arms and had freckles on my nose. In a pillbox I had found in the cobhouse I had the forked tongue of a sandpiper, along with three copper shell casings from the bullets I had shot at the rabbit. At the Warnerville station Harry asked me who my father was married to now. I said I didn't know. He didn't ask me to come again, or wait to see if the train came and stopped for me, but got his Ford turned around, bucking in forward, then drove off in a cloud of dust. There was no wind at all to move it. When it finally settled there was nothing to see.

1. How does Morris establish that his younger self is someone quite unfamiliar with farm life?

2. What kinds of experience make the greatest impression on the boy? Does any one of his senses seem more acute than the others?

3. How does Morris characterize his relatives? Does he suggest that farm life has influenced their behavior? If so, how?

4. How would you compare the boy's arrival at the farm with his departure? What similarities do you see? What differences?

5. How is this descriptive selection different from one concerned with an urban setting? In the city, would the boy have to be observant in different ways? Or have to call upon different powers of description?

∽ George Orwell ∽

(1903-1950)

See the biographical note on page 53. Orwell spent several months in Morocco (September, 1938–March, 1939) while working on the manuscript of a novel, Coming Up for Air; *it was his first visit to the country. He wrote "Marrakech" in the spring of 1939.*

MARRAKECH

As the corpse went past the flies left the restaurant table in a cloud and rushed after it, but they came back a few minutes later.

The little crowd of mourners—all men and boys, no women —threaded their way across the market-place between the piles of pomegranates and the taxis and the camels, wailing a short chant over and over again. What really appeals to the flies is that the corpses here are never put into coffins, they are merely wrapped in a piece of rag and carried on a rough wooden bier on the shoulders of four friends. When the friends get to the burying-ground they hack an oblong hole a foot or two deep, dump the body in it and fling over it a little of the dried-up, lumpy earth, which is like broken brick. No gravestone, no name, no identifying mark of any kind. The burying-ground is merely a huge waste of hummocky earth, like a derelict building-lot. After a month or two no one can even be certain where his own relatives are buried.

When you walk through a town like this—two hundred thousand inhabitants, of whom at least twenty thousand own literally nothing except the rags they stand up in—when you see how the people live, and still more how easily they die, it is always difficult to believe that you are walking among human beings. All colonial empires are in reality founded upon that fact. The people have brown faces—besides, there are so many of them! Are they really the same flesh as yourself? Do they even have names? Or are they merely a kind of undifferentiated brown stuff, about as individual as bees or coral insects? They rise out of the earth, they sweat and starve for a few years, and then they sink back into the nameless mounds of the graveyard and nobody notices that they are gone. And even the graves themselves soon fade back into the soil. Sometimes, out for a walk, as you break your way through the prickly pear, you notice that it is rather bumpy underfoot, and only a certain regularity in the bumps tells you that you are walking over skeletons.

I was feeding one of the gazelles in the public gardens.

Gazelles are almost the only animals that look good to eat when they are still alive, in fact, one can hardly look at their hindquarters without thinking of mint sauce. The gazelle I was feeding seemed to know that this thought was in my mind, for though it took the piece of bread I was holding out it obviously did not like me. It nibbled rapidly at the bread, then lowered its head and tried to butt me, then took another nibble and then butted again. Probably its idea was that if it could drive me away the bread would somehow remain hanging in mid-air.

An Arab navvy working on the path nearby lowered his heavy hoe and sidled slowly towards us. He looked from the gazelle to the bread and from the bread to the gazelle, with a sort of quiet amazement, as though he had never seen anything quite like this before. Finally he said shyly in French:

"*I* could eat some of that bread."

I tore off a piece and he stowed it gratefully in some secret place under his rags. This man is an employee of the Municipality.

When you go through the Jewish quarters you gather some idea of what the medieval ghettoes were probably like. Under their Moorish rulers the Jews were only allowed to own land in certain restricted areas, and after centuries of this kind of treatment they have ceased to bother about overcrowding. Many of the streets are a good deal less than six feet wide, the houses are completely windowless, and sore-eyed children cluster everywhere in unbelievable numbers, like clouds of flies. Down the centre of the street there is generally running a little river of urine.

In the bazaar huge families of Jews, all dressed in the long black robe and little black skull-cap, are working in dark fly-infested booths that look like caves. A carpenter sits cross-legged at a prehistoric lathe, turning chair-legs at lightning speed. He works the lathe with a bow in his right hand and guides the chisel with his left foot, and thanks to a lifetime of sitting in this position his left leg is warped out of shape. At his side his grandson, aged six, is already starting on the simpler parts of the job.

I was just passing the coppersmiths' booths when somebody noticed that I was lighting a cigarette. Instantly, from the dark holes all round, there was a frenzied rush of Jews, many of them old grandfathers with flowing grey beards, all clamouring for a cigarette. Even a blind man somewhere at the back of one of the booths heard a rumour of cigarettes and came crawling out, groping in the air with his hand. In about a minute I had used up the whole packet. None of these people, I suppose, works less than twelve hours a day, and every one of them looks on a cigarette as a more or less impossible luxury.

As the Jews live in self-contained communities they follow the same trades as the Arabs, except for agriculture. Fruit-sellers, potters, silversmiths, blacksmiths, butchers, leather-workers, tailors, water-carriers, beggars, porters—whichever way you look you see nothing but Jews. As a matter of fact there are thirteen thousand of them, all living in the space of a few acres. A good job Hitler wasn't here. Perhaps he was on his way, however. You hear the usual dark rumours about the Jews, not only from the Arabs but from the poorer Europeans.

"Yes, mon vieux, they took my job away from me and gave it to a Jew. The Jews! They're the real rulers of this country, you know. They've got all the money. They control the banks, finance—everything."

"But," I said, "isn't it a fact that the average Jew is a labourer working for about a penny an hour?"

"Ah, that's only for show! They're all moneylenders really. They're cunning, the Jews."

In just the same way, a couple of hundred years ago, poor old women used to be burned for witchcraft when they could not even work enough magic to get themselves a square meal.

All people who work with their hands are partly invisible, and the more important the work they do, the less visible they are. Still, a white skin is always fairly conspicuous. In northern Europe, when you see a labourer ploughing a field, you probably give him a second glance. In a hot country, anywhere south of Gibraltar or east of Suez, the chances are that you don't even see him. I have noticed this again and again. In a tropical landscape one's eye takes in everything except the human beings. It takes in the dried-up soil, the prickly pear, the palm tree and the distant mountain, but it always misses the peasant hoeing at his patch. He is the same colour as the earth, and a great deal less interesting to look at.

It is only because of this that the starved countries of Asia and Africa are accepted as tourist resorts. No one would think of running cheap trips to the Distressed Areas. But where the human beings have brown skins their poverty is simply not noticed. What does Morocco mean to a Frenchman? An orange-grove or a job in Government service. Or to an Englishman? Camels, castles, palm trees, Foreign Legionnaires, brass trays, and bandits. One could probably live there for years without noticing that for nine-tenths of the people the reality of life is an endless, back-breaking struggle to wring a little food out of an eroded soil.

Most of Morocco is so desolate that no wild animal bigger than a hare can live on it. Huge areas which were once covered with forest have turned into a treeless waste where the soil is exactly like broken-up brick. Nevertheless a good deal of it is cultivated, with frightful labour. Everything is done by hand. Long lines of women, bent double like inverted capital L's, work their way slowly across the fields, tearing up the prickly weeds with their hands, and the peasant gathering lucerne for fodder pulls it up stalk by stalk instead of reaping it, thus saving an inch or two on each stalk. The plough is a wretched wooden thing, so frail that one can easily carry it on one's shoulder, and fitted underneath with a rough iron spike which stirs the soil to a depth of about four inches. This is as much as the strength of the animals is equal to. It is usual to plough with a cow and a donkey yoked together. Two donkeys would not be quite strong enough, but on the other hand two cows would cost a little more to feed. The peasants possess no harrows, they merely plough the soil several times over in different directions, finally leaving it in rough furrows, after which the whole field has to be shaped with hoes into small oblong patches to conserve water. Except for a day or two after the rare rainstorms there is never enough water. Along the edges of the fields channels are hacked out to a depth of thirty or forty feet to get at the tiny trickles which run through the subsoil.

Every afternoon a file of very old women passes down the road outside my house, each carrying a load of firewood. All of them are mummified with age and the sun, and all of them are tiny. It seems to be generally the case in primitive communities that the women, when they get beyond a certain age, shrink to the size of children. One day a poor old creature who could not have been more than four feet tall crept past me under a vast load of wood. I stopped her and put a five-sou piece (a little more than a farthing) into her hand. She answered with a shrill wail, almost a scream, which was partly gratitude but mainly surprise. I suppose that from her point of view, by taking any notice of her, I seemed almost to be violating a law of nature. She accepted her status as an old woman, that is to say as a beast of burden. When a family is travelling it is quite usual to see a father and a grown-up son riding ahead on donkeys, and an old woman following on foot, carrying the baggage.

But what is strange about these people is their invisibility. For several weeks, always at about the same time of day, the file of old women had hobbled past the house with their firewood, and though they had registered themselves on my eyeballs I cannot truly say that I had seen them. Firewood was passing—that was how I saw it. It was only that one day I happened to be walking behind them, and the curious up-and-down motion of a load of wood drew my attention to the human being beneath it. Then for the first time I noticed the poor old earth-coloured bodies, bodies reduced to bones and leathery skin, bent double under the crushing weight. Yet I suppose I had not been five minutes on Moroccan soil before I noticed the overloading of the donkeys and was infuriated by it. There is no question that the donkeys are damnably treated. The Moroccan donkey is hardly bigger than a St. Bernard dog, it carries a load which in the British Army would be considered too much for a fifteen-hands mule, and very often its pack-saddle is not taken off its back for weeks together. But what is peculiarly pitiful is that it is the most willing creature on earth, it follows its master like a dog and does not need either bridle or halter. After a dozen years of devoted work it suddenly drops dead, whereupon its master tips it into the ditch and the village dogs have torn its guts out before it is cold.

This kind of thing makes one's blood boil, whereas—on the whole—the plight of the human beings does not. I am not commenting, merely pointing to a fact. People with brown skins are next door to invisible. Anyone can be sorry for the donkey with its galled back, but it is generally owing to some kind of accident if one even notices the old woman under her load of sticks.

As the storks flew northward the Negroes were marching southward—a long, dusty column, infantry, screw-gun batteries, and then more infantry, four or five thousand men in all, winding up the road with a clumping of boots and a clatter of iron wheels.

They were Senegalese, the blackest Negroes in Africa, so black that sometimes it is difficult to see whereabouts on their necks the hair begins. Their splendid bodies were hidden in reach-me-down khaki uniforms, their feet squashed into boots that looked like blocks of wood, and every tin hat seemed to be a couple of sizes too small. It was very hot and the men had marched a long way. They slumped under the weight of their packs and the curiously sensitive black faces were glistening with sweat.

As they went past a tall, very young Negro turned and caught my eye. But the look he gave me was not in the least the kind of look you might expect. Not hostile, not contemptuous, not sullen, not even inquisitive. It was the shy, wide-eyed Negro look, which actually is a look of profound respect. I saw how it was. This wretched boy, who is a French citizen and has therefore been dragged from the forest to scrub floors and catch syphilis in garrison towns, actually has feelings of reverence before a white skin. He has been taught that the white race are his masters, and he still believes it.

But there is one thought which every white man (and in this connection it doesn't matter twopence if he calls himself a socialist) thinks when he sees a black army marching past. "How much longer can we go on kidding these people? How long before they turn their guns in the other direction?"

It was curious, really. Every white man there had this

thought stowed somewhere or other in his mind. I had it, so had the other onlookers, so had the officers on their sweating chargers and the white N.C.O.'s marching in the ranks. It was a kind of secret which we all knew and were too clever to tell; only the Negroes didn't know it. And really it was like watching a flock of cattle to see the long column, a mile or two miles of armed men, flowing peacefully up the road, while the great white birds drifted over them in the opposite direction, glittering like scraps of paper.

1. *Why do you think Orwell begins his essay with the account of the funeral and burial? After reading the entire essay, do you think it is a good introduction to Orwell's view of Marrakech? What difference would it make if he added more specific details—for example, gave the name of the dead man and the site of the burial ground, or described the faces of the friends?*
2. *Whom do you think Orwell sees as his audience? For example, do you think he is addressing natives of Morocco or people who are deciding on their next vacation trip? Explain what details in the description help you define the audience.*
3. *Orwell relies on a series of scenes to create his view of Marrakech—the zoo, the ghetto, the women carrying firewood, the Senegalese troops. Why does he include each of these scenes and how are they related to one another?*
4. *What is Orwell's own role in his account? What is the vantage point from which he describes the scenes in Marrakech? To what kinds of details does Orwell as an observer seem particularly sensitive. Do you think his primary interest is in describing Marrakech itself?*
5. *Why do you think Orwell concludes with the scene involving the Senegalese troops? How would it change his account if he had concluded a page earlier with the scene involving the old women?*

Possibilities for Writing

1. Accumulate a list of details describing a place that you remember vividly, then go over the list and decide how all of these details might best fit together. See also if there might be any opportunity for something other than visual memory to play a part in your description. When you have finished the description, exchange your essay with someone else in the class and compare what you were attempting to convey with what your reader finds memorable.

2. Write a description of a place you remember that has now changed in very noticeable ways. Concentrate on trying to capture the difference between what it was and what it is and on trying to convey whatever shifts in your feelings and your interest have occurred as a result.

3. Write a description of a reasonably large geographical area —for example, a city block, a particular district in a town— any place that would include a considerable variety of people and activities and sights. Make your description express a significant pattern within all this variety, one that would express what you feel is the essence of this particular place.

4. Write an analysis of the kind of community Alfred Kazin grew up in, and the attitude he had toward that community, based on the specific details he uses in his description of "the block and beyond."

CHAPTER FIVE

PEOPLE

Introduction: Concreteness and Generalization

An autobiographical record invariably tells not only what happened and where, but with whom. In most accounts of personal experience much of what a writer has to say about himself emerges through what he says about his relationships with other people. An autobiographer introduces other characters in order to create a context for his own life, since his role as principal actor would make very little sense if the rest of the stage always remained empty. But any revelations about other people also constitute a form of self-revelation. When we characterize a friend, an enemy, even some slight acquaintance, there is always an implicit element of self-characterization, for we are revealing what we value in another person, what we distrust or even abhor, whom we depend upon and why.

Characterization also introduces a new dimension in the autobiographical writer's method of organizing his experience. Narration leads us immediately to think about time, description about space. But characterization depends much more upon the isolation of qualities that strike us through recurrence; it requires us to sort out the habitual from the occasional as a way of identifying who we think another person really is. Of course we often rely on narration or description to create the portrait of a particular human being. We may dramatize a moment of generosity or heroism or affection as a vivid illustration of character, or we may provide a detailed description of someone's face or style of dress as a significant confirmation of their basic qualities. But each time we do, we are usually calling upon our memories of other particular occasions as well, using them as a basis for judging the representativeness of the moment we are dramatizing or describing.

Our sense of what characterization is may be warped by memories of articles about "The Most Unforgettable Person I Ever Met," articles that relied on the drama of single chance meetings or sudden unexpected revelations. In such accounts, a vivid character stands out, like The Lone Ranger, as someone who does his impressive deed and then disappears into the sunset. It is much more likely, however, that the persons who get considerable attention in our autobiographies will be those about whom we feel deeply and with whom we have relations of long standing, not someone who reveals himself in a single moment of dramatic crisis. Personal memories usually involve parents, relatives, lovers, husbands or wives, close friends, professional associates—a whole range of people whose characters emerge for us through a long cumulative experience. As a result many writers tend to emphasize recurrent events and habitual conduct. Compare, for example, the methods used in the selections that follow when a writer is remembering his or her own father. The writers may begin in their own minds with memories of specific moments, but they select those memories that they identify as part of a persistent pattern in their father's behavior.

The selection by Frank O'Connor illustrates the writer's use of representative conduct as a basis for characterization. O'Connor provides a series of sketches of his father's activities at home—reading the paper after work, writing letters about his pension, fixing his pipe, making fumbling attempts to do repair work. In every instance, O'Connor stresses how he is telling us of things his father did habitually, actions that the writer can visualize in great detail but that he refuses to locate at a specific moment. O'Connor never says "One morning in May" or "On the day of my sixth birthday"; he prefers "often" or "usually" or "whenever." He will frequently introduce an account of his father's behavior with a sentence establishing a general trait of his father's character; then whatever follows gives us details that are specific examples and yet not single instances of that trait.

> Nothing could ever persuade Father that he was anything but a naturally home-loving body—which, indeed, for a great part of the time, he was. Nobody but himself could lock up the house for the night, and he had a big bolt for the back door and two bolts for the front, and only he could properly check the catch on the window, wind the alarm on the clock, and see that the lamp was out before we retired.

The process by which an autobiographical writer characterizes another person, then, is often similar to the one used by O'Connor. The writer sifts the random memories of his relations with someone in order to find some pattern of recurrence that leads him to make generalizations. In effect, he uses a cluster of separate events or descriptions involving that person and begins to bind them together according to some common theme. O'Connor, for example, may have begun with mental images of his father doing a whole series of ordinary tasks. These memories all showed the father taking comfort and pleasure in being at home and willingly performing a number of household chores. As a result, O'Connor creates a generalization, a statement that expresses the common ground shared by these memories. The generalization establishes the father as a "naturally home-loving body" (we will discuss the qualifications in O'Connor's sentence a bit later) and provides a focus for specific memories that serve in the quoted passage to substantiate the father's characteristic of being home-loving.

The passage also illustrates how, although we organize our experiences by moving from a particular impression to a larger generalization, we are likely to reverse this movement in our written account. We can usually see our own way more clearly and direct the reader more forcefully if, like O'Connor, we begin with a statement general enough to include the more particular impressions that follow: "any project of Father's . . . involved preparation on a major scale"; "he was one of the most awkward men who ever handled a tool."

Whether generalizations precede or follow the specific memories that foster them remains the writer's own decision, but the interrelationship of the two determines the effectiveness of the writer's characterization. Any generalization represents a conclusion based on some evidence, and if it is an important conclusion—one the writer wishes his readers to take note of and agree with—he must be careful to include some of the evidence that led to it. His task is to be both convincing and economical; not all of the evidence is required, only the most compelling. O'Connor might have decided to narrate a single dramatic event to "prove" his father a homebody or to present a single detailed description of his father comfortably settled in his chair next to the hearth with his pipe and paper. Instead he provides several brief examples, all of which contribute to the cumulative impression of his father that fits the general term O'Connor introduced at the start.

Although as writers we frequently rely on narration and description to give body to more general statements we wish to make, we are not restricted only to these two methods. We may find we can communicate our sense of someone's character more clearly by thinking of him in relation to someone else (father as a homebody in contrast to his well-traveled brother). Again, our memories can shift away from the immediate subject to focus on our associations with it (O'Connor's characterization of his father going through his discharge papers: "he would be moved like an old novelist re-reading a review of his first talented book"). In such cases we would still be making our generalizations clearer by particularizing them, but we would be moving away from memories of a specific moment or scene from the past and instead making use of comparison or analogy to create images that indirectly illuminate our subject. Whatever kind of particularization we choose—narrative illustration, descriptive illustration, a sequence of examples, comparison, analogy, or some combination among them—we are reassuring the reader that our generalizations are based on actual experience.

Our generalizations themselves and the relationships we find among them provide the basis for the overall shape of our biographical account. In other words, the general terms that we have used in naming the qualities of a person's character become in their turn the bases for developing a larger pattern of organization. We can see that O'Connor has such a larger pattern firmly in mind when he begins by first saying, not that his father was a "naturally home-loving body," but rather that nobody could persuade his father he wasn't this type of person. After we have read the entire selection, we realize that O'Connor qualifies the generalization about his father as home-loving because he will later show us how his father, when out of control on an alcoholic binge, will quite literally strip the house bare, pawning everything saleable in order to pay for his drinks. O'Connor wants to begin his portrait with an account of his father's domestic feelings partially to create a sense of ironic contrast with what he later reveals, partially to introduce a more winning and kindly side of his father's character before he tells of the destructive side. If we learned of the father's drinking and its impact on the home at the outset of O'Connor's characterization, we might refuse any sympathetic attention to the father's more attractive human qualities.

Studying the examples of characterization in this section shows us how autobiographical writing can remain autobiographical and yet move away from the temporal organization of narrative and the spatial organization of description (forms of organization that dominated the two preceding chapters). As we have seen, narration and description often contribute to characterization, but they are subordinated to a pattern of ideas about general qualities that reveal the nature of the character. We may think of a person as energetic, friendly, hard-working, ambitious, quick-tempered, efficient; then we must decide which of these impressions should be used in our characterization and in what order and relationship they should be introduced. We obviously would not adopt a simple narrative organization, telling of each quality as it first manifested itself in the character's actions, nor would we rely only on describing the character at home, at work, at the beach, on the tennis court. What we do instead is to establish a sequence of relationships among the concepts that we have associated with the other person, a sequence that makes us feel we have communicated something significant about the other person's nature as it touched our own. The result may be a classification of features in the order of their importance, or a division into public and private, or a contrast between the life-enhancing and the self-destructive. We may define the person the way N. Scott Momaday presents his grandmother, placing her within the traditions of American Indian experience and making her represent an entire cultural tradition. Or we may create another kind of comparison by using another person's attitudes and characteristics as a way of revealing our own values, as Lillian Hellman does in her memoir of Dashiell Hammett. Another possibility is to select one or two extraordinary traits and to emphasize their persistence in a range of situations, as James Thurber does, with wonderful comic effect, in telling the story of Doc Marlowe.

Since characterization involves the writer in a search for patterns of recurrence and relationship, it makes him particularly aware of the need for some kind of general organization that would govern the account of his life. Because it can follow whatever direction an individual life may take, autobiography is an especially permissive form, and a writer may feel a sense of relief that with autobiography he does not have to maintain the rigorous logic demanded by an argumentative or expository essay. But the autobiographer cannot simply reproduce on paper the random images of an evening's reverie; although he may begin with disconnected memories, he must discover some comprehensible shape that will make these memories communicable to others. For example, Joan Baez decides to organize her memories of her father around his ethical character and, although she touches on many aspects of her father's life, she keeps returning to ways in which he provided her with valuable moral counsel and example. Studying such characterizations created by other writers can help us to characterize ourselves and others and can prepare us to search for an appropriate design within the rich tangle of our memories.

∿ Frank O'Connor ∿

(1903-1966)

See the biographical note on page 29. O'Connor wrote two autobiographies, An Only Child *(1958), about his early life in Cork, from which this selection is taken, and* My Father's Son *(1968), about his emergence into the literary world and his friendships with other Irish writers.*

CHILD, I KNOW YOU'RE GOING TO MISS ME

Father was a really fine-looking man. He was a six-footer and built to match, and years of work as a navvy had not affected the soldierly erectness of bearing he had picked up as a young man in the Army. He had a long Scandinavian head, but because of the slightly Mongolian cast of feature he had inherited from Grandmother, the lines of his face were horizontal instead of vertical. At the same time the bulge of the brows and the height of the cheekbones, instead of making his eyes seem weak, made them look as though they were twinkling. He was extraordinarily like certain photographs of the young Maxim Gorky. He dressed carefully, in the manner of an old-fashioned tradesman, in a blue serge suit with the cuffs of the trousers turned down over the heels, a bowler hat cocked a little to one side, and a starched shirt-front. Dressing him for Mass on Sunday was a serious task for any woman, for his fingers were all thumbs. He could rarely fasten his own studs, and it sometimes ended with his stamping and cursing before the big mirror, and Mother's grabbing at a stool to stand on, so that she could reach up to him, and begging him for the Lord's sake to keep quiet and let her do it for him. Then he put an open white handkerchief, casually disposed, in his breast pocket, and went down the road, graciously bowing and raising his hat to any woman he met, a fine figure of a man, and as vain as a child in his first sailor suit. In the "tall tales" he loved to tell of his soldiering days there was a great favourite of his about a review held by Queen Victoria during which she said: "And tell me, General, who is that distinguished-looking man in the second rank?" to which the general replied: "That, Your Majesty, is Michael O'Donovan, one of the best-looking men in your whole army."

Nothing could ever persuade Father that he was anything but a naturally home-loving body—which, indeed, for a great part of the time, he was. Nobody but himself could lock up the house for the night, and he had a big bolt for the back door and two bolts for the front, and only he could properly check the catch on the window, wind the alarm on the clock, and see that the lamp was out before we retired. Often he would be up first in the morning, give Mother a cup of tea in bed, and have a tremendous wash-up under the tap in the yard, winter and summer. Indeed, if there was snow he rubbed himself all over with it because it prevented chilblains. It was a bitter disappointment to him that I was a sissy, and he made angry comments when I drew a basin of water and then poured hot water from the kettle into it. When he got in from work in the evening, he usually had a more leisurely, noisy wash, changed into old trousers and "slippers" that were old boots cut down and hacked in all directions so that the leather did not press on his corns, and, with his cap on to protect his head from drafts, sat at the head of the table by the window to read the evening *Echo* aloud to Mother, with comments that went on longer than the news. He began with the Police Court news to put him into good humour, and reserved for the last the political meetings, which made him scowl and mutter. "Oh, that unspeakable scut, George Crosbie!" I liked that till I began to read myself, but even then it did not disturb me much, for I was always too involved in what I read even to notice when neighbours dropped in.

This was just as well, because any project of Father's, from cutting his corns to writing to Whitehall about his pension, involved preparation on a major scale and something like general mobilization, and in any detail of this he could become entirely lost. For instance, when he wrote to Whitehall—this usually meant no more than filling out some form to show he was still alive—he had first of all to get the penny bottle of ink, and a new nib for the pen, and a bit of blotting-paper, and lay them all out on the table before him; then he had to get his papers, which were in a locked tin trunk in the bedroom, and he could never take one of these out without re-reading the lot: and on going through his discharge papers and discovering again what a model soldier he had been, he would be moved like an old novelist re-reading a review of his first talented book, and would have to bring them down and read them all over again to Mother, who knew them by heart. Every question on a questionnaire he read over several times before replying to it, because he knew it had been drafted by an old and cunning hand with the deliberate intention of catching him out. When he spotted the trap—and there nearly always was a trap—his whole face lit up with approval and he explained the problem carefully to Mother while he considered how best to handle it. He liked a subtle enemy because it enabled him to show how subtle he could be himself. He was a born hob-lawyer, always laying down the law about regulations, and greatly looked up to by other old soldiers, like Bill Heffernan, who were too humble even to pretend that they knew what the War Office wanted of them. When the form was filled out and in its envelope on the mantelpiece, and Mother had been warned that she must post it with her own hand and not entrust it to me, he would become emotional again about the goodness of the British Government and its consideration for its old servants—unlike the gnats of employers he worked for in Cork, who would see an old workman dying in the streets and not lift a hand to help him. The pension meant much more to him than the trifle of money it represented. It gave him a personal interest in the British Government. A Liberal Government might be good for the Irish cause, but a Conservative one would be better for. the pension. It gave him wild dreams, because no quarter passed without his toying with the idea of compounding it for a capital sum, the size of which staggered imagination. It gave him the prospect of a happy old age, for when Mother died he could hand it in in return for provision in one of the military hospitals like Chelsea or Kilmainham where every day for the rest of his life he would get his pint of beer for nothing.

When the time came to cut his corns, he got a chair and rooted about on top of the wardrobe, which was his hidey-hole, well out of my reach, or intended to be; and after contemplating his many treasures, he took down his current razor, wrapped in oiled cloth, and a couple of other, older razors that he had either abandoned or picked up from those who had no further use for them but that could be trusted to do the rough work of corn-cutting. Then he got the wash-basin, and a jug of cold water, and a kettle of boiling water, and a bottle of corn cure, and a paper of some sort to read while his feet soaked, and a hand mirror to see the parts of his feet that were normally hard to see, and anything else that could conceivably be of use to him, and then, with Mother or myself lined up to hold the mirror, he was set for the evening. Not that I ever remember his doing it without cutting himself.

Or else it was an evening with his pipes. He was an inveterate magpie, and everything that anyone else threw away Father would pick up, in the full conviction that if you kept it for seven years it would be bound to come in useful, while the person who had discarded it would probably pay for his improvidence by dying in the workhouse. Old broken pipes were a tremendous temptation to him, and he had a large collection of bowls and stems, all of which needed only careful handling to turn them into brand-new pipes of the most expensive kind. This task would have been considerably easier if he had ever had anything like a gimlet handy, but as he rarely did, he had to make a tool. Usually, the treasure chest yielded some sort of blade, and some sort of handle, and the blade had to be heated and set in the handle, and then the handle usually burst and had to be bound with a bit of string or wax-end. Then the improvised tool had to be heated again, and the bowl or the stem burned till the two pieces could be joined. I can still remember the rancid smell of burned amber. The result was usually most peculiar—a delicate bowl joined to a colossal stem or a delicate stem to a rural bowl—but Father puffed it with great satisfaction, in the belief that he had cheated some ruffian of a tobacco merchant out of the price of a brand-new pipe.

Father was, I think, a naturally melancholy man; though he was always pleased when people called, he rarely called on anybody himself; and, like all melancholy men, he made his home his cave, and devoted a great deal of thought to its beauty and utility. Unfortunately, he was one of the most awkward men who ever handled a tool, and it is a subject I can speak on with some authority, for I have inherited his awkwardness. Along with the razors, the pipe bowls and stems and the rest, he had a peculiar hoard of tools and equipment, mostly stored on top of the wardrobe. They had been lovingly accumulated over the years in the conviction that eventually they would be bound to come in useful. Prior to tackling any major job, all this had to be unloaded onto the kitchen table, and Father put on his glasses and studied it affectionately in the way in which he studied the documents in the tin trunk, forgetting whatever he was supposed to be looking for as he recited the history of hinges, bolts, screws, wooden handles, blades, clock springs, and mysterious-looking bits of machinery that had probably fallen out of a railway engine in process of dissolution, and wondered what some of them could be used for.

Finally, having selected his equipment—the nice bit of timber that would nearly do for a shelf, and the brackets that didn't quite match, and the screws or nails that were either a bit too long or a bit too short, and the old chisel that would do for a screw-driver, and the hammer with the loose head—Father set to work. He had lined up my mother and myself as builder's mates, to hold the plank and the hammer, the saw that needed setting, and the nails and screws. Before he had been at work for five minutes, the top of the hammer would have flown off and hit him in the face, or the saw would have cut the chair instead of the plank, or the nail that was to have provided the setting for the screw would have carried away inches of the plank with the unmerciful wallops he gave it. Father had the secret of making inanimate objects appear to possess a secret, malevolent life of their own, and sometimes it was hard to believe that his tools and materials were not really in a conspiracy against him.

His first reaction to this behaviour was chagrin that, for all his love and care, they were turning on him again, but this soon changed to blind rage and an autocratic determination to put them in their places. Hacking away great chunks of the plaster, he nailed in the brackets any old way, while Mother and I, our hearts in our mouths, stood by with anything we thought might come in handy. He swore bloody murder, exactly as he did when the studs in his shirt-front turned against him before Mass on Sunday and it became a toss-up whether, to spite them, he might not go to Mass at all; and in the same gentle voice Mother besought him to let it alone and not to be upsetting himself like that. And when it was all over, and the kitchen a wreck, he would sit down with gloomy pride to read a paper he could not concentrate on, obsessed by the image of himself as a good man and kind father on whom everybody and everything turned.

That was why, in spite of the fact that he had a cobbler's last among his treasures, and that I was forever hacking the good boots that were bought for me with his money, he didn't often try his hand at cobbling. A man who could hardly hit a three-inch nail with a large hammer could not be expected to do much with a shoemaker's tack. Most often it was Mother who did the cobbling, buying a patch or a pair of half-soles in town and tacking them on herself. But I seem to remember that his hoarding instinct betrayed him once when he discovered a large strip of fan-belting from a factory, made of some extraordinary material which he maintained was stronger than leather and would save us a fortune, and he did cut strips off this and nail them to his working boots, on which they looked like pieces of board. On the other hand, he liked rough tailoring, and was perfectly happy sewing a patch onto his working trousers.

But I never minded Father as a handyman the way I minded him as a barber. He always had one pair of clippers, and sometimes two, wrapped in oil rags among the other treasures, and, according to him, these clippers had saved him untold expense. Given a pencil and paper, he could even work it out, as he worked out the amount he saved by being a teetotaller. He was a great man for saving. "My couple of ha'pence," he used to call it. Mother, I suspect, never knew how much he really earned, and when he was sober he usually had a substantial sum in the locked trunk in the bedroom. When he was feeling depressed, he went upstairs by way of consulting his documents and counted it softly, but not so softly that we couldn't hear the chink of the coins as he caressed them. He was a bit of a skinflint and disliked the improvident way Mother bought me sweets, biscuits, or boys' weeklies, not to mention toys at Christmas—a season that seemed to have been specially invented for his mortification. Father, of course, was only providing for the rainy day.

So, on a sunny afternoon, he would take down the clippers, pull off the oily rags, adjust the blades, set a chair in the back yard, and, with a towel round his neck, let Mother cut his hair. There was no great difficulty about this, since all Father wanted was the equivalent to a close shave. According to him, this was excellent for the growth of the hair, and one of his ambitions was to double his savings by protecting my hair as well. I didn't want my hair protected, though he assured me angrily that I would be bald before I was grown up at all; neither did Mother want it, and so, the moment it grew a bit too long and she saw Father casting brooding glances at it, she gave me tuppence to go to the barber. This made Father furious, for not only had she again demonstrated her fundamental improvidence, but Curtin, the barber, would have left me with what Father called "a most unsightly mop." It was like the business of wanting me to wash under the tap. But no matter how carefully she watched over me, he sometimes caught me with the clippers in his hand, and I had to sit on a chair in the back yard, sobbing and sniffling, while he got to work on me and turned me into a laughing-stock for the neighbourhood. He went about it in exactly the same way that he went about cutting his corns or putting up a shelf. "Wisha, is it the way you want to make the child look like a convict?" Mother would cry indignantly, and Father would stamp and curse and pull at a whole chunk of hair till I screamed, and then curse again and shout: "It's your own fault, you little puppy, you! Why can't you stop quiet?"

Then one evening Father would be late, and Mother and I would sit over the fire, half crazy with panic, and I would say prayers to the Sacred Heart and the Blessed Virgin to look after him. I can never remember that my prayers had any effect. Finally, he would come in, full of fallacious good humour, and stand at the door, rubbing his palms and puckering up his lips in a sly grin. He expressed great—indeed, undue—surprise at the lateness of the hour. He had been detained talking to a man he hadn't met for fifteen years—not since the funeral of poor Jack Murphy of the Connaught Rangers in September '98, which he remembered distinctly because Tim O'Connor, God rest him, had been there as well, and the three of them had left the funeral together and spent the evening in a pub called Keohane's that used to be at the corner of Windmill Road but had since been torn down. He would ramble on like that for half an hour, in loosely related clauses that gave the impression of coherence but were difficult to follow, and toward ten o'clock would decide to take a little stroll. That was the end of Father in his role as a home-loving body. Next evening he would slink upstairs to the locked trunk where he kept his savings, and then go out again. The rainy day had at last arrived. He would return in a state of noisy amiability that turned to sullenness when it failed to rouse a response. I was most often to blame for this because, in spite of Mother's appeals to me not to answer him back, I could not bear his maudlin attentions, which made him so like my grandmother, and, like her, he was offended, and snarled that I was "better fed than taught." The day after, he would not go to work and at twelve or one would be at the trunk again and off for a longer carouse.

The savings usually lasted him for a week or ten days. When they were exhausted, Mother had to go to the pawnshop with his best blue suit. So that the neighbours would not see what she was doing, she would put on her long black shawl. I hated the very sight of that shawl, even though I knew that it suited her long, thin, virginal face; it meant an immediate descent in the social scale from the "hatties" to the "shawlies"— the poorest of the poor. I also hated the pawning of the blue suit, because it meant that Father stopped going for walks or to Mass—especially to Mass, for he would not have dreamed of worshipping God in anything less dignified than blue serge— and it meant that we had him all day about the house, his head swollen, his eyes bloodshot, sitting by the fire and shivering in the fever of alcoholism or getting up and walking to and fro, unable to read, unable to work, unable to think of anything except drink. Home was no longer a refuge for him. It had become a prison and a cage, and the only hope of escaping from it was more money. When Mother returned from town and put the five or six shillings on the table with the pawn tickets, he sometimes turned on her with an angry "Lord God, was that all you got on it?" It was not so much that he expected more as that staging a quarrel at this point meant that she would not dare to ask him for money for food, or the rent, or the insurance, or Levin the peddler, who had sold her a suit for me.

Two days later she would be off again with one of the two clocks—her own clock from the bedroom, which did not have an alarm. After that came the clock with the alarm, which was no longer necessary as he did not go to work, and then his silver watch. "In God's name, Mick Donovan, do you want to put us on the street?" she would cry, and he would stamp and shout like a madman. He didn't know what being put on the street meant as she, the orphan, did. Then her blue costume went, and his military medals, and, lastly, his "ring paper"— so called because it was printed in a series of small circles intended for the post-office date stamp—his authority for drawing his Army pension. Though the transaction was illegal, the security was excellent. Even then he would be greedily eying the wedding ring on her finger and whining at her to pawn this as well, "just for a couple of days till I steady up," but it was only when she was really desperate that she let this go, and it took precedence of everything else when the time came to reclaim the little bits of married life. By this time all the money coming into the house would be the ninepence or shilling she earned as a charwoman, and he would be striding like a caged tiger up and down the kitchen in the dusk, waiting for her to come in from work so that he could get this from her.

"Come on!" he would say with forced joviality. "Tuppence is all I want. Me entrance fee!"

"And where am I to get the child's dinner?" she would cry in despair. "Or is it the way you want us to starve?"

"Look, it's all over now. No one is going to starve. Can't you see I'm steadying up? Come on, woman, give us the money!"

"Stay here, then, and I'll go and get it for you!"

"I don't want you to get it for me," he would say, turning nasty. "Getting it for him" was a later stage, which occurred only when he had completely exhausted his credit and old friends cleared out when he came red-eyed and fighting mad into the pub. With his "entrance fee," as he called it, he had not only the price of a drink but the chance of cadging more, either from the barmaid, if the publican was out, or from one of his old cronies.

If he did not get the money immediately, his tone would change again and he would become whining and maudlin. As night came on and his chances of a real debauch diminished, he would grow vicious. "Jesus Christ, I'll put an end to this!" he would mutter, and take down his razor. His threats were never empty, as I well knew since the night when I was an infant and he flung the two of us out into Blarney Lane in our night clothes, and we shivered there in the roadway till some neighbours took us in and let us lie in blankets before the fire. Whenever he brandished the razor at Mother, I went into hysterics, and a couple of times I threw myself on him, beating him with my fists. That drove her into hysterics, too, because she knew that at times like that he would as soon have slashed me as her. Later, in adolescence, I developed pseudo-epileptic fits that were merely an externalization of this recurring nightmare, and though I knew they were not real, and was ashamed of myself for indulging in them at all, I could not resist them when once I had yielded to the first nervous spasm.

In those days, the house would be a horror. Only when he had money for drink would we have peace for an hour, and sometimes Mother borrowed it just to get him out of the house. When I was old enough to go to school, I would come back at three o'clock and scout round to make sure that he was not at home. If he wasn't, I would sneak in and hastily make myself a cup of tea. If he was, I did without the tea and wandered round the rest of the afternoon, waiting till it was time to intercept Mother on her way home from work. I never went near my grandmother. From the moment Father began his drinking bout, you could feel her disapproval of Mother and me—the two heartless creatures who did not sympathize with her darling son. This, she seemed to say, all came of Father's mistake in marrying a woman who did not know her place, a would-be lady. When I talked of him to Mother, I always called him "he" or "him," carefully eschewing the name of "Father" which would have seemed like profanation to me. "You must not speak like that of your father, child," Mother would say severely. "Whatever he does, he's still your father." I resented her loyalty to him. I wanted her to talk to me about him the way I knew the neighbours talked. They could not understand why she did not leave him. I realize now that to do so she would have had to take a job as housekeeper and put me into an orphanage—the one thing in the world that the orphan child could not do.

It always ended in the same way—only when we were completely destitute; when the shop-keepers refused Mother even a loaf of bread, and the landlord threatened us with eviction, and Father could no longer raise the price of a single pint. At that point only did he give in—"cave in" better describes what really happened to him. Sour and savage and silent, he began to look for another job. He rarely went back to the job he had left, and in those days I believed it was because he had lost it. Now I am certain that he was far too good a workman to be put off because of a drinking bout, however prolonged, and that he was too humiliated to go back. To have done that would have been to admit his weakness and guilt. He was, as I have said, a proud man, and he would never have admitted to the other poor labourers, whom he despised, that he had sunk so low. And because something had to be done about the mass of debt that had accumulated in the meantime, he and Mother would have to go to the loan office in Paul Street, accompanied by some friend to act as guarantor. Mother had to go with him, because even at this stage he would still have taken the money and drunk it along with the rest. I was very impressed by the big interest we had to pay, and it struck me that if only I could accumulate a little capital and lend them the money myself, it would be an excellent way both of getting rich and of saving Mother anxiety—the money would, at least, be in the family. But my own savings usually evaporated in the first few days of strain, and I realized that I would need a more settled background before I could set up in business as a money-lender.

With the aid of the loan, Father would take out his "ring paper" and draw his pension, and out of that he would release his best suit, so that he could again worship God on Sundays in the Dominican Church on the Sand Quay. Then would come the clocks and the watch and chain and the military medals, and finally Mother's blue costume. It was characteristic of him that when he started to put money aside again, it was to pay the publicans. He preferred to let Mother work for a shilling a day rather than defer the payment of his drinking debts. It would seem to be obvious that he was only preparing the way for another debauch—because this, in fact, was the ultimate effect of it—and yet I should still say that this was untrue. I am sure it was pride that moved him. I don't think Mother had much pride. Gay people have no need of pride because gaiety is merely the outward sign of inward integrity, but Father had no integrity; as with all mentally sick people, the two sides of his nature hardly communicated and were held together by pins and Hail Marys, and pride was one of the ways in which he protected the false conception of his own character that was one side.

And once again the little house was reconstituted about that incomplete conception of Father as a home-loving body, and a new cycle began. Brisk and cheerful, he rose in the early morning to wash under the tap and bring Mother a cup of tea in bed, and in the evenings he read the *Echo* to her while I sat in some corner, absorbed in my own boys' weekly, and a wind blew up the river and seemed to isolate us as on a ship at sea. On such evenings, no one could doubt his love for her or hers for him, but I, who had no other security, knew better than she did what he was really like, and watched him suspiciously, in the way that only a child can watch, and felt that all authority was only a pretense and that God Himself was probably not much better, and directed my prayers not to Him, but to His mother, who had said nothing but merely suffered.

Because I was jealous of him, I knew that there was real devotion between that strangely assorted pair, and yet I often wonder what really went on in Mother's mind during those terrible years. I think when she wasn't entirely desperate, pity was what was uppermost in her mind, pity for this giant of a man who had no more self-knowledge or self-control than a baby. The least pain could bewilder and madden him and even a toothache could drive him to drink. He died as he had lived, wandering about Cork, looking for drink when he was in the last stages of pneumonia, and I, who might have controlled him, was not informed because it would upset me too much, and besides Mother felt I wouldn't understand. Even God wouldn't understand. Whenever his anniversary came round, she withdrew into herself for weeks, and, without a word to anyone, the offering for Masses was sent to the Cistercians at Mount Melleray, because God might fail to realize that poor Father really was at heart a home-loving body and a good husband and father, and might keep him too long in Purgatory, a place he would not be happy in at all because he could not stand pain, and even a toothache would drive him mad.

Once only did she say anything significant, and that was while she was raving. I was a grown man and living in Dublin, and I came back to Cork on holiday to find her desperately ill, and poor Father—the world's most hopeless man with his hands—devotedly nursing her with nothing but neat whisky. I blasted him for not wiring for me, and he snarled back: "How could I, when she wouldn't let me?" And then he sat over the fire, flapping his hands and snivelling: "What would I do without her?" When I had made her comfortable for the night, I sat with her, holding her hand, and heard her muttering about me as though I were not there.

"God! God!" she whispered. "He raised me from the gutter

where the world threw me. He raised me from the gutter where the world threw me!"

1. *What kind of household jobs does O'Connor describe his father as doing? How do they help characterize the man?*

2. *O'Connor writes at length of several of his father's habitual activities (filling out a government form, cutting his corns, mending a pipe), activities that would ordinarily strike a reader as trivial and not worth mentioning. Why do you think O'Connor presents them in detail? How does he make them of greater interest than you might expect?*

3. *When and how does O'Connor introduce the subject of his father's drinking? What sort of attitude does O'Connor have toward his father? How is his attitude toward his mother different? Do you think O'Connor seems detached or emotionally involved in the story of his family?*

4. *How does O'Connor manage to give variety and pace to his account of his father's behavior? What sustains your interest through this lengthy characterization?*

5. *Read the interview with O'Connor in the first section of this book. In what ways do his comments there about his values and his methods as a writer help you to understand what he has done here?*

∽ Joan Baez ∽

(1941-   )

Joan Baez began singing publicly in coffee shops and at folk concerts around Boston. She became nationally known during the 1960s, both because of her talents as a singer and because of her strong opposition to American military involvement in Vietnam. Today she continues a highly successful career as a songwriter, performer, and recording artist. Her autobiography, Daybreak *(1966), deals with her early life, her strong family ties, and her political, social, and musical interests.*

MY FATHER

My father is short, honest, dark, and very handsome. He's good, he's a good man. He was born in Mexico, and brought up in Brooklyn. His father was a Mexican who left the Catholic church to become a Methodist minister. My father worked hard in school. He loved God and the church and his parents. At one time in his life he was going to be a minister, but the hypocrisy of the church bothered him and he became a scientist instead. He has a vision of how science can play the major role in saving the world. This vision puts a light into his eyes. He is a compulsive worker, and I know that he will never stop his work long enough to have a look at some of the things in his life which are blind and tragic. But it's not my business to print. About me and my father I don't know. I keep thinking of how hard it was for him to say anything nice about me to my face. Maybe he favored me and felt guilty about it, but he couldn't say anything nice. A lot of times I thought he would break my heart. Once he complimented me for something I was wearing. "You ought to wear that kind of thing more often," he said, and I looked into the mirror and I was wearing a black dress which I hated. I was fourteen then and I remember thinking, "Hah. I remind him of his mother in this thing."

My father is the saint of the family. You work at something until you exhaust yourself, so that you can be good at it, and with it you try to improve the lot of the sad ones, the hungry ones, the sick ones. You raise your children trying to teach them decency and respect for human life. Once when I was about thirteen he asked me if I would accept a large sum of money for the death of a man who was going to die anyway. I didn't quite understand. If I was off the hook, and just standing by, and then the man was killed by someone else, why shouldn't I take a couple of million? I told him sure, I'd take the money, and he laughed his head off. "That's immoral," he said. I didn't know what immoral meant, but I knew something was definitely wrong taking money for a man's life.

Once in my life I spent a month alone with my father. In 1950, when he was assigned to a project in Baghdad, Iraq, for UNESCO, my sisters got jaundice, and couldn't leave the States. My father left on schedule, for a month of briefing in Paris before going to Baghdad. I had jaundice too, but I didn't tell anyone. I wanted very badly to go to Paris. So despite bad pains in my stomach and black urine which I flushed in a hurry so he wouldn't see, and a general yellow hue which was creeping over my skin, and sometimes seemed to be tinting everything I looked at, I took full advantage of that time with my old man in Gay Paree. We bicycled everywhere, and bought long fresh bread and cheese and milk. We sat in outdoor cafés and had tea, and while he was busy at UNESCO house, I would run the elevators and visit secretaries and draw pictures of everyone and go off to feed pigeons in the park. Neither of us spoke French, but we faked it. One night in a restaurant, we couldn't understand anything on the dessert menu, so my father took a gamble and said, *"Ça, s'il vous plaît,"* pointing to the word *"Confiture,"* and they brought him a dish of strawberry jam, which he ate.

Once the family was together in Baghdad, I developed a terrible fear that my father was going to die. The fact is he almost killed himself tampering with the stupid brick oven which had to be lit in order to get hot bath water. He was "experimenting" with it—trying to determine how fast he could get the fire going by increasing the flow of kerosene into the oven. It exploded in his face, setting his clothes on fire and giving him third degree burns on his hands and face. He covered his eyes instinctively, or he would probably have been blinded, but his eyelashes and eyebrows were burned off anyway. Pauline passed out after telling Mother that "Popsy is on fire," and Mother wrapped him up in a sheet and called the English hospital for an ambulance. While we waited for the ambulance, my father tapped his feet in rhythm on the kitchen tiles, and cleared his throat every four or five seconds. He smelled terrible, and except for Mother, we just stood there. I was probably praying. Mother took me to the hospital to see him once, and I felt bad because I got dizzy when I saw his hands. They had big pussy blisters on them, and his face looked like a Rice Krispie, and I wanted to make him feel better, but I also wanted to go stick my head out the window and get some fresh air. When he came home from the hospital he was bandaged so that all you could see were his eyes and his ears. He held classes for his students at home. He is a brilliant teacher, and they loved him. I know they loved him, because the room smelled so awful from burnt flesh and Middle East medication that I felt sick every time I passed his door. And they came every day to learn and to see him.

My father teaches physics. He is a Ph.D. in physics, and we all wish he'd had just one boy who wasn't so opposed to school, to degrees, to formal education of any kind. One child to show some interest when he does physics experiments at the dinner table. But then it must be partly because we felt obligated to be student-types that we have all rebelled so completely. I can barely read. That is to say, I would rather do a thousand things before sitting down to read.

He used to tell us we should read the dictionary. He said it was fun and very educational. I've never gotten into it.

When we lived in Clarence Center, New York (it was a town of eight hundred people, and as far as they knew, we were niggers; Mother says that someone yelled out the window to me, "Hey, nigger!" and I said, "You ought to see me in the summertime!"), my father had a job working in Buffalo. It was some kind of armaments work. I just knew that it was secret, or part of it was secret, and that we began to get new things like a vacuum cleaner, a refrigerator, a fancy coffee pot, and one day my father came home with a little Crosley car. We were so excited about it that we drove it all over the front lawn, around the trees and through the piles of leaves. He was driving, Mother was in the front seat, and we three kids were in the back. The neighbors knew we were odd to begin with, but this confirmed it. Mother was embarrassed and she kept clutching my father's arm and saying, "Oh, Abo!" but he would take a quick corner around a tree and we'd all scream with laughter and Mother gave up and had hysterics.

Then something started my father going to Quaker meetings. We all had to go. It meant we had to sit and squelch giggles for about twenty minutes, and then go off with some kind old lady who planted each of us a bean in a tin can, and told us it was a miracle that it would push its little head up above the damp earth and grow into a plant. We knew it was a miracle, and we knew she was kind, but we made terrible fun of her the entire time and felt guilty about it afterwards.

While we were in the side room with the kind old lady, watching our beans perform miracles, my father was in the grown-up room, the room where they observe silence for a whole hour, and he was having a fight with his conscience. It took him less than a year of those confrontations with himself in that once a week silence to realize that he would have to give up either the silences or his job. Next thing I knew we were packing up and moving across the country. My father had taken a job as a professor of physics at the University of Redlands for about one-half the pay, and one-tenth the prestige—against the advice of everyone he knew except my mother. Since leaving Buffalo in 1947, he's never accepted a job that had anything to do with armaments, offense, defense, or whatever they prefer to call it. Last night I had a dream about him. I dreamed he was sitting next to himself in a theater. One of him was as he is now, and the other was the man of thirty years ago. I kept trying to get him to look at himself and say hello. Both faces smiled very understandingly, but neither would turn to greet the other.

I don't think he's ever understood me very well. He's never understood my compulsiveness, my brashness, my neuroses, my fears, my antinationalism (though he's changing on that), my sex habits, my loose way of handling money. I think often I startle him, and many times I please him. Sometimes I have put him through hell, like when I decided to live with Michael when I was twenty. "You mean you're going to . . . *live* with him?" "Yes," I said, and my father took a sleeping bag and went to the beach for two days, because Michael was staying in the house. Years later he sent me an article by Bertrand Russell, whom he respects very much, underlining the part which said that if young people could have a chance at "experimental marriages" while they were in college, they might know more about what it's all about before they actually got married. My father wrote that it always amazed him how I came to conclusions intuitively which took him years to realize.

· · ·

Lately my father has told me, off and on, that he is 100 percent behind me in the things I do. I think that's hard for him to say, for lots of reasons, one being the reason I mentioned earlier—that he has trouble telling me nice things about myself or what I do. Another is that he hasn't always gone along with my radical ideas of nonviolence and antinationalism, or my feelings that formal education is meaningless at best, and that universities are baby-sitting operations. Even though he was peace-marching long before I was, when I swung, I swung all the way, and left my father looking and acting, in my opinion, fairly moderate. But he has changed very much in the last five years, and I know that when my mother and Mimi and I went to jail for doing Civil Disobedience at the Army induction center, he had no doubts that we were doing the right thing, and he took over the Institute for Non-Violence for the weekend seminars. I think that all the while he was working with UNESCO in Paris, traveling around the world, trying to help find ways of teaching science in underdeveloped countries, he was more concerned than he admitted to himself about two problems: One was how he could teach people the wonders of science and at the same time keep them from simply trying to ape the powerful nations of the world and race to discover new scientific ways to destroy themselves and each other. The temptation for power is so great, and unfortunately, what power has always meant is one's ability and efficiency to murder one's neighbor. The other problem that haunted my father had to do with UNESCO itself: It was filled with power-hungry and money-hungry individuals, and he never wanted to admit it. My mother told me of a time when they were at a dinner party of UNESCO science division men and their wives. Some of the men were loosening up on wine and my father was talking about his difficulties in South America. His colleagues were not really interested in his successes or failures in teaching science to Brazilians, and that fact became more and more apparent. Finally, one of them said something to the effect of, "Aw c'mon, Baez, you don't really give a damn about science teaching methods, do you?" My mother was completely floored by this, and she said, "That's what we're here for," and asked the man why *he* was with UNESCO. He had a publishing job, the man said, and it hadn't really paid much:

UNESCO paid a hell of a lot more, plus you got to travel, so he had gone to work for UNESCO and ended up in Paris. Not a bad deal all the way around. He went on kidding my father, who was struck dumb; and Mother did something she doesn't do unless she's in a state of shock or fury—she gave something resembling a speech. "My husband was an idealist when he came to work for UNESCO. He's a pacifist. He's concerned about the fact that people are starving to death and he thought the best way he could help out would be through UNESCO, to spread the uses of science to people who need it. Maybe we're just crazy, but I never imagined anyone came to work here for any other reason."

While he was with UNESCO, he seemed to lose his sense of humor. When I would visit them in Paris, sometimes it seemed that all I ever heard him say was, "I have this deadline . . . You know I just have to keep to this schedule . . ." He was trying to finish a book, which took him eight years to write. A basic text in physics. I seriously thought he would not ever complete that book, that it was like an eternally incomplete project he had to have to keep himself worn out. And I thought he was afraid to get it printed. But it was published while he was still in Paris. It's beautiful. The introduction is preceded by a picture of a huge rock suspended over the ocean. The picture makes you want to sit down heavily on the floor, or throw a paperweight out the window and watch it hit the sidewalk. There are little bits of human philosophy preceding each chapter, over eight hundred pictures, and the book is dedicated to "my wife, Joan, and my three daughters, Pauline, Joanie, and Mimi." And on page 274 there is a drawing which illustrates how an image is projected onto a television screen, and the image being projected is of a familiar-looking girl with long black hair, who stands holding a guitar.

In my estimation, my old man got his sense of humor back when he left Paris, and returned to the States. Toward the end of a course he was teaching at Harvard, a crash summer course, based on his book, he gave what he later described to me as the "demonstration of the century." He told the class that he was going to give an example of jet propulsion. He had a little red wagon brought in, and then he took the fire extinguisher off the wall and sat down in the wagon and jet propelled himself in circles around the front of the room, explaining, at the top of his voice, exactly what was happening technically. The students stood on their chairs and gave him an ovation, and it was all so overwhelming that he repeated the experiment. He shouted halfway through it for someone to open the door, and shot himself out into the hall, and disappeared. When he came back the bell had rung and the class was still there, cheering.

Right now, in 1967, my mother has planted my father and herself in a beautiful place in Carmel Valley, about one mile from my house, and not far from Pauline. A while after they began to be settled, I asked him if he could give himself permission to enjoy the luxury of his new home, his swimming pool, the endless beauty of the hills around. He tried to avoid my question by making a joke, but I said I was serious. We were sitting on the floor on a nice carpet, and he smoothed his hands over it as he leaned back against the wall. He looked very brown and Mexican in that moment, and I watched his profile against the valley hills as he struggled with himself. He said something about other people in the world, and about hunger. Then he looked up and gave me a smile of such a combination of things. "Yes, honey," he said, "I think I can enjoy it . . . if I keep myself busy enough . . ."

1. *After reading the selection, how would you explain what Baez means when she says of her father, "He's good, he's a good man"?*
2. *Are there incidents in the narrative that help explain why Baez says she thinks "formal education is meaningless," even though her father is a professor? Are there aspects of her style and her way of organizing her autobiography that would identify her as someone reacting against academic training?*

3. Does Baez tend to rely on telling you about things her father did habitually or about experiences that only happened once? Identify at least two or three anecdotes about unique events and show how they contribute to the portrait.

4. To what extent does Baez concentrate on her personal relationship with her father? How does she present that relationship to you?

5. How does Baez relate her interest in presenting a family portrait with her political and social concerns? Which do you think dominates the selection?

∽ Patricia Hampl ∽

(1946-   )

Patricia Hampl grew up in St. Paul, Minnesota, graduated from the University of Minnesota, where she now teaches, and studied at the Iowa Writer's Workshop. Her book A Romantic Education *(1981) tells of her life in St. Paul and her stay in Prague, the city she associates with her Czech grandmother. In this selection, Hampl recalls visiting her grandmother for Sunday dinners in St. Paul.*

[GRANDMOTHER'S SUNDAY DINNER]

Food was the potent center of my grandmother's life. Maybe the immense amount of time it took to prepare meals during most of her life accounted for her passion. Or it may have been her years of work in various kitchens on the hill and later, in the house of Justice Butler: after all, she was a professional. Much later, when she was dead and I went to Prague, I came to feel the motto I knew her by best—*Come eat*—was not, after all, a personal statement, but a racial one, the *cri de coeur* of Middle Europe.

Often, on Sundays, the entire family gathered for dinner at her house. Dinner was 1 P.M. My grandmother would have preferred the meal to be at the old time of noon, but her children had moved their own Sunday dinner hour to the more fashionable (it was felt) 4 o'clock, so she compromised. Sunday breakfast was something my mother liked to do in a big way, so we arrived at my grandmother's hardly out of the reverie of waffles and orange rolls, before we were propped like rag dolls in front of a pork roast and sauerkraut, dumplings, hot buttered carrots, rye bread and rollikey, pickles and olives, apple pie and ice cream. And coffee.

Coffee was a food in that house, not a drink. I always begged for some because the magical man on the Hills Brothers can with his turban and long robe scattered with stars and his gold slippers with pointed toes, looked deeply happy as he drank from his bowl. The bowl itself reminded me of soup, Campbell's chicken noodle soup, my favorite food. The distinct adultness of coffee and the robed man with his deep-drinking pleasure made it clear why the grownups lingered so long at the table. The uncles smoked cigars then, and the aunts said, "Oh, those cigars."

My grandmother, when she served dinner, was a virtuoso hanging on the edge of her own ecstatic performance. She seemed dissatisfied, almost querulous until she had corralled everybody into their chairs around the table, which she tried to do the minute they got into the house. No cocktails, no hors d'oeuvres (pronounced, by some of the family, "horse's ovaries"), just business. She was a little power crazed: she had us and, by God, we were going to eat. She went about it like a goose breeder forcing pellets down the gullets of those dumb birds.

She flew between her chair and the kitchen, always finding more this, extra that. She'd given you the *wrong* chicken breast the first time around; now she'd found the *right* one: eat it too, eat it fast, because after the chicken comes the rhubarb pie. Rhubarb pie with a thick slice of cheddar cheese that it was imperative every single person eat.

We had to eat fast because something was always out there in the kitchen panting and charging the gate, champing at the bit, some mound of rice or a Jell-O fruit salad or vegetable casserole or pie was out there, waiting to be let loose into the dining room.

She had the usual trite routines: the wheedlings, the silent pout ("What! You don't like my brussels sprouts? I thought

you liked *my* brussels sprouts," versus your wife's/sister's/
mother's. "I made that pie just for you," etc., etc.). But it was
the way she tossed around the old cliches and the overused
routines, mixing them up and dealing them out shamelessly,
without irony, that made her a pro. She tended to peck at her
own dinner. Her plate, piled with food, was a kind of stage
prop, a mere bending to convention. She liked to eat, she was
even a greedy little stuffer, but not on these occasions. She was
a woman possessed by an idea, given over wholly to some
phantasmagoria of food, a mirage of stuffing, a world where
the endless chicken and the infinite lemon pie were united at
last at the shore of the oceanic soup plate that her children and
her children's children alone could drain . . . if only they
would try.

She was there to bolster morale, to lead the troops, to give
the sharp command should we falter on the way. The futility
of saying no was supreme, and no one ever tried it. How could
a son-in-law, already weakened near the point of imbecility
by the once, twice, thrice charge to the barricades of pork and
mashed potato, be expected to gather his feeble wit long
enough to ignore the final call of his old commander when she
sounded the alarm: "Pie, Fred?"

Just when it seemed as if the food-crazed world she had
created was going to burst, that she had whipped and frothed
us like a sack of boiled potatoes under her masher, just then
she pulled it all together in one easeful stroke like the pro
she was.

She stood in the kitchen doorway, her little round Napo-
leonic self sheathed in a cotton flowered pinafore apron, the
table draped in its white lace cloth but spotted now with gravy
and beet juice, the troops mumbling indistinctly as they
waited at their posts for they knew not what. We looked up at
her stupidly, weakly. She said nonchalantly, "Anyone want
another piece of pie?" No, no more pie, somebody said. The
rest of the rabble grunted along with him. She stood there
with the coffeepot and laughed and said, "Good! Because there
isn't any more pie."

No more pie. We'd eaten it all, we'd put away everything in that kitchen. We were exhausted and she, gambler hostess that she was (but it was her house she was playing), knew she could offer what didn't exist, knew us, knew what she'd wrought. There was a sense of her having won, won something. There were no divisions among us now, no adults, no children. Power left the second and third generations and returned to the source, the grandmother who reduced us to mutters by her art.

That wasn't the end of it. At 5 P.M. there was "lunch"—sandwiches and beer; the sandwiches were made from the leftovers (mysteriously renewable resources, those roasts). And at about 8 P.M. we were at the table again for coffee cake and coffee, the little man in his turban and his coffee ecstasy and his pointed shoes set on the kitchen table as my grandmother scooped out the coffee and dumped it into a big enamel pot with a crushed eggshell. By then everyone was alive and laughing again, the torpor gone. My grandfather had been inviting the men, one by one, into the kitchen during the afternoon where he silently (the austere version of memory—but he must have talked, must have said *something*) handed them jiggers of whiskey, and watched them put the shot down in one swallow. Then he handed them a beer, which they took out in the living room. I gathered that the *little* drink in the tiny glass shaped like a beer mug was some sort of antidote for the *big* drink of beer. He sat on the chair in the kitchen with a bottle of beer on the floor next to him and played his concertina, allowing society to form itself around him—while he lived he was the center—but not seeking it, not going into the living room. And not talking. He held to his music and the kindly, medicinal administration of whiskey.

By evening, it seemed we could eat endlessly, as if we'd had some successful inoculation at dinner and could handle anything. I stayed in the kitchen after they all reformed in the dining room at the table for coffee cake. I could hear them, but the little man in his starry yellow robe was on the table in the kitchen and I put my head down on the oil cloth very near the curled and delighted tips of his pointed shoes, and I slept. Whatever laughter there was, there was. But something sweet and starry was in the kitchen and I lay down beside it, my stomach full, warm, so safe I'll live the rest of my life off the fat of that vast family security.

1. How is the grandmother described as a cook and hostess? What other occupations does Hampl associate with her grandmother and how do such analogies help you understand the way the grandmother behaves?

2. How is the food itself described? In what ways do these descriptions do more than inform you of what people ate?

3. What roles do other members of the family play in Hampl's account? How does she present her own behavior at these family gatherings? How does her description of such a gathering compare with your own memories of family occasions?

4. What is Hampl's attitude toward her grandmother? Does Hampl's account convey to you the "vast family security" she mentions at the end of the selection?

5. How would you compare the Sunday dinner scene in this selection with the scene portrayed by Russell Baker elsewhere in this chapter?

∽ N. Scott Momaday ∽

(1934-   )

*N. Scott Momaday is a Kiowa Indian raised on Indian reserva-
tions in the southwestern United States. He is now a Professor
of English and Comparative Literature at the University of
California, Berkeley. He has published essays on American
literature and was awarded the Pulitzer Prize in 1969 for his
first novel,* House Made of Dawn. *The following selection is
the autobiographical preface to his collection of Indian legends and folk tales,* The Way to Rainy Mountain *(1969).*

[A KIOWA GRANDMOTHER]

A single knoll rises out of the plain in Oklahoma, north and
west of the Wichita Range. For my people, the Kiowas, it is an
old landmark, and they gave it the name Rainy Mountain.
The hardest weather in the world is there. Winter brings bliz-
zards, hot tornadic winds arise in the spring, and in summer
the prairie is an anvil's edge. The grass turns brittle and
brown, and it cracks beneath your feet. There are green belts
along the rivers and creeks, linear groves of hickory and pecan,
willow and witch hazel. At a distance in July or August the
steaming foliage seems almost to writhe in fire. Great green
and yellow grasshoppers are everywhere in the tall grass, popping up like corn to sting the flesh, and tortoises crawl about
on the red earth, going nowhere in the plenty of time. Loneliness is an aspect of the land. All things in the plain are isolate;

there is no confusion of objects in the eye, but *one* hill or *one* tree or *one* man. To look upon that landscape in the early morning, with the sun at your back, is to lose the sense of proportion. Your imagination comes to life, and this, you think, is where Creation was begun.

I returned to Rainy Mountain in July. My grandmother had died in the spring, and I wanted to be at her grave. She had lived to be very old and at last infirm. Her only living daughter was with her when she died, and I was told that in death her face was that of a child.

I like to think of her as a child. When she was born, the Kiowas were living the last great moment of their history. For more than a hundred years they had controlled the open range from the Smoky Hill River to the Red, from the headwaters of the Canadian to the fork of the Arkansas and Cimarron. In alliance with the Comanches, they had ruled the whole of the southern Plains. War was their sacred business, and they were among the finest horsemen the world has ever known. But warfare for the Kiowas was preeminently a matter of disposition rather than of survival, and they never understood the grim, unrelenting advance of the U.S. Cavalry. When at last, divided and ill-provisioned, they were driven onto the Staked Plains in the cold rains of autumn, they fell into panic. In Palo Duro Canyon they abandoned their crucial stores to pillage and had nothing then but their lives. In order to save themselves, they surrendered to the soldiers at Fort Sill and were imprisoned in the old stone corral that now stands as a military museum. My grandmother was spared the humiliation of those high gray walls by eight or ten years, but she must have known from birth the affliction of defeat, the dark brooding of old warriors.

Her name was Aho, and she belonged to the last culture to evolve in North America. Her forebears came down from the high country in western Montana nearly three centuries ago. They were a mountain people, a mysterious tribe of hunters whose language has never been positively classified in any major group. In the late seventeenth century they began a long migration to the south and east. It was a journey toward the dawn, and it led to a golden age. Along the way the Kiowas were befriended by the Crows, who gave them the culture and religion of the Plains. They acquired horses, and their ancient nomadic spirit was suddenly free of the ground. They acquired Tai-me, the sacred Sun Dance doll, from that moment the object and symbol of their worship, and so shared in the divinity of the sun. Not least, they acquired the sense of destiny, therefore courage and pride. When they entered upon the southern Plains they had been transformed. No longer were they slaves to the simple necessity of survival; they were a lordly and dangerous society of fighters and thieves, hunters and priests of the sun. According to their origin myth, they entered the world through a hollow log. From one point of view, their migration was the fruit of an old prophecy, for indeed they emerged from a sunless world.

Although my grandmother lived out her long life in the shadow of Rainy Mountain, the immense landscape of the continental interior lay like memory in her blood. She could tell of the Crows, whom she had never seen, and of the Black Hills, where she had never been. I wanted to see in reality what she had seen more perfectly in the mind's eye, and traveled fifteen hundred miles to begin my pilgrimage.

Yellowstone, it seemed to me, was the top of the world, a region of deep lakes and dark timber, canyons and waterfalls. But, beautiful as it is, one might have the sense of confinement there. The skyline in all directions is close at hand, the high wall of the woods and deep cleavages of shade. There is a perfect freedom in the mountains, but it belongs to the eagle and the elk, the badger and the bear. The Kiowas reckoned their stature by the distance they could see, and they were bent and blind in the wilderness.

Descending eastward, the highland meadows are a stairway to the plain. In July the inland slope of the Rockies is luxuriant with flax and buckwheat, stonecrop and larkspur. The

earth unfolds and the limit of the land recedes. Clusters of
trees, and animals grazing far in the distance, cause the vision
to reach away and wonder to build upon the mind. The sun
follows a longer course in the day, and the sky is immense beyond all comparison. The great billowing clouds that sail
upon it are shadows that move upon the grain like water, di-
viding light. Farther down, in the land of the Crows and
Blackfeet, the plain is yellow. Sweet clover takes hold of the
hills and bends upon itself to cover and seal the soil. There the
Kiowas paused on their way; they had come to the place where
they must change their lives. The sun is at home on the plains.
Precisely there does it have the certain character of a god.
When the Kiowas came to the land of the Crows, they could
see the dark lees of the hills at dawn across the Bighorn River,
the profusion of light on the grain shelves, the oldest deity
ranging after the solstices. Not yet would they veer southward
to the caldron of the land that lay below; they must wean their
blood from the northern winter and hold the mountains a
while longer in their view. They bore Tai-me in procession to
the east.

A dark mist lay over the Black Hills, and the land was like
iron. At the top of a ridge I caught sight of Devil's Tower up-
thrust against the gray sky as if in the birth of time the core of
the earth had broken through its crust and the motion of the
world was begun. There are things in nature that engender an
awful quiet in the heart of man; Devil's Tower is one of them.
Two centuries ago, because they could not do otherwise, the
Kiowas made a legend at the base of the rock. My grandmother
said:

Eight children were there at play, seven sisters and their
brother. Suddenly the boy was struck dumb; he trembled and
began to run upon his hands and feet. His fingers became
claws, and his body was covered with fur. Directly there was
a bear where the boy had been. The sisters were terrified; they
ran, and the bear after them. They came to the stump of a
great tree, and the tree spoke to them. It bade them climb upon

*it, and as they did so it began to rise into the air. The bear
came to kill them, but they were just beyond its reach. It
reared against the tree and scored the bark all around with its
claws. The seven sisters were borne into the sky, and they
became the stars of the Big Dipper.*

From that moment, and so long as the legend lives, the Kiowas
have kinsmen in the night sky. Whatever they were in the
mountains, they could be no more. However tenuous their
well-being, however much they had suffered and would suffer
again, they had found a way out of the wilderness.

My grandmother had a reverence for the sun, a holy regard
that now is all but gone out of mankind. There was a wariness
in her, and an ancient awe. She was a Christian in her later
years, but she had come a long way about, and she never for-
got her birthright. As a child she had been to the Sun Dances;
she had taken part in those annual rites, and by then she had
learned the restoration of her people in the presence of Tai-me.
She was about seven when the last Kiowa Sun Dance was held
in 1887 on the Washita River above Rainy Mountain Creek.
The buffalo were gone. In order to consummate the ancient
sacrifice—to impale the head of a buffalo bull upon the medicine tree—a delegation of old men journeyed into Texas, there
to beg and barter for an animal from the Goodnight herd. She
was ten when the Kiowas came together for the last time as a
living Sun Dance culture. They could find no buffalo; they
had to hang an old hide from the sacred tree. Before the dance
could begin, a company of soldiers rode out from Fort Sill
under orders to disperse the tribe. Forbidden without cause the
essential act of their faith, having seen the wild herds slaugh-
tered and left to rot upon the ground, the Kiowas backed away
forever from the medicine tree. That was July 20, 1890, at the
great bend of the Washita. My grandmother was there. Without bitterness, and for as long as she lived, she bore a vision
of deicide.

Now that I can have her only in memory, I see my grandmother in the several postures that were peculiar to her: stand-

ing at the wood stove on a winter morning and turning meat in a great iron skillet; sitting at the south window, bent above her beadwork, and afterwards, when her vision failed, looking down for a long time into the fold of her hands; going out upon a cane, very slowly as she did when the weight of age came upon her; praying. I remember her most often at prayer. She made long, rambling prayers out of suffering and hope, having seen many things. I was never sure that I had the right to hear, so exclusive were they of all mere custom and company. The last time I saw her she prayed standing by the side of her bed at night, naked to the waist, the light of a kerosene lamp moving upon her dark skin. Her long, black hair, always drawn and braided in the day, lay upon her shoulders and against her breasts like a shawl. I do not speak Kiowa, and I never understood her prayers, but there was something inherently sad in the sound, some merest hesitation upon the syllables of sorrow. She began in a high and descending pitch, exhausting her breath to silence; then again and again—and always the same intensity of effort, of something that is, and is not, like urgency in the human voice. Transported so in the dancing light among the shadows of her room, she seemed beyond the reach of time. But that was illusion; I think I knew then that I should not see her again.

Houses are like sentinels in the plain, old keepers of the weather watch. There, in a very little while, wood takes on the appearance of great age. All colors wear soon away in the wind and rain, and then the wood is burned gray and the grain appears and the nails turn red with rust. The windowpanes are black and opaque; you imagine there is nothing within, and indeed there are many ghosts, bones given up to the land. They stand here and there against the sky, and you approach them for a longer time than you expect. They belong in the distance; it is their domain.

Once there was a lot of sound in my grandmother's house, a lot of coming and going, feasting and talk. The summers there were full of excitement and reunion. The Kiowas are a summer people; they abide the cold and keep to themselves, but when the season turns and the land becomes warm and vital they cannot hold still; an old love of going returns upon them. The aged visitors who came to my grandmother's house when I was a child were made of lean and leather, and they bore themselves upright. They wore great black hats and bright ample shirts that shook in the wind. They rubbed fat upon their hair and wound their braids with strips of colored cloth. Some of them painted their faces and carried the scars of old and cherished enmities. They were an old council of warlords, come to remind and be reminded of who they were. Their wives and daughters served them well. The women might indulge themselves; gossip was at once the mark and compensation of their servitude. They made loud and elaborate talk among themselves, full of jest and gesture, fright and false alarm. They went abroad in fringed and flowered shawls, bright beadwork and German silver. They were at home in the kitchen, and they prepared meals that were banquets.

There were frequent prayer meetings, and great nocturnal feasts. When I was a child I played with my cousins outside, where the lamplight fell upon the ground and the singing of the old people rose up around us and carried away into the darkness. There were a lot of good things to eat, a lot of laughter and surprise. And afterwards, when the quiet returned, I lay down with my grandmother and could hear the frogs away by the river and feel the motion of the air.

Now there is a funeral silence in the rooms, the endless wake of some final word. The walls have closed in upon my grandmother's house. When I returned to it in mourning, I saw for the first time in my life how small it was. It was late at night, and there was a white moon, nearly full. I sat for a long time on the stone steps by the kitchen door. From there I could see out across the land; I could see the long row of trees by the creek, the low light upon the rolling plains, and the stars of the Big Dipper. Once I looked at the moon and caught sight of a strange thing. A cricket had perched upon the handrail, only a few inches away from me. My line of vision was such that the creature filled the moon like a fossil. It had gone there, I thought, to live and die, for there, of all places, was its small definition made whole and eternal. A warm wind rose up and purled like the longing within me.

The next morning I awoke at dawn and went out on the dirt road to Rainy Mountain. It was already hot, and the grasshoppers began to fill the air. Still, it was early in the morning, and the birds sang out of the shadows. The long yellow grass on the mountain shone in the bright light, and a scissortail hied above the land. There, where it ought to be, at the end of a long and legendary way, was my grandmother's grave. Here and there on the dark stones were ancestral names. Looking back once, I saw the mountain and came away.

1. To what extent is Momaday interested in describing what his grandmother did or said and what she looked like? How is his method of characterization different from that of other writers represented in this chapter?

2. Identify two or three passages where Momaday writes about specific memories he has of his grandmother and explain why you think he includes these particular memories in his sketch.

3. Momaday was raised on Indian reservations in the southwestern United States. How do his concerns as a member of a distinctive culture shape his story? What attitudes does he have toward Indian people and Indian traditions? How is his portrait of his grandmother related to those attitudes?

4. The selection printed here serves as an introduction to a book in which Momaday retells the legends and stories of the Kiowa. Does the portrait of his grandmother strike you as an appropriate introduction to such a book? Why or why not?

5. Unlike most of the other selections in this chapter, Momaday's account does not begin by discussing himself or his family. How does his opening paragraph serve as an introduction to what he wants to tell his readers?

∽ Russell Baker ∽

(1925-   )

*Russell Baker has written a regular column, "The Observer,"
for* The New York Times *since 1962; his writing is now syndi-
cated to many other newspapers and in 1975 he won a Pulitzer
Prize for journalism. Baker was born in Virginia, but he was
brought up by his widowed mother in Baltimore, where his
family struggled through the Depression and where Baker
eventually attended Johns Hopkins University. The selection
that follows, from Baker's autobiography,* Growing Up *(1982),
describes how he introduced the woman he later married to
his mother.*

[MOTHER AND MIMI]

Three months passed before I mustered the courage to introduce Mimi at Marydell Road. Sunday dinner seemed the ideal
occasion. Sunday dinner had become a family ritual for my
mother, as it had once been with Ida Rebecca, a time when
family was expected to gather round and celebrate its unity in
food and table talk. It weekly confirmed my mother's pleasure
in having given us "a home of our own." It was always a
command appearance for me. Doris, now nineteen, helped
with the hours of cooking. My mother would preside at one
end of the table, and Herb would sit at the other straining to
hear the Washington Senators baseball game on the living-
room radio while flattering my mother on the crispness of the
fried chicken, the texture of the gravy, the excellence of the

devil's food cake, the coconut cake, and the apple pie with which the dinner always ended. Their child, Mary Leslie, was big enough now to sit at the table on a pile of books. Uncle Harold and Aunt Sister came frequently, and there were always other guests with blood ties to my mother's family, to Herb's, or to the Bakers.

It seemed the logical occasion for presenting Mimi. Sunday dinner put my mother in her most gracious mood. With so many people present there would be no chance of matters getting out of hand. I knew Mimi would have instant allies in Doris, who was broad-minded; in Uncle Harold, who liked women; and in Aunt Sister, who liked meeting people.

"I've invited a girl I know to dinner Sunday," I told my mother. "I hope you don't mind."

"Your friends are always welcome here, Buddy. What's her name?"

"Mimi."

"I've never heard you mention a Mimi before."

"You'll like her."

"I'm sure I'll like her if you like her. My boy has good taste."

"She's a lot like you. She's had to make her own way in the world."

"Did you meet her at Hopkins?"

"She's not in school," I said. "She's got a job."

"What does she do?"

"Works in a department store."

"Selling?"

"Sort of."

"Well, I've got nothing against a girl making her own way in this world. Lord knows, I had to do it long enough."

"You'll like her," I said.

"Have you met her family?"

"She doesn't have any family. I guess you could call her an orphan."

"Where does she live if she doesn't have a family?"

"She's got an apartment downtown with another girl."

"Two girls living alone in an apartment?"

"They're both nice girls."

"Have you been there?"

"Once or twice," I lied.

"I see," my mother said, and I suspected she did. She couldn't help but wonder why I had stayed out so many times in recent weeks until four o'clock in the morning. She must have worried about where I might be on those nights, but she hadn't asked. "I look forward to meeting her" was all she said, though.

"You'll like her," I said.

I hadn't told Mimi much about my mother. "You'll like her," I'd said. I suspected neither would like the other, but I was praying.

On Sunday Mimi came out to Marydell Road. I met her, and when she stepped off the streetcar, I felt a pang of uneasiness. Excited about being received into a family, eager to make a fine impression, she had dressed elaborately. She had bought a new dress, a pink clinging fabric that molded itself seductively to her body. She had had her hair done the day before by a hairdresser who, after lightening it with streaks of bleach, had chosen an upsweep suggestive of a Hollywood sex goddess. To present a proper face, she'd spared no expense at the cosmetics counter. Gazing at her, I thought her the most beautiful woman I'd ever seen and knew it was all wrong for Marydell Road.

"Do I look all right?" she asked.

"Terrific," I assured her.

The other guests hadn't arrived, and my mother was waiting alone on the porch when Mimi and I came up the steps. It wasn't until next day that my mother said, "Mimi wouldn't be a bad-looking girl if she didn't use so much makeup," but Mimi understood everything that Sunday night when I took her home on the streetcar. "Your mother didn't like me," she said.

"How can you say that? Of course she liked you."

In fact she had taken pains to be pleasant to Mimi all afternoon. I'd been happily surprised by that.

"She doesn't like me," Mimi said. "She'll never like me."

I was unwilling to believe this even after the next day's "Mimi wouldn't be a bad-looking girl if she didn't use so much makeup." I insisted Mimi come back for another Sunday dinner, and another, and another, and she did. Uncle Harold and Aunt Sister became fond of her. So did Herb. So did Doris. My mother saw only menace. She began clocking my movements.

No matter how quietly I came creeping in at three or four o'clock in the morning, I could count on my mother to be awake. "Is that you, Buddy?" she would whisper from her bedroom.

"Uh-huh."

"What time is it?"

"I don't know. Not too late."

Once in a while: "Where've you been?"

"Out with George," I'd whisper, closing the bedroom door behind me.

One morning, tiptoeing in just before dawn, I found her sitting in the dark in the living room. "Do you know what time it is? I've been waiting up all night for you."

"Is something wrong?"

"There's plenty wrong and you know what it is."

I didn't know how to answer that, so didn't.

"Don't you ever want to amount to anything, Russell?"

I was scheduled to graduate from college in a few months. "I'm not doing too bad," I said. "Let's turn in."

"I've worked and slaved to help you make something of yourself someday," she said. "Now you're throwing everything away because of that girl. She's got you hypnotized."

"That's silly."

"Oh, is it? Where've you been all night?"

"Out with George," I said.

"George doesn't stay out all night. He's in medical school,

he's trying to make something of himself. You've been with Mimi, haven't you?"

"Come on, Mom, you're tired. Let's go to bed."

She turned on the light instead. "You never used to lie to me, Russell. Now you lie all the time. Can't you see what she's done to you?"

"What do you want me to do?" In anger at being treated like a child, I was ready to burn bridges.

"I'm only interested in your own good, Buddy. Don't think your mother is interfering."

"That's a fine thing to say. Of course you're interfering. Well, if you want to know—yes, I have been at Mimi's. Does that satisfy you?"

Her face went slack, expressionless. She stared beyond me at something five thousand miles away. "It's in the blood," she said, speaking to herself now.

"What's in the blood?" I asked.

She focused again on me, and, with a look as close to hate as she'd ever given me, she cried, "You're just like your father was. Just like your father."

It was said with loathing. Had she hated him, then? I'd spent most of a lifetime with her and she had rarely told me anything about my father, rarely even mentioned him. It was as if she wanted to erase him from my life. But now, in that hate-filled cry—"Just like your father"—she lit up an entirely different landscape of the heart. There had been some taint in my father's blood. She had reared me in dread that it might reappear in mine. Maybe that had been her reason for taking me out of Morrisonville and away from my father's people before the funeral meats were cold. Maybe she had hoped I could escape the taint of the blood by growing up far away from it among her own people.

I didn't know then nor for many years later that I'd been conceived before she and my father were married. Not knowing that, I couldn't grasp the complex emotions behind her cry: "Just like your father." She must have seen life repeating itself as a macabre dance. It must have seemed that I was reliving with Mimi my father's affair with her, that she was reliving Ida Rebecca's struggle against a foolish son and a wayward girl, and that I was in danger of reliving the disaster that love had made of her own life. She had overcome that and had transformed me from the agent of her disaster into a promise of a triumph for herself. Now the taint had surfaced to threaten everything, and, looking on me for that one terrible moment, she must have seen me as disaster recurring.

"Just like your father!"

After that, Mimi no longer came to Sunday dinner. Lines of battle had been drawn. The time for conciliation had passed.

1. Baker uses a great deal of dialogue in presenting this portrait of his mother and of his relation to her. What do you think are the most revealing things his mother says and what do they reveal about her?

2. What particular occasions does Baker choose to dramatize? Do they seem to you best suited to his story and his characters? Are there other moments you think should have been dramatized? Explain your reasons.

3. Toward the end of this selection, Baker refers back to much earlier incidents in his life: the time when his father and mother, first married, lived across the road from his father's strong-willed mother, Ida Rebecca, in the tiny rural town of Morrisonville, Virginia. Why does he allude to the past in this way? Are those passages related to his conclusion "The time for conciliation had passed"?

4. What attitude does Baker express toward his mother? Do you sympathize with him or with her? Why?

～ James Thurber ～

(1894-1961)

James Thurber was born and brought up in Columbus, Ohio. Thurber worked as a newspaperman for various papers until he finally joined the staff of The New Yorker *magazine in 1927. From that time on, the bulk of Thurber's work— sketches, reminiscences, cartoons, short stories, and essays— was written for the magazine, and it established him as one of America's great humorists. His portrait of Doc Marlowe comes from* Let Your Mind Alone *(1937), a collection of his magazine pieces from the middle Nineteen Thirties.*

DOC MARLOWE

I was too young to be other than awed and puzzled by Doc Marlowe when I knew him. I was only sixteen when he died. He was sixty-seven. There was that vast difference in our ages and there was a vaster difference in our backgrounds. Doc Marlowe was a medicine-show man. He had been a lot of other things, too: a circus man, the proprietor of a concession at Coney Island, a saloon-keeper; but in his fifties he had traveled around with a tent-show troupe made up of a Mexican named Chickalilli, who threw knives, and a man called Professor Jones, who played the banjo. Doc Marlowe would come out after the entertainment and harangue the crowd and sell bottles of medicine for all kinds of ailments. I found out all this about him gradually, toward the last, and after he died.

From James Thurber: *Let Your Mind Alone*. Published by Harper & Row. Copyright © 1937 by James Thurber, copyright © 1965 by Helen W. Thurber and Rosemary Thurber Sauers. Originally printed in *The New Yorker*. Reprinted by permission of Mrs. James Thurber.

When I first knew him, he represented the Wild West to me, and there was nobody I admired so much.

I met Doc Marlowe at old Mrs. Willoughby's rooming house. She had been a nurse in our family, and I used to go and visit her over week-ends sometimes, for I was very fond of her. I was about eleven years old then. Doc Marlowe wore scarred leather leggings, a bright-colored bead vest that he said he got from the Indians, and a ten-gallon hat with kitchen matches stuck in the band, all the way around. He was about six feet four inches tall, with big shoulders, and a long, drooping mustache. He let his hair grow long, like General Custer's. He had a wonderful collection of Indian relics and six-shooters, and he used to tell me stories of his adventures in the Far West. His favorite expressions were "Hay, boy!" and "Hay, boy-gie!," which he used the way some people now use "Hot dog!" or "Doggone!" He told me once that he had killed an Indian chief named Yellow Hand in a tomahawk duel on horseback. I thought he was the greatest man I had ever seen. It wasn't until he died and his son came on from New Jersey for the funeral that I found out he had never been in the Far West in his life. He had been born in Brooklyn.

Doc Marlowe had given up the road when I knew him, but he still dealt in what he called "medicines." His stock in trade was a liniment that he had called Snake Oil when he traveled around. He changed the name to Blackhawk Liniment when he settled in Columbus. Doc didn't always sell enough of it to pay for his bed and board, and old Mrs. Willoughby would sometimes have to "trust" him for weeks at a time. She didn't mind, because his liniment had taken a bad kink out of her right limb that had bothered her for thirty years. I used to see people whom Doc had massaged with Blackhawk Liniment move arms and legs that they hadn't been able to move before he "treated" them. His patients were day laborers, wives of streetcar conductors, and people like that. Sometimes they would shout and weep after Doc had massaged them, and several got up and walked around who hadn't been able to walk before. One man hadn't turned his head to either side for seven years before Doc soused him with Blackhawk. In half an hour he could move his head as easily as I could move mine. "Glory be to God!" he shouted. "It's the secret qualities in the ointment, my friend," Doc Marlowe told him, suavely. He always called the liniment ointment.

News of his miracles got around by word of mouth among the poorer classes of town—he was not able to reach the better people (the "tony folks," he called them)—but there was never a big enough sale to give Doc a steady income. For one thing, people thought there was more magic in Doc's touch than in his liniment, and, for another, the ingredients of Blackhawk cost so much that his profits were not very great. I know, because I used to go to the wholesale chemical company once in a while for him and buy his supplies. Everything that went into the liniment was standard and expensive (and well-known, not secret). A man at the company told me he didn't see how Doc could make much money on it at thirty-five cents a bottle. But even when he was very low in funds Doc never cut out any of the ingredients or substituted cheaper ones. Mrs. Willoughby had suggested it to him once, she told me, when she was helping him "put up a batch," and he had got mad. "He puts a heap of store by that liniment being right up to the mark," she said.

Doc added to his small earnings, I discovered, by money he made gambling. He used to win quite a few dollars on Saturday nights at Freck's saloon, playing poker with the market-men and the railroaders who dropped in there. It wasn't for several years that I found out Doc cheated. I had never heard about marked cards until he told me about them and showed me his. It was one rainy afternoon, after he had played seven-up with Mrs. Willoughby and old Mr. Peiffer, another roomer of hers. They had played for small stakes (Doc wouldn't play cards unless there was some money up, and Mrs. Willoughby wouldn't play if very much was up). Only twenty or thirty cents had changed hands in the end. Doc had won it all. I remember my astonishment and indignation when it dawned on me that Doc had used the marked cards in playing the old lady and the old man. "You didn't cheat *them*, did you?" I asked him. "Jimmy, my boy," he told me, "the man that calls the turn wins the money." His eyes twinkled and he seemed to enjoy my anger. I was outraged, but I was helpless. I knew I could never tell Mrs. Willoughby about how Doc had cheated her at seven-up. I liked her, but I liked him, too. Once he had given me a whole dollar to buy fireworks with on the Fourth of July.

I remember once, when I was staying at Mrs. Willoughby's, Doc Marlowe was roused out of bed in the middle of the night by a poor woman who was frantic because her little girl was sick. This woman had had the sciatica driven out of her by his liniment, she reminded Doc. He placed her then. She had never been able to pay him a cent for his liniment or his "treatments," and he had given her a great many. He got up and dressed, and went over to her house. The child had colic, I suppose. Doc couldn't have had any idea what was the matter, but he sopped on liniment; he sopped on a whole bottle. When he came back home, two hours later, he said he had "relieved the distress." The little girl had gone to sleep and was all right the next day, whether on account of Doc Marlowe or in spite of him I don't know. "I want to thank you, Doctor," said the mother, tremulously, when she called on him that afternoon. He gave her another bottle of liniment, and he didn't charge her for it or for his "professional call." He used to massage, and give liniment to, a lot of sufferers who were too poor to pay. Mrs. Willoughby told him once that he was too generous and too easily taken in. Doc laughed—and winked at me, with the twinkle in his eye that he had had when he told me how he had cheated the old lady at cards.

Once I went for a walk with him out Town Street on a Saturday afternoon. It was a warm day, and after a while I said I wanted a soda. Well, he said, he didn't care if he took something himself. We went into a drugstore, and I ordered a chocolate soda and he had a lemon phosphate. When we had finished, he said, "Jimmy, my son, I'll match you to see who pays for the drinks." He handed me a quarter and he told me to toss the quarter and he would call the turn. He called heads and won. I paid for the drinks. It left me with a dime.

I was fifteen when Doc got out his pamphlets, as he called them. He had eased the misery of the wife of a small-time printer and the grateful man had given him a special price on two thousand advertising pamphlets. There was very little in them about Blackhawk Liniment. They were mostly about Doc himself and his "Life in the Far West." He had gone out to Franklin Park one day with a photographer—another of his numerous friends—and there the photographer took dozens of pictures of Doc, a lariat in one hand, a six-shooter in the other. I had gone along. When the pamphlets came out, there were the pictures of Doc, peering around trees, crouching behind bushes, whirling the lariat, aiming the gun. "Dr. H. M. Marlowe Hunting Indians" was one of the captions. "Dr. H. M. Marlowe after Hoss-Thieves" was another one. He was very proud of the pamphlets and always had a sheaf with him. He would pass them out to people on the street.

Two years before he died Doc got hold of an ancient, wheezy Cadillac somewhere. He aimed to start traveling around again, he said, but he never did, because the old automobile was so worn out it wouldn't hold up for more than a mile or so. It was about this time that a man named Hardman and his wife came to stay at Mrs. Willoughby's. They were farm people from around Lancaster who had sold their place. They got to like Doc because he was so jolly, they said, and they enjoyed his stories. He treated Mrs. Hardman for an old complaint in the small of her back and wouldn't take any money for it. They thought he was a fine gentleman. Then there came a day when they announced that they were going to St. Louis, where they had a son. They talked some of settling in St. Louis. Doc Marlowe told them they ought to buy a nice auto cheap and drive out, instead of going by train—it wouldn't cost much and they could see the country, give themselves a treat. Now, he knew where they could pick up just such a car.

Of course, he finally sold them the decrepit Cadillac—it had been stored away somewhere in the back of a garage whose owner kept it there for nothing because Doc had relieved his mother of a distress in the groins, as Doc explained it. I don't know just how the garage man doctored up the car, but he did. It actually chugged along pretty steadily when Doc took the Hardmans out for a trial spin. He told them he hated to part with it, but he finally let them have it for a hundred dollars. I knew, of course, and so did Doc, that it couldn't last many miles.

Doc got a letter from the Hardmans in St. Louis ten days later. They had had to abandon the old junk pile in West Jefferson, some fifteen miles out of Columbus. Doc read the letter aloud to me, peering over his glasses, his eyes twinkling, every now and then punctuating the lines with "Hay, boy!" and "Hay, boy-gie!" "I just want you to know, Dr. Marlowe," he read, "what I think of low-life swindlers like you [Hay, boy!] and that it will be a long day before I put my trust in a two-faced lyer and imposture again [Hay, boy-gie!]. The garrage man in W. Jefferson told us your old rattle-trap had been doctored up just to fool us. It was a low down dirty trick as no swine would play on a white man [Hay, boy!]." Far from being disturbed by the letter, Doc Marlowe was plainly amused. He took off his glasses, after he finished it and laughed, his hand to his brow and his eyes closed. I was pretty mad, because I had liked the Hardmans, and because they had liked him. Doc Marlowe put the letter carefully back into its envelope and tucked it away in his inside coat pocket, as if it were something precious. Then he picked up a pack of cards and began to lay out a solitaire hand. "Want to set in a little seven-up game, Jimmy?" he asked me. I was furious. "Not with a cheater like you!" I shouted, and stamped out of the room, slamming the door. I could hear him chuckling to himself behind me.

The last time I saw Doc Marlowe was just a few days before he died. I didn't know anything about death, but I knew that he was dying when I saw him. His voice was very faint and his face was drawn; they told me he had a lot of pain. When I got ready to leave the room, he asked me to bring him a tin box that was on his bureau. I got it and handed it to him. He poked around in it for a while with unsteady fingers and finally found what he wanted. He handed it to me. It was a quarter, or rather it looked like a quarter, but it had heads on both sides. "Never let the other fella call the turn, Jimmy, my boy," said Doc, with a shadow of his old twinkle and the echo of his old chuckle. I still have the two-headed quarter. For a long time I didn't like to think about it, or about Doc Marlowe, but I do now.

1. Why do you think Thurber wants to write about Doc Marlowe?

2. Thurber frequently tells you of particular phrases that Doc Marlowe used. What is his point in drawing your attention to Marlowe's language?

3. Thurber tells of Marlowe cheating an old lady at cards in one paragraph and then of his helping someone in the middle of the night at no charge in the next paragraph. What is his purpose in putting these two stories together? What sense of Marlowe's character does it give you?

4. How does Thurber's story of Doc Marlowe and the Hardmans fit into this portrait?

5. What does the last line of the sketch mean? How does it help to express Thurber's attitude? Do you see a difference between his interest in Doc Marlowe as a youngster and his interest now?

∽ Lillian Hellman ∽

(1907-   )

Lillian Hellman was born and brought up in New Orleans and educated at New York University and Columbia University. Her career as a playwright began with the New York success of The Children's Hour *(1934). Her dramas have received many awards, and such plays as* The Little Foxes *(1940),* Watch On The Rhine *(1941), and* Toys In The Attic *(1960) have been great popular successes, both on Broadway and in later film versions. Among her autobiographical volumes are* An Unfinished Woman *(1969) and* Pentimento *(1973), both filled with portraits of the memorable people in her life. In this selection, she writes of her relationship with Dashiell Hammett, the creator of such classic works of detective fiction as* The Maltese Falcon *and* The Thin Man.

DASHIELL HAMMETT

For years we made jokes about the day I would write about him. In the early years, I would say, "Tell me more about the girl in San Francisco. The silly one who lived across the hall in Pine Street."

And he would laugh and say, "She lived across the hall in Pine Street and was silly."

"Tell more than that. How much did you like her and how—?"

He would yawn. "Finish your drink and go to sleep."

But days later, maybe even that night, if I was on the find-out kick, and I was, most of the years, I would say, "O.K., be stubborn about the girls. So tell me about your grandmother and what you looked like as a baby."

"I was a very fat baby. My grandmother went to the movies every afternoon. She was very fond of a movie star called Wallace Reid and I've told you all this before."

I would say I wanted to get everything straight for the days after his death when I would write his biography and he would say that I was not to bother writing his biography because it would turn out to be the history of Lillian Hellman with an occasional reference to a friend called Hammett.

The day of his death came on January 10, 1961. I will never write that biography because I cannot write about my closest, my most beloved friend. And maybe, too, because all those questions through all the thirty-one on and off years, and the sometime answers, got muddled, and life changed for both of us and the questions and answers became one in the end, flowing together from the days when I was young to the days when I was middle-aged. And so this will be no attempt at a biography of Samuel Dashiell Hammett, born in St. Mary's County, Maryland, on May 27, 1894. Nor will it be a critical appraisal of his work. In 1966 I edited and published a collection of his stories. There was a day when I thought all of them very good. But all of them are not good, though most of them, I think, are very good. It is only right to say immediately that by publishing them at all I did what Hammett did not want to do: he turned down all offers to republish the stories, although I never knew the reason and never asked. I did know, from what he said about "Tulip," the unfinished novel that I included in the book, that he meant to start a new literary life and maybe didn't want the old work to get in the way. But sometimes I think he was just too ill to care, too worn out to listen to plans or read contracts. The fact of breathing, just breathing, took up all the days and nights.

In the First World War, in camp, influenza led to tuberculosis and Hammett was to spend years after in army hospitals.

He came out of the Second World War with emphysema, but how he ever got into the Second World War at the age of forty-eight still bewilders me. He telephoned me the day the army accepted him to say it was the happiest day of his life, and before I could finish saying it wasn't the happiest day of mine and what about the old scars on his lungs, he laughed and hung up. His death was caused by cancer of the lungs, discovered only two months before he died. It was not operable—I doubt that he would have agreed to an operation even if it had been—and so I decided not to tell him about the cancer. The doctor said that when the pain came, it would come in the right chest and arm, but that the pain might never come. The doctor was wrong: only a few hours after he told me, the pain did come. Hammett had had self-diagnosed rheumatism in the right arm and had always said that was why he had given up hunting. On the day I heard about the cancer, he said his gun shoulder hurt him again, would I rub it for him. I remember sitting behind him, rubbing the shoulder and hoping he would always think it was rheumatism and remember only the autumn hunting days. But the pain never came again, or if it did he never mentioned it, or maybe death was so close that the shoulder pain faded into other pains.

He did not wish to die and I like to think he didn't know he was dying. But I keep from myself even now the possible meaning of a night, very late, a short time before his death. I came into his room, and for the only time in the years I knew him there were tears in his eyes and the book was lying unread. I sat down beside him and waited a long time before I could say, "Do you want to talk about it?"

He said, almost with anger, "No. My only chance is not to talk about it."

And he never did. He had patience, courage, dignity in those last, awful months. It was as if all that makes a man's life had come together to prove itself: suffering was a private matter and there was to be no invasion of it. He would seldom even ask for anything he needed, and so the most we did—my secretary and Helen, who were devoted to him, as most women always had been—was to carry up the meals he barely touched, the books he now could hardly read, the afternoon coffee, and the martini that I insisted upon before the dinner that wasn't eaten.

One night of that last year, a bad night, I said, "Have another martini. It will make you feel better."

"No," he said, "I don't want it."

I said, "O.K., but I bet you never thought I'd urge you to have another drink."

He laughed for the first time that day. "Nope. And I never thought I'd turn it down."

Because on the night we had first met he was getting over a five-day drunk and he was to drink very heavily for the next eighteen years, and then one day, warned by a doctor, he said he would never have another drink and he kept his word except for the last year of the one martini, and that was my idea.

We met when I was twenty-four years old and he was thirty-six in a restaurant in Hollywood. The five-day drunk had left the wonderful face looking rumpled, and the very tall thin figure was tired and sagged. We talked of T. S. Eliot, although I no longer remember what we said, and then went and sat in his car and talked at each other and over each other until it was daylight. We were to meet again a few weeks later and, after that, on and sometimes off again for the rest of his life and thirty years of mine.

Thirty years is a long time, I guess, and yet as I come now to write about them the memories skip about and make no pattern and I know only certain of them are to be trusted. I know about that first meeting and the next, and there are many other pictures and sounds, but they are out of order and out of time, and I don't seem to want to put them into place. (I could have done a research job, I have on other people, but I didn't want to do one on Hammett, or to be a bookkeeper of my own life.) I don't want modesty for either of us, but I ask myself now if it can mean much to anybody but me that my second sharpest memory is of a day when we were living on a small island off the coast of Connecticut. It was six years after we had first met: six full, happy, unhappy years during which I had, with help from Hammett, written *The Children's Hour*, which was a success, and *Days to Come*, which was not. I was returning from the mainland in a catboat filled with marketing and Hammett had come down to the dock to tie me up. He had been sick that summer—the first of the sicknesses—and he was even thinner than usual. The white hair, the white pants, the white shirt made a straight, flat surface in the late sun. I thought: Maybe that's the handsomest sight I ever saw, that line of a man, the knife for a nose, and the sheet went out of my hand and the wind went out of the sail. Hammett laughed as I struggled to get back the sail. I don't know why, but I yelled angrily, "So you're a Dostoevsky sinner-saint. So you are." The laughter stopped, and when I finally came in to the dock we didn't speak as we carried up the packages and didn't speak through dinner.

Later that night, he said, "What did you say that for? What does it mean?"

I said I didn't know why I had said it and I didn't know what it meant.

Years later, when his life had changed, I did know what I had meant that day: I had seen the sinner—whatever is a sinner—and sensed the change before it came. When I told him that, Hammett said he didn't know what I was talking about, it was all too religious for him. But he did know what I was talking about and he was pleased.

But the fat, loose, wild years were over by the time we talked that way. When I first met Dash he had written four of the five novels and was the hottest thing in Hollywood and New York. It is not remarkable to be the hottest thing in either city—the hottest kid changes for each winter season—but in his case it was of extra interest to those who collect people that the ex-detective who had bad cuts on his legs and an indentation in his head from being scrappy with criminals was gentle in manner, well educated, elegant to look at, born of early settlers, was eccentric, witty, and spent so much money on women that they would have liked him even if he had been none of the good things. But as the years passed from 1930 to 1948, he wrote only one novel and a few short stories. By 1945, the drinking was no longer gay, the drinking bouts were longer and the moods darker. I was there off and on for most of those years, but in 1948 I didn't want to see the drinking anymore. I hadn't seen or spoken to Hammett for two months until the day when his devoted cleaning lady called to say she thought I had better come down to his apartment. I said I wouldn't, and then I did. She and I dressed a man who could barely lift an arm or a leg and brought him to my house, and that night I watched delirium tremens, although I didn't know what I was watching until the doctor told me the next day at the hospital. The doctor was an old friend. He said, "I'm going to tell Hammett that if he goes on drinking he'll be dead in a few months. It's my duty to say it, but it won't do any good." In a few minutes he came out of Dash's room and said, "I told him. Dash said O.K., he'd go on the wagon forever, but he can't and he won't."

But he could and he did. Five or six years later, I told Hammett that the doctor had said he wouldn't stay on the wagon.

Dash looked puzzled. "But I gave my word that day."

I said, "Have you always kept your word?"

"Most of the time," he said, "maybe because I've so seldom given it."

He had made up honor early in his life and stuck with his rules, fierce in the protection of them. In 1951 he went to jail because he and two other trustees of the bail bond fund of the Civil Rights Congress refused to reveal the names of the contributors to the fund. The truth was that Hammett had never been in the office of the Congress, did not know the name of a single contributor.

The night before he was to appear in court, I said, "Why don't you say that you don't know the names?"

"No," he said, "I can't say that."

"Why?"

"I don't know why. I guess it has something to do with keeping my word, but I don't want to talk about that. Nothing much will happen, although I think we'll go to jail for a while, but you're not to worry because"—and then suddenly I couldn't understand him because the voice had dropped and the words were coming in a most untypical nervous rush. I said I couldn't hear him, and he raised his voice and dropped his head. "I hate this damn kind of talk, but maybe I better tell you that if it were more than jail, if it were my life, I would give it for what I think democracy is, and I don't let cops or judges tell me what I think democracy is." Then he went home to bed, and the next day he went to jail.

1. Near the beginning of this selection, Hellman says that she is not writing a biography of Hammett or a critical appraisal of his work. How would you describe what she has accomplished here?

2. Why do you think Hellman begins her account with a brief dialogue between herself and Hammett? What are they talking about and how is it important to this piece?

3. In the paragraph beginning "Thirty years is a very long time . . ." Hellman denies following any particular order in writing about her relationship with Hammett. What kind of sequence or shape do you think the selection does have?

4. What sense of Hellman herself do you get from her recollections? Does she reveal herself in the things she admires about Hammett? In her conversations with him?

∿ Ralph Ellison ∿

(1914-   )

Ralph Ellison is best known as the author of Invisible Man
*(1952), a rich and complex novel about the experience of be-
ing black in America. He has written essays and reviews about
various aspects of American society and culture. Ellison was
born and raised in Oklahoma City, where in the late 1920s
many gifted black musicians were developing their art. The
following selection, from* Shadow and Act *(1964), presents
Ellison's memories of hearing Jimmy Rushing, one of the
greatest male jazz singers, before Rushing became nationally
famous as the vocalist with Count Basie and his Orchestra.*

REMEMBERING JIMMY

In the old days the voice was high and clear and poignantly
lyrical. Steel-bright in its upper range and, at its best, silky
smooth, it was possessed of a purity somehow impervious to
both the stress of singing above a twelve-piece band and the
urgency of Rushing's own blazing fervor. On dance nights,
when you stood on the rise of the school grounds two blocks
to the east, you could hear it jetting from the dance hall like
a blue flame in the dark; now soaring high above the trum-
pets and trombones, now skimming the froth of reeds and
rhythm as it called some woman's anguished name—or demanded in a high, thin, passionately lyrical line, "Baaaaay-
bay, Bay-aaaay-bay! Tell me what's the matter now!"—above
the shouting of the swinging band.

Nor was there need for the by now famous signature line: "If anybody asks you who sang this song / Tell 'em / it was little Jimmy Rushing / he's been here and gone"—for everyone on Oklahoma City's "East Side" knew that sweet, high-floating sound. "Deep Second" was our fond nickname for the block in which Rushing worked and lived, and where most Negro business and entertainment were found, and before he went to cheer a wider world his voice evoked the festive spirit of the place. Indeed, he was the natural herald of its blues-romance, his song the singing essence of its joy. For Jimmy Rushing was not simply a local entertainer, he expressed a value, an attitude about the world for which our lives afforded no other definition. We had a Negro church and a segregated school, a few lodges and fraternal organizations, and beyond these there was all the great white world. We were pushed off to what seemed to be the least desirable side of the city (but which some years later was found to contain one of the state's richest pools of oil), and our system of justice was based upon Texas law, yet there was an optimism within the Negro community and a sense of possibility which, despite our awareness of limitation (dramatized so brutally in the Tulsa riot of 1921), transcended all of this; and it was this rock-bottom sense of reality, coupled with our sense of the possibility of rising above it, which sounded in Rushing's voice.

And how it carried! In those days I lived near the Rock Island roundhouse, where, with a steady clanging of bells and a great groaning of wheels along the rails, switch engines made up trains of freight unceasingly. Yet often in the late-spring night I could hear Rushing as I lay four blocks away in bed, carrying to me as clear as a full-bored riff on "Hot Lips" Page's horn. Heard thus, across the dark blocks lined with locust trees, through the night throbbing with the natural aural imagery of the blues, with high-balling trains, departing bells, lonesome guitar chords simmering up from a shack in the alley—it was easy to imagine the voice as setting the pattern to which the instruments of the Blue Devils Orchestra

RALPH ELLISON

and all the random sounds of night arose, affirming, as it were, some ideal native to the time and to the land. When we were still too young to attend night dances, but yet old enough to gather beneath the corner street lamp on summer evenings, anyone might halt the conversation to exclaim "Listen, they're raising hell down at Slaughter's Hall," and we'd turn our heads westward to hear Jimmy's voice soar up the hill and down, as pure and as miraculously unhindered by distance and earthbound things as is the body in youthful dreams of flying.

"Now, that's the Right Reverend Jimmy Rushing preaching now, man," someone would say. And rising to the cue another would answer, "Yeah, and that's old Elder 'Hot Lips' signifying along with him; urging him on, man." And, keeping it building, "Huh, but though you can't hear him out this far, Ole Deacon Big-un [the late Walter Page] is up there patting his foot and slapping on his big belly [the bass viol] to keep those fools in line." And we might go on to name all the members of the band as though they were the Biblical four-and-twenty elders, while laughing at the impious wit of applying church titles to a form of music which all the preachers assured us was the devil's potent tool.

Our wit was true, for Jimmy Rushing, along with the other jazz musicians whom we knew, had made a choice, had dedicated himself to a mode of expression and a way of life no less "righteously" than others dedicated themselves to the church. Jazz and the blues did not fit into the scheme of things as spelled out by our two main institutions, the church and the school, but they gave expression to attitudes which found no place in these and helped to give our lives some semblance of wholeness. Jazz and the public jazz dance was a third institution in our lives, and a vital one; and though Jimmy was far from being a preacher, he was, as official floor manager or master-of-the-dance at Slaughter's Hall, the leader of a public rite.

He was no Mr. Five-by-five in those days, but a compact,

305

debonair young man who dressed with an easy elegance. Much later, during theatre appearances with Basie's famous band, he sometimes cut an old step from slavery days called "falling off the log" for the sheer humor provided by the rapid, and apparently precarious, shifting of his great bulk, but in the Oklahoma days he was capable of an amazing grace of movement. A nineteenth-century formality still clung to public dances at the time, and there was quite a variety of steps. Jimmy danced them all, gliding before the crowd over the polished floor, sometimes with a girl, sometimes with a huge megaphone held chest-high before him as he swayed. The evenings began with the more formal steps, to popular and semi-classical music, and proceeded to become more expressive as the spirit of jazz and the blues became dominant. It was when Jimmy's voice began to soar with the spirit of the blues that the dancers—and the musicians—achieved that feeling of communion which was the true meaning of the public jazz dance. The blues, the singer, the band and the dancers formed the vital whole of jazz as an institutional form, and even today neither part is quite complete without the rest. The thinness of much of the so-called "modern jazz" is especially reflective of this loss of wholeness, and it is quite possible that Rushing retains his vitality simply because he has kept close to the small Negro public dance.

1. *Ellison does not begin his essay by telling his readers who Jimmy Rushing is or by reminding them of what he accomplished during his career. How does he begin the essay and how would you explain his choice of an opening?*
2. *What kinds of details does Ellison introduce to describe what a performance by Rushing was like? According to this selection, what are Rushing's most compelling qualities as a performer?*
3. *Why does Ellison refer to "the Right Reverend Jimmy Rushing"? Is the connection between the singer and a minister something that Ellison takes seriously?*

4. Ellison does not indicate in his essay that he ever knew Rushing personally. Why then does he still remember the experience of hearing him sing many years before he writes this essay? Does the fact that both the writer and the singer are black affect the kind of importance Ellison gives to Rushing?

5. Do you have memories of having a singer, a dancer, or a musician make a great impact upon you? How would you explain the reasons for that impact? Are they similar to or different from Ellison's reasons?

Possibilities for Writing

1. Choose a person you would find interesting to write about and make a list, as long as you can, of qualities, actions, gestures, physical characteristics, habits, interests, possessions, etc., that you associate with the person. Then write a character sketch based on some of the material on your list. In class, discuss how you used the list: what items you selected and why, what order you used them in and why.

2. Sometimes a single incident can confirm or enlarge our sense of the personality and character of someone we know well. Write a character sketch based on such an incident, in which you make clear how the incident communicated so much about this other person. You might compare your method of presenting an incident with that of Joan Baez, who uses this technique in discussing her father.

3. Write a character sketch of someone you have known for some time and have seen frequently (a close friend or a relative, perhaps). Then write a sketch of someone who impresses or interests you, but whom you have met only once or twice or whom you have only read about and seen on television. In class, compare your two characterizations and discuss what you, as a writer, have done differently in each piece.

4. Write an essay discussing how James Thurber makes you aware that as a young boy he thought differently about Doc

Marlowe than he does now. What attracts the young Thurber to Marlowe? In what ways does he have difficulty understanding Marlowe's behavior? What explains the change in feelings that Thurber mentions in the last sentence of the sketch?

5. Write an essay comparing what Patricia Hampl found memorable about her grandmother with what N. Scott Momaday found memorable about his grandmother. What special kind of dignity or authority is associated with each grandparent? What feelings does each writer express about the grandparent? Which writer is more interested in conveying a child's point of view?

CHAPTER SIX

PERSPECTIVES ON EXPERIENCE

Introduction: Generalizing from Experience

As every self-portrait in this anthology makes clear, the pur-
pose of autobiography is not simply to create a record of our
lives, but to create a meaningful record. We have seen that the
act of remembering and putting memories on paper is inseparable from a process of conscious and unconscious selection in
which we choose to include some things because they are relevant or meaningful and to exclude others. The same process of
selection that governs what we perceive and what we remember also applies to the language we use to convey such perceptions and memories—our words inevitably involve us in
creating and revealing meanings. The sum of these selections
becomes a point of view, a particular way of seeing meanings
in the world and expressing them in words.

We have also discovered that a further way of creating
meaning is through our ability to generalize. We are never
content to exist simply as custodians of the separate moments
of our past; we want to organize our experiences, grouping
them so that we can see pattern and relationship and can make
sense of them at last. In the preceding chapter we discussed
how generalizations could substitute for or serve as the culmi-
nation of a number of separate perceptions, binding those perceptions together into a characterization. Now it is necessary
to make a further distinction between two complementary
methods of enlarging upon a single moment of experience.
One method—generalization—carries us beyond that single

moment by placing its elements in broader or more general categories. We can gain some sense of how generalization works if we look at four related sentences, introduced here to illustrate stages of generalization. The first refers to a single specific event: (1) "On Tuesday John tried to impress Nancy by taking her to the most expensive restaurant in New York." The second sentence still focuses on John, but now includes many actions of a type similar to the specific event mentioned in the first sentence: (2) "John always tries to impress women by taking them to expensive places." The third sentence generalizes further by placing John himself in a larger category: (3) "American men show their interest in women by spending money on them." The fourth sentence goes furthest of all, since it claims to apply to all men universally: (4) "All men believe that their bank account has sex appeal."

As we have seen, these four sentences follow an ascending order of generalization. Sentence 2 generalizes in a very limited way, since it refers to only one person and to only one facet of his behavior. Because of its limited scope, such a statement is often called a low-level generalization; Frank O'Connor relied on generalizations of this type in his characterization of his father (Ch. 5). High-level generalizations take in a wider spectrum of human agents and their actions; at their most inclusive, as in sentence 4, general statements do not include any qualifying context. As the level of generalization increases, the statements made need more careful support if they are to be convincing. We might accept sentence 2 as representing a fairly familiar kind of male chauvinism, but we would probably be skeptical of the accuracy of sentence 3, without some careful qualification. Sentence 4 is clearly too broad to be persuasive and, like most extreme generalizations, tells us much more about the values of the writer than it does about the subject matter. Taken together the sentences show how every writer needs to be aware of the degree to which he is generalizing and of the degree to which he needs to support each generalization.

The second method of enlarging an individual moment of experience is abstraction. Abstraction separates a quality or characteristic from the concrete instances that embody it. John's behavior toward Nancy, in our earlier example, could be summarized by the abstraction "extravagant" or "self-promoting," words which are broader in their reference than the specific action by John that they describe. Another writer (John himself, perhaps) might use other abstractions, such as "generous" or "discriminating," to summarize the qualities that define John's behavior. Abstractions, like generalizations, are forceful markers of the writer's values and point of view. For this reason, a writer must be careful to use such language with precision, knowing not only how widely it applies but also what kind of judgments it reveals.

When we attempt to define and illustrate generalization and abstraction, they can sound like complicated activities that only mature and highly trained people engage in. In fact, all of us generalize and abstract continually, without giving it any particular thought. If we look back to the opening selection in this book, we find Harry Truman saying, "I always liked the underdogs better than the high hats," a generalization about people that is both casual and understandable. In other words, the reason the subject needs discussion in this chapter is to remind ourselves of what we have already been doing, and to teach ourselves to use generalizations and abstractions more accurately.

In a way, writing that begins from a strong autobiographical impulse is less likely to tempt a writer to do much generalizing. If we want to re-create some vivid past experience, our generalizations will be limited ones. Suppose, for example, that you were in a grocery store when a holdup took place. If you decided to write about this memorable event, you would probably emphasize its separate stages and what you saw, did, and felt. However, if your purpose was to write about a broader, less personal subject—fear of crime in your neighborhood or crime and gun control laws—the holdup might serve you as a powerful example. Many of the selections in this section introduce personal experience in this second way; the writer has initially been thinking of some large issue and then finds compelling testimony concerning that issue in his personal memories. James Baldwin, for example, does not write his essay primarily to tell us about his life in a tiny Swiss village; his concern is the place of black people in Western societies shaped entirely by white cultural traditions; as he thinks about that subject, his own experience in Switzerland strikes him as relevant and he then chooses to make it a prominent part of his story.

Any writer needs to concern himself with the fit between his personal experience and the generalization he wishes to link with it. His initial questions should be: How broad or narrow is the range of personal experience I am drawing on? How high or low is the level of the generalization I am presenting? If the holdup represented your single personal encounter with crime, it would be too limited a base to support a high-level generalization about gun control laws; it would serve much more comfortably if you wrote about a relatively low-level generalization—the fear of crime in your own neighborhood. If your range of relevant personal experience was much broader (if, for example, you were a police officer or a ballistics expert), you might write effectively about gun control laws, relying almost entirely on what you yourself have experienced. Richard Rodriguez demonstrates this point in his essay. He begins with this sentence: "Supporters of bilingual education today imply that students like me miss a great deal by not being taught in their family's language." The remainder of Rodriguez' essay explores this generalization, which applies to all students whose native language is other than English and who are nevertheless instructed exclusively in English. Rodriguez can confine himself to personal recollections in the course of his essay because his entire experience since he came to be of school age involves being a learner in a second language. He can therefore draw on many varied memories, both in the classroom and at home with his family, and his experiences give him a sense of the complexity of the issue and a special authority in addressing it.

As a writer, you need to recognize that being present at one holdup does not mean you can persuade a reader that you know about gun control. Nevertheless, you should not simply abandon either the subject or your autobiographical experience. You can still make use of the holdup, perhaps as a dramatic starting point for your essay, as long as you assemble more evidence (the experiences of friends, public news reports, statistical data, the testimony of some recognized experts) which can follow or be interwoven with your own story. Part of the task of revision is to judge how well you have made personal experience and generalization fit together. If that fit disappoints you, you can make changes in one of two directions. You can scale down the generalization until your autobiographical testimony will strike the reader as both representative and convincing. Alternatively, you can expand the range of nonautobiographical testimony until your generalization has either the support or the qualification it needs to be accepted by the reader.

The reason that generalization and abstraction are important concepts for the autobiographer is that they enable him to form explicit patterns from the specific memories of his earlier life. One of the great attractions of our personal past for us as writers is that it is both familiar and finished; we know it but are not enveloped in it, as we are in the changing and uncertain condition of our present life. Since we possess a degree of detachment toward our past, we often want to make some explicit interpretation of our experience. To do that we need to introduce abstractions and larger generalizations and introduce them with some frequency. In other words, there may be times when we want to convey the special savor of some moment in our lives as only we could have experienced it, concretely and particularly, but there may be other times when we want to represent our experience as a member of some class or group—as a student, say, or as an adolescent, or as an American. We have already seen how

Frank O'Connor made generalizations that were limited because they applied only to his father. But O'Connor might have written of these same memories and seen them within a pattern that would apply to many other people as well as to his father. For example, he might have wanted to assert that alcoholism invariably destroys human dignity, enlarging his own memories through such an abstraction. Or he might have used his memories to comment on drinking among Irish working-class men or to illustrate the effects that an alcoholic parent has on the lives of the rest of the family. As "my father" becomes included in words that refer to larger categories, the writer moves to some higher level of generalization (Irish working-class men or alcoholic parents).

THE PURPOSES OF GENERALIZATION

When we generalize about ourselves we invariably demonstrate a degree of detachment about our own lives. If we convert one of O'Connor's descriptions of his father to the first person ("I was a naturally melancholy man; though I was always pleased when people called, I rarely called on anybody myself"), we can see that using limited generalizations about oneself creates a necessary separation between the writer and the person who is being written about. Such generalizations remind us that autobiography is indeed about another person: ourselves as we were at some past moment. From our vantage point in the present we can see that past moment and place it as something significant in our understanding of who we are.

Even though generalizations and abstractions about ourselves cost us some degree of intimacy and spontaneity in autobiography, we use them because we wish to show that we understand the meaning of our own lives. Not only do we want to determine the shape of our lives by deciding what memories we will include, but we also want to demonstrate that we have thought out our experiences and connected them with other times and other places in our lives. Any autobiographer generalizes to some extent about his own past because he recognizes that his authority as a writer depends on convincing his reader that he is presenting a considered account of what has happened to him.

The other reason most writers try to generalize from their personal experience is to place themselves in some broad category with which their audience can associate. When James Baldwin writes about living through the winter in a tiny Swiss village, an experience which very few of his readers could ever have shared, he sees his situation as that of a black American in an uncomprehending environment. His experience becomes that of a black man facing the non-African world and his anguish and rage become the feelings endured by anyone alien and misunderstood. Generalization is Baldwin's way of transforming an autobiographical experience that might initially seem to us quite limited and specialized into something that touches on the concerns of our quite different lives. By generalizing in the way that he does, Baldwin's account can awaken the interest of a great range of potential readers—not just American blacks, or whites anxious for a better understanding of racial relations, but anyone concerned by the issue of how human beings treat whatever they think of as alien to their own culture. When a writer like Baldwin generalizes about some aspect of his past, he is simply trying to insist that his life does have relevance for other people whose lives may be quite different from his own. Generalization is one vehicle by which the writer can identify himself with some area of shared human concern.

At the same time, however, a writer who places too much emphasis on generalizations about his life or fails to support them is in danger of obscuring whatever is uniquely interesting about himself and becoming too much of a representative man. We are all familiar with the kind of person who is always identifying himself with some vast general class: "As a believer in the democratic system, I would like to say . . ." or

"My experience has taught me that man must and will prevail." Such statements usually strike us as pompous and empty, concealing rather than revealing any kind of personal vision. Some writers think of these windy examples when they imagine themselves generalizing about their lives, and they sensibly want to avoid that kind of meaningless assertion. As a result, many writers see higher-level generalizations as a prerogative of the very old and feel that only an autobiographer safely retired from participation in the world's activities can make general pronouncements without embarrassment.

It is true that "conclusions" and "reflections" do seem most appropriate from someone whose lengthy and varied life justifies a large view of the human condition, but a much younger writer has a perfect right to generalize from his experience, so long as he is careful to make his experiences create a proper context for his generalizations. The point becomes clearer when we return to the Baldwin essay, published when he was twenty-nine years old. Here is a characteristic passage: "The rage of the disesteemed is personally fruitless, but it is also absolutely inevitable; this rage, so generally discounted, so little understood even among the people whose daily bread it is, is one of the things that makes history." Baldwin is using very large generalizations indeed—"the disesteemed," "history"—but we cannot judge them simply by their inclusiveness and wonder what a twenty-nine-year-old can know about "history." We have to see whether such large statements float unattached in the essay or whether they seem to be bound up with the particulars of the personal experience that Baldwin is presenting. The issue is not whether the generalization is valid, but whether it is apt, whether it fits the specific circumstances the writer has included and is a suitable response to them. Furthermore, the level of generalization the writer uses must be maintained with some consistency. We are probably willing to accept Baldwin's large statement about history for two reasons: first, he has managed to show how daily incidents in his life in the village provoke the generalization; second, he has established himself from the beginning of his essay as someone who reflects broadly on his experience. His life in the village makes him think of his generally isolated state among white people, and makes him speculate on his relation to the whole tradition of white European culture—Dante, Shakespeare, Michelangelo—so his comment on "history" follows appropriately enough from these other reflections.

Baldwin demonstrates that a writer of any age or circumstances can convincingly generalize from his experience as long as the generalization keeps some mooring in the world of the tangible and the specific. Because of the necessary interdependence of the particular and the general, the concrete and the abstract, writing about ourselves effectively does not entail a step-by-step mastery, first of narration, then of description, and so on, until we finally succeed in producing a sentence or a paragraph of vast generalization. Although the chapters in this book necessarily follow a sequence, the goal in writing is the integration of all the skills that have been discussed. Ideally, each writer should try to strike some congenial balance in which he is able to reproduce past experience vividly, and at the same time take advantage of his distance from that past moment to explain it more fully. There may be occasions when he emphasizes narrative flow or descriptive accuracy to the exclusion of anything else, but usually he will also need abstraction and generalization to show how particular experiences contribute to the meaning of his autobiography.

AUTOBIOGRAPHY AND OTHER FORMS OF WRITING

Personal experience, furthermore, can give substance to other kinds of writing besides formal autobiography. A writer can often make autobiographical material serve a valuable but subordinate role within the framework of a general argument about an issue or an idea. Jessica Mitford, for example, is not primarily interested in being autobiographical in the excerpt from *Kind and Unusual Punishment*. Instead, she wishes to draw upon personal memories to support and clarify her statements about the penal system in America. As a result, her account is not consistently an account of personal experience: often she is describing prison procedures which she will never have to undergo, or interviewing prisoners in order to document aspects of prison life she will never see. Mitford's distinctive purposes do not make this selection different in kind from others in the chapter, but they do create a special emphasis, one which makes the reader more aware of a life being used for illustrative purposes. Her recollections make us conscious of the degradation of the lives of inmates in a typical "detention center," and of the failures and inequities of the system she describes, rather than making us see her own life in a more vivid or comprehensible way.

Mitford's general views have undoubtedly been influenced by events in her personal past, but many times a writer needs to discuss matters that have little or nothing to do with his own life. In these circumstances, generalization and abstraction provide him with a way to write about ideas and issues that do not derive directly from his own experience. Such conceptual language enables him to write about capital punishment although he has never been inside a prison or about divorce although he has never signed a marriage license. However, when a writer turns away from the concrete details provided by personal experience, he cannot simply assert his general views without specific support; he must find other forms of documentation or illustration to validate his statements. On some occasions a writer will combine personal and impersonal evidence to establish his authority, as V. S. Pritchett gracefully introduces historical data about other autobiographers along with his recollections of the frustrations involved in writing his own autobiography. On other occasions, including a good number of writing situations in college, a writer will wish to establish a viewpoint of unquestioned objectivity and will eliminate any reference to personal experience or personal feelings, using as evidence only the work of published authorities and being careful to balance the comments of several such authorities when introducing a controversial issue. This is not cowardice, only an appropriate choice for the writer when his purpose makes him wish to have his readers trust his detachment.

Clearly, then, we will not find ourselves being autobiographical in everything we write, but we will always be making use of the skills we can learn especially well through writing about ourselves. Autobiography makes us narrate our experiences, describe our environments, characterize our friends, explain our behavior, analyze our feelings and motives, argue for our beliefs, and summarize our accomplishments—in short, it may at any given moment call upon us to adopt one or another of the techniques any good writer has to master. Simultaneously, autobiography gives each of us the chance to root our language first and foremost in our own self-awareness, and from this source fashion a personal voice in our writing, one that should survive as identifiably ours even when we turn to more impersonal topics. We should therefore value autobiography highly because it endows us with two gifts that all writers cherish: the freedom to choose among diverse ways of presenting our subject and the opportunity to speak for it with authority.

∽ Marilyn Young ∽

(1937-   )

Marilyn Young was born and grew up in Brooklyn, where her father worked as a postal clerk and her mother as a school secretary. She attended Vassar and did graduate work in history at Harvard. Her general area of interest was Far Eastern history, and her special concern has been Sino-American relations. After having two children and living the life of a faculty wife, she returned to teaching at the University of Michigan, where she is an Associate Professor of History. This selection is from Working It Out *(1977), an anthology of essays by women in various fields, looking back over their early lives and the beginnings of their professional careers.*

[LOOKING BACK AT COLLEGE]

Perhaps because I am a historian, the only way I can understand the contradictory and ambivalent relationship I have to the work I do (or even to work as such) is historically. As it happens with most people, my first idea of what work is came from my family. Work was hard, usually tedious, always ill-paid. It was what men did so that women and children could eat. My father worked. The first job I remember my father having was in the Railway Mail Service, a now defunct unit of the post office. When I was very young he worked "on the road," sorting mail as the train moved from New York to mythical places like Chicago, Washington, Buffalo. He would be away overnight and we'd get post cards. I only remember one: a picture of Niagara Falls labeled hot and cold with a message claiming that he'd had a fine shower there that morning. I can distinctly recall the sensation of believing and not believing simultaneously. His job was not without a certain romance and danger; when he came home he would talk about the split-second timing needed to hook the mailbag from the station as the train passed through barely slowing down. There were regular civil service tests that he studied for with an elaborate system of index cards and large egg cartons into which, chanting the names of the stations, he would toss the appropriate card. I don't know how many stations he had to memorize—thousands, it seemed—but my first sense of the power of words, any words, came from hearing his voice calling out the towns of America as I fell asleep. Later he worked in the office at Grand Central and Penn stations. It was, I suppose, a kind of promotion. But the work was routine and boring to a degree that seemed sometimes to strain his mind beyond bearing.

For a time my mother also had an outside job, but I remember little about it. I am told that my maternal grandmother took care of me when my mother was working—easy enough since we lived in the same building. But my grandfather objected, there was no alternative child-care, and she was forced to quit. From that point until I was about thirteen my mother "didn't work." Then, when my younger sister was six or seven, she passed the necessary exams and took a job as a school secretary. We got by through an elaborate system of juggled schedules—which became even more complex when my mother gave birth to yet another daughter—a system that involved my father working nights, my dropping the baby off at an aunt's house on the way to high school, my mother taking my middle sister to school with her, and so on.

Two peculiar characteristics were associated with my mother's working. First, as opposed to my father's having a job, her working was bad for us. It was "common wisdom" at the time that juvenile delinquents flowed from working mothers as the night the day. This notion had a significant impact on my younger sister and was mildly upsetting to me as well, though it was clear that neither of us was cut out for delinquency. Second, my mother's job was defined as interfering with her primary responsibilities to us and my father. Before she started on the job, all our family fights centered around money—or rather, the lack of it. These were terrible, bitter explosions, difficult to explain if you haven't experienced what a lack of money (which is not the same thing as poverty) can do to people in America. The foolish spending of some trifling amount provoked monumental, irrational fury. With my mother working for pay, the issue was different. Now there was much more money around. The problem was that she "brought her work home," that dinner might be late, or the laundry undone. "You owe them nothing," my father would shout. "It's just a job." Of course since she didn't get overtime, the office work she did after hours was indeed exploitative, and he was right to be angry. But there was something else involved too. It was as if the school work she did at home was on *his* time—and he wasn't paying her to do P.S. 183's final payroll, but to take care of us.

In a sense, I was raised with the hope that I wouldn't have to work, because I would become a professional—a doctor or a lawyer. The irony of this is that my father had the utmost contempt for the American medical and legal professions, a contempt I had no difficulty sharing, then or since. What marked such people was not only their high incomes, but the fact that what they did to earn them was not, in our sense, "work" at all. Work was what my father wrote to me about my first year away at college. His job, he said, was a prison. He went to it as one goes to death. He was doing time, a thirty-year sentence. Yet what was his crime? I would become enraged at the human waste explicit in those letters. The mindlessness of his job, the years and years of it stretching ahead of him, the viciousness of a world (later I would learn to call it a system, and name that system capitalism) that condemned

326

people like my father to lives of nearly intolerable frustration made the experience of the elite woman's college I attended more than mildly contradictory.

How I got to Vassar College is a separate but related topic. Although all I knew of private high schools came from the back pages of the Sunday *Times* magazine section, my father—in pursuit of the medical or legal chimera—had often talked to me about private colleges. Vassar, he said, was where the children of Hollywood stars went. For scholarship, Barnard and Bryn Mawr were the best; there were, he told me, scholarship funds for good students, and if I also won a New York State Regents fellowship, it might be possible to swing Barnard. By my senior year in high school the discussion changed; now he said that Brooklyn College was "plenty good enough" and, in one furious battle, told me I should go to work and "give money into the house the way other children do." Part of the problem was the application fee each college required. This was a gamble in which the family stood to lose as much as fifty dollars if I failed to get admitted *and* receive scholarship funds. And we didn't fool around with fifty dollars. In any event, a high school guidance counselor put pressure on my parents to fill out the forms. I am certain they would have done so anyhow. My father wrote, in my name, truly touching appeals for financial aid. I went to a series of terrifying interviews—wearing, as per the guidance counselor's instructions, a small borrowed hat and a pair of gloves. The only catastrophe occurred when I looked down at my shoes in the full light of Saratoga Avenue's elevated subway stop and discovered I was wearing one brown and one blue suede pump. But it was too late to go home and change.

Vassar came through with enough money so that with the Regents fellowship and a five-hundred-dollar loan, I could attend. Given what it would have cost to commute from my neighborhood to Barnard, it almost seemed cheaper to live away from home. By my sophomore year a clerical error resulted in my receiving thirty-five dollars in cash over and above the scholarship. Summer work paid for clothes, books, vacation trips home. Clothes were a problem. That first year my mother took me to the College Shop at Abraham & Straus and also, if I remember correctly, Lord & Taylor—the latter an incredible journey beyond our accustomed turf. I got a polo coat (blue—which was, that year, quite the wrong color), several pairs of flannel Bermuda shorts, some shirts, a collar pin (again, an arrow—when small gold circles were proper), and, most disastrously, a pair of unspeakably collegiate plaid pajamas. On one of my first nights at college a knowledgeable freshman said with a laugh, "I bet you got those specially for college." I never wore them in public again.

The trouble was, I did not want to be a doctor. When, as a direct result of an inability to work a balance scale, I dropped freshman chemistry after two weeks, my family reluctantly agreed that there must be other ways to earn a living. At first I threatened to major in English literature, but I was deterred by my parents' depression-born conviction that that would prepare me to clerk in a shoe store and nothing else. (Were shoe stores specially staffed with English B.A.'s in the thirties? Or is it just Brooklyn folklore?) Later I majored in history, which for reasons still obscure, seemed to all three of us a more responsible choice.

College cut my world in half. At sixteen, I moved from a working-class Jewish neighborhood in Brooklyn, where you took a subway to look at the grass, to this residential park called Vassar College. And yet, despite an almost unnamable pleasure at what was happening to my mind, I related to college as *work*. Only one letter home survives from my freshman year; I can hardly believe a real person wrote it:

Dear Folks,
Today is a very busy day. I'm sitting in on Miss Nevins' class at 1:30. At 2:30 I get my first painting lesson from one of the talented freshmen here, who also teaches painting at Martha's Vineyard in the summer. Then I'll squeeze in some homework. At 4:30 the Davison baseball team gets out on the field for some practice. To-night at 8:15 the Writers Club meets and I shall read my po-etry . . . All this activity will just leave me time for my History

and French homework, if that (both not due till Monday). Friday night there is a meeting of the Human Rights Committee. This means both Friday and Saturday nights will be occupied. My English paper will be worked on every waking hour in between then. Sandy Spatt got me a blind date (for several weeks hence). However I would much rather spend that weekend with you (hate blind dates anyhow). If you can't come up, I shall probably turn that date down anyhow since my 1500 w. English paper is due that week (but I shall finish it that weekend) and my 25 page History paper—with only 17 days to work on it—starts that weekend. At any rate, if you decide to come up great, I'll squeeze the work in somewhere. If not I shall have a wonderful weekend of research in the libe about some obscure 19th century topic. (I mean it about wonderful, I told you I love that sort of thing.)

The letter ends with a request for them to let me know if they want me to go to a seder with a Jewish family in town—this, to relieve anxieties aroused earlier in the year that I might convert out of a deep infatuation with the literary merits of the Gospel According to St. John.

Look at it. I want them to understand—no, *admit*—that I too am *working*, not playing. Only then could I bear the guilt. Here I was, really, doing nothing but pleasuring myself in the library. I knew they didn't think it was work; I didn't think so myself. So I had to transform it *into* work. That first year I reported every paper and course grade I got. I brought home final grades like salary checks. In high school we had all "worked for grades." What other medium of exchange was there? In Brooklyn we knew each other's grade-point average to the second decimal point; if those points were truly earned, and not the result of a teacher's favoritism, we respected the person the way the Chinese do "advanced producers" in agriculture and industry. For the first year I openly did the same at Vassar. There were embarrassments of course. Coming out of our first French test, I turned to Marcia Kennedy and asked her the classic Brooklyn high school question: "Whadja get?" To which she scornfully replied: "We don't do that here. This is a *college*, not a high school."

Gradually I was made to feel ashamed of the way I worked.

I learned that one was not supposed to work for grades, or for anything other than the sheer pleasure of learning. We were not preparing ourselves for a world of work or wages. We were, it seemed, engaged in some other enterprise altogether, and if I was to belong there, I must discover what it was. I don't think I ever did. Instead, I tried to learn proper manners. Though burning to know, I rarely asked a fellow student her grades, and I disguised (to some degree) just how many hours I put in. But the more I accepted, however superficially, this ruling-class view of women's education, the more guilty I felt about what I had left behind at home. For how could I justify to myself what I was doing at college if it did not, in some measure, compare with the efforts my parents made, every day of their lives, to survive. Bad enough that I could experience quintessential springs at Vassar while my sisters mucked about in the dreariness of East Flatbush. Only some demonstration that I too toiled relieved me.

Summers were somewhat easier because they were less confused. Each June I would lie my way into a fairly well-paid secretarial job, swearing on all that was holy (and faking an occasional document) that I had no intention of going to college in the fall; and each fall I would sadly inform the boss that my family was "moving to Florida" and I would have to quit. (Once I suffered the acute embarrassment of being given a goodbye party and gifts from the other "girls" in my typing pool.) For those three months or so, I found myself in the familiar world of my parents. This was real work. I hated the job, the boss, the subway, the heat. That's what working was all about: a stubborn hatred, a reluctant resignation, and, somewhere in it too, pleasure in my typing skill, my friendships with co-workers, the way the thing ended at a certain hour, the weekend. Finally, I knew I didn't have an indeterminate sentence, merely a straight ninety days. Anyone can do ninety days.

By my junior year, my parents and I had made a not inconsiderable discovery. College professors, less munificently rewarded than doctors or lawyers, still seemed to be able to lead the good life without seriously working. This realization crystallized one weekend when my parents came to visit and we all had lunch with a favorite history teacher. He and his wife and two children lived in a substantial white house near the campus. They were clearly comfortably off, he loved what he was doing, his wife seemed content, and the kids had the run of the campus. What puzzles me now is whether my parents envisioned that I would be the professor or the wife? I had other models at college, but even to discuss them briefly with my parents led to terrible fights. I was much enamored, for example, of the life of another history professor. She was I suppose in her late fifties and shared a house with a woman colleague. She seemed to lead a life of enviable completeness, deeply involved in both her teaching and her research. In a word more commonly used in the fifties than it is now, my roommate and I thought of her as "fulfilled." My sense (and admiration) of this teacher enraged (and frightened) my parents, especially my mother. And what of marriage? And children? How could a little white-haired old maid seem anything but pathetic to me? This was most confusing; clearly I could never become the male history professor, but it seemed equally obvious that I *should* not become the female one. So, mouthing pieties about combining "marriage and career," I went to graduate school.

1. At the beginning of her essay, Young says her way of thinking about her work is shaped by her professional role as a historian. In what ways do you find this selection shaped by the perspective of a historian?

2. What differences do you see between the various kinds of work that Young talks about in this selection? Consider, for example, her father's work, her mother's work, the work Young did to earn money as a college student, and, finally, Young's work as a college student.

3. Why does Young choose to reproduce a long passage from a letter she wrote home when she was a college freshman? What does the letter tell you about Young and about her relationship with her parents? Does Young see the letter in a different perspective many years later as she is writing this essay?

4. How does going to college affect Young? Does she experience college in a distinctive way because her parents are not affluent?

∽ Richard Rodriguez ∽

(1944-   )

Richard Rodriguez grew up in Sacramento, California, and attended Stanford University on a scholarship. After achieving his degree with honors in English, he went on to do graduate work at Columbia University, the Warbourg Institute (London), and the University of California at Berkeley. He has written essays about literary subjects as well as reflections on his early life. This selection, from Rodriguez' collection of autobiographical essays Hunger of Memory *(1982), comments on the different claims of the English-speaking parochial school he attended and his Spanish-speaking home.*

[PRIVATE AND PUBLIC LANGUAGE]

Supporters of bilingual education today imply that students like me miss a great deal by not being taught in their family's language. What they seem not to recognize is that, as a socially disadvantaged child, I considered Spanish to be a private language. What I needed to learn in school was that I had the right—and the obligation—to speak the public language of *los gringos.* The odd truth is that my first-grade classmates could have become bilingual, in the conventional sense of that word, more easily than I. Had they been taught (as upper-middle-class children are often taught early) a second language like Spanish or French, they could have regarded it simply as that: another public language. In my case such bilingualism could not have been so quickly achieved. What I did not believe was that I could speak a single public language.

Without question, it would have pleased me to hear my teachers address me in Spanish when I entered the classroom. I would have felt much less afraid. I would have trusted them and responded with ease. But I would have delayed—for how long postponed?—having to learn the language of public society. I would have evaded—and for how long could I have afforded to delay?—learning the great lesson of school, that I had a public identity.

Fortunately, my teachers were unsentimental about their responsibility. What they understood was that I needed to speak a public language. So their voices would search me out, asking me questions. Each time I'd hear them, I'd look up in surprise to see a nun's face frowning at me. I'd mumble, not really meaning to answer. The nun would persist, "Richard, stand up. Don't look at the floor. Speak up. Speak to the entire class, not just to me!" But I couldn't believe that the English language was mine to use. (In part, I did not want to believe it.) I continued to mumble. I resisted the teacher's demands. (Did I somehow suspect that once I learned public language my pleasing family life would be changed?) Silent, waiting for the bell to sound, I remained dazed, diffident, afraid.

Because I wrongly imagined that English was intrinsically a public language and Spanish an intrinsically private one, I easily noted the difference between classroom language and the language of home. At school, words were directed to a general audience of listeners. ("Boys and girls.") Words were meaningfully ordered. And the point was not self-expression alone but to make oneself understood by many others. The teacher quizzed: "Boys and girls, why do we use that word in this sentence? Could we think of a better word to use there? Would the sentence change its meaning if the words were differently arranged? And wasn't there a better way of saying much the same thing?" (I couldn't say. I wouldn't try to say.)

Three months. Five. Half a year passed. Unsmiling, ever watchful, my teachers noted my silence. They began to connect my behavior with the difficult progress my older sister and brother were making. Until one Saturday morning three nuns arrived at the house to talk to our parents. Stiffly, they sat on the blue living room sofa. From the doorway of another room, spying the visitors, I noted the incongruity—the clash of two worlds, the faces and voices of school intruding upon the familiar setting of home. I overheard one voice gently wondering, "Do your children speak only Spanish at home, Mrs. Rodriguez?" While another voice added, "That Richard especially seems so timid and shy."

That Rich-heard!

With great tact the visitors continued, "Is it possible for you and your husband to encourage your children to practice their English when they are home?" Of course, my parents complied. What would they not do for their children's well-being? And how could they have questioned the Church's authority which those women represented? In an instant, they agreed to give up the language (the sounds) that had revealed and accentuated our family's closeness. The moment after the visitors left, the change was observed. *"Ahora,* speak to us *en inglés,"* my father and mother united to tell us.

At first, it seemed a kind of game. After dinner each night, the family gathered to practice "our" English. (It was still then *inglés,* a language foreign to us, so we felt drawn as strangers to it.) Laughing, we would try to define words we could not pronounce. We played with strange English sounds, often over-anglicizing our pronunciations. And we filled the smiling gaps of our sentences with familiar Spanish sounds. But that was cheating, somebody shouted. Everyone laughed. In school, meanwhile, like my brother and sister, I was required to attend a daily tutoring session. I needed a full year of special attention. I also needed my teachers to keep my attention from straying in class by calling out, *Rich-heard—* their English voices slowly prying loose my ties to my other name, its three notes, *Ri-car-do.* Most of all I needed to hear my mother and father speak to me in a moment of seriousness in broken—suddenly heartbreaking—English. The scene was inevitable: One Saturday morning I entered the kitchen where my parents were talking in Spanish. I did not realize that they were talking in Spanish however until, at the moment they saw me, I heard their voices change to speak English. Those *gringo* sounds they uttered startled me. Pushed me away. In that moment of trivial misunderstanding and profound insight, I felt my throat twisted by unsounded grief. I turned quickly and left the room. But I had no place to escape to with Spanish. (The spell was broken.) My brother and sisters were speaking English in another part of the house.

Again and again in the days following, increasingly angry, I was obliged to hear my mother and father: "Speak to us *en inglés.*" (*Speak.*) Only then did I determine to learn classroom English. Weeks after, it happened: One day in school I raised my hand to volunteer an answer. I spoke out in a loud voice. And I did not think it remarkable when the entire class understood. That day, I moved very far from the disadvantaged child I had been only days earlier. The belief, the calming assurance that I belonged in public, had at last taken hold.

Shortly after, I stopped hearing the high and loud sounds of *los gringos.* A more and more confident speaker of English, I didn't trouble to listen to *how* strangers sounded, speaking to me. And there simply were too many English-speaking people in my day for me to hear American accents anymore. Conversations quickened. Listening to persons who sounded eccentrically pitched voices, I usually noted their sounds for an initial few seconds before I concentrated on *what* they were saying. Conversations became content-full. Transparent. Hearing someone's *tone* of voice—angry or questioning or sarcastic or happy or sad—I didn't distinguish it from the words it expressed. Sound and word were thus tightly wedded. At the end of a day, I was often bemused, always relieved, to realize how "silent," though crowded with words, my day in public had been. (This public silence measured and quickened the change in my life.)

At least, seven years old, I came to believe what had been technically true since my birth: I was an American citizen.

But the special feeling of closeness at home was diminished by then. Gone was the desperate, urgent, intense feeling of being at home; rare was the experience of feeling myself individualized by family intimates. We remained a loving family, but one greatly changed. No longer so close; no longer bound tight by the pleasing and troubling knowledge of our public separateness. Neither my older brother nor sister rushed home after school anymore. Nor did I. When I arrived home there would often be neighborhood kids in the house. Or the house would be empty of sounds.

Following the dramatic Americanization of their children, even my parents grew more publicly confident. Especially my mother. She learned the names of all the people on our block. And she decided we needed to have a telephone installed in the house. My father continued to use the word *gringo*. But it was no longer charged with the old bitterness or distrust. (Stripped of any emotional content, the word simply became a name for those Americans not of Hispanic descent.) Hearing him, sometimes, I wasn't sure if he was pronouncing the Spanish word *gringo* or saying gringo in English.

Matching the silence I started hearing in public was a new quiet at home. The family's quiet was partly due to the fact that, as we children learned more and more English, we shared fewer and fewer words with our parents. Sentences needed to be spoken slowly when a child addressed his mother or father. (Often the parent wouldn't understand.) The child would need to repeat himself. (Still the parent misunderstood.) The young voice, frustrated, would end up saying, "Never mind"—the subject was closed. Dinners would be noisy with the clinking of knives and forks against dishes. My mother would smile softly between her remarks; my father at the other end of the table would chew and chew at his food, while he stared over the heads of his children.

My *mother!* My *father!* After English became my primary language, I no longer knew what words to use in addressing my parents. The old Spanish words (those tender accents of sound) I had used earlier—*mamá* and *papá*—I couldn't use anymore. They would have been too painful reminders of how much had changed in my life. On the other hand, the words I heard neighborhood kids call *their* parents seemed equally unsatisfactory. *Mother* and *Father*; *Ma, Papa, Pa, Dad, Pop* (how I hated the all-American sound of that last word especially)—all these terms I felt were unsuitable, not really terms of address for *my* parents. As a result, I never used them at home. Whenever I'd speak to my parents, I would try to get their attention with eye contact alone. In public conversations, I'd refer to "my parents" or "my mother and father."

My mother and father, for their part, responded differently, as their children spoke to them less. She grew restless, seemed troubled and anxious at the scarcity of words exchanged in the house. It was she who would question me about my day when I came home from school. She smiled at small talk. She pried at the edges of my sentences to get me to say something more. (What?) She'd join conversations she overheard, but her intrusions often stopped her children's talking. By contrast, my father seemed reconciled to the new quiet. Though his English improved somewhat, he retired into silence. At dinner he spoke very little. One night his children and even his wife helplessly giggled at his garbled English pronunciation of the Catholic Grace before Meals. Thereafter he made his wife recite the prayer at the start of each meal, even on formal occasions, when there were guests in the House. Hers became the public voice of the family. On official business, it was she, not my father, one would usually hear on the phone or in stores, talking to strangers. His children grew so accustomed to his silence that, years later, they would speak routinely of his shyness. (My mother would often try to explain. Both his parents died when he was eight. He was raised by an uncle who treated him like little more than a menial servant. He was never encouraged to speak. He grew up alone. A man of few words.) But my father was not shy, I realized, when I'd watch him speaking Spanish with relatives. Using Spanish, he was quickly effusive. Especially when talking with other men, his voice would spark, flicker, flare alive with sounds. In Spanish, he expressed ideas and feelings he rarely revealed in English. With firm Spanish sounds, he conveyed confidence and authority English would never allow him.

The silence at home, however, was finally more than a literal silence. Fewer words passed between parent and child, but more profound was the silence that resulted from my inattention to sounds. At about the time I no longer bothered to listen with care to the sounds of English in public, I grew careless about listening to the sounds family members made when they spoke. Most of the time I heard someone speaking at home and didn't distinguish his sounds from the words people uttered in public. I didn't even pay much attention to my parents' accented and ungrammatical speech. At least not at home. Only when I was with them in public would I grow alert to their accents. Though, even then, their sounds caused me less and less concern. For I was increasingly confident of my own public identity.

I would have been happier about my public success had I not sometimes recalled what it had been like earlier, when my family had conveyed its intimacy through a set of conveniently private sounds. Sometimes in public, hearing a stranger, I'd hark back to my past. A Mexican farmworker approached me downtown to ask directions to somewhere. "¿Hijito . . . ?" he said. And his voice summoned deep longing. Another time, standing beside my mother in the visiting room of a Carmelite convent, before the dense screen which rendered the nuns shadowy figures, I heard several Spanish-speaking nuns—their busy, singsong overlapping voices—assure us that yes, yes, we were remembered, all our family was remembered in their prayers. (Their voices echoed faraway family sounds.) Another day, a dark-faced old woman—her hand light on my shoulder—steadied herself against me as she boarded a bus. She murmured something I couldn't quite comprehend. Her Spanish voice came near, like the face of a never-before-seen relative in the instant before I was kissed.

Her voice, like so many of the Spanish voices I'd hear in public, recalled the golden age of my youth. Hearing Spanish then, I continued to be a careful, if sad, listener to sounds. Hearing a Spanish-speaking family walking behind me, I turned to look. I smiled for an instant, before my glance found the Hispanic-looking faces of strangers in the crowd going by.

Today I hear bilingual educators say that children lose a degree of "individuality" by becoming assimilated into public society. (Bilingual schooling was popularized in the seventies, that decade when middle-class ethnics began to resist the process of assimilation—the American melting pot.) But the bilingualists simplistically scorn the value and necessity of assimilation. They do not seem to realize that there are *two* ways a person is individualized. So they do not realize that while one suffers a diminished sense of *private* individuality by becoming assimilated into public society, such assimilation makes possible the achievement of *public* individuality.

The bilingualists insist that a student should be reminded of his difference from others in mass society, his heritage. But they equate mere separateness with individuality. The fact is that only in private—with intimates—is separateness from the crowd a prerequisite for individuality. (An intimate draws me apart, tells me that I am unique, unlike all others.) In public, by contrast, full individuality is achieved, paradoxically, by those who are able to consider themselves members of the crowd. Thus it happened for me: Only when I was able to think of myself as an American, no longer an alien in *gringo* society, could I seek the rights and opportunities necessary for full public individuality. The social and political advantages I enjoy as a man result from the day that I came to believe that my name, indeed, is *Rich-heard Road-ree-guess*. It is true that my public society today is often impersonal. (My public society is usually mass society.) Yet despite the anonymity of the crowd and despite the fact that the individuality I achieve in public is often tenuous—because it depends on my being one in a crowd—I celebrate the day I acquired my new name. Those middle-class ethnics who scorn assimilation seem to me filled with decadent self-pity, obsessed by the burden of public life. Dangerously, they romanticize public separateness and they trivialize the dilemma of the socially disadvantaged.

My awkward childhood does not prove the necessity of bilingual education. My story discloses instead an essential myth of childhood—inevitable pain. If I rehearse here the changes in my private life after my Americanization, it is finally to emphasize the public gain. The loss implies the gain: The house I returned to each afternoon was quiet. Intimate sounds no longer rushed to the door to greet me. There were other noises inside. The telephone rang. Neighborhood kids ran past the door of the bedroom where I was reading my schoolbooks—covered with shopping-bag paper. Once I learned public language, it would never again be easy for me to hear intimate family voices. More and more of my day was spent hearing words. But that may only be a way of saying that the day I raised my hand in class and spoke loudly to an entire roomful of faces, my childhood started to end.

1. In much of his essay, Rodriguez focuses on the distinguishing characteristics of the two languages he hears and speaks. What are some of the ways he claims English and Spanish were different experiences for him?

2. How does Rodriguez find himself beginning to learn English? What prompts him to learn?

3. Why does Rodriguez frequently use the terms "public language" and "private language" in his essay? Does he find one of these languages more valuable than the other, or do they simply perform different functions?

4. What does Rodriguez mean when he says that on the day he first raised his hand in class and said something, "my childhood started to end"?

5. Rodriguez separates the last three paragraphs of this selection from the preceding part of the essay. How is the final section related to what has preceded it? Do you see any reason for Rodriguez' decision to separate the final section from the rest?

6. If your parents are English-speaking, do you still see ways in which Rodriguez' story might have similarities with your own experience as a young child going to school?

∽ Jessica Mitford ∽

(1917-   )

Born into a titled family in England, Jessica Mitford developed left-wing political sympathies and left England when she was nineteen to participate in the Spanish Civil War. She has lived in the United States since 1939. She did not begin writing until she was nearly forty, and her books reflect her strong interest in exposing injustice and corruption in various aspects of American life. Kind and Usual Punishment *(1973) is a highly critical study of the United States' penal system; in this selection Mitford reports on her experiences playing the role of a prisoner for just a few hours.*

WOMEN IN CAGES

Our domicile was a short and narrow corridor on one side of which are the cells, at the far end a dining room with television set. Women were standing in desultory knots in the corridor, sitting in their cells, or watching TV. The overall impression: a combination of college dorm (silly jokes, put-downs, occasional manifestations of friendliness), lunatic asylum (underlying sense of desolate futility), a scene from *The Threepenny Opera* (graffiti on the walls: "Welcome to the Whores' Paradise!"). I was struck by the number of little-girl faces, kids who except for their funny-looking clothes could be part of a high-school class, and by one or two sad, vacant old faces. The median age here is twenty-five.

As we entered, our names were called out, we were handed sheets and led to our assigned cells, tiny cubicles with two beds, a dresser, and a clothesline for hanging coats and dresses (the prison, like most, is fearfully overcrowded and now holds more than twice its intended capacity). My cellmate was a pleasant-faced black woman in her early thirties, named Della. She welcomed me like a good hostess, helped me make my bed, and apologized for the stale, dead smell compounded of people, food, and disinfectant that pervaded our quarters: "We used to have at least some breeze, but they've cut off the air. There's a new rule against opening the corridor window because they claim the inmates were letting down rope to haul up contraband brought by their boyfriends. Now, does that make any sense? With the officers watching you like a hawk every minute of the day and night?"

From Della I learned that, as I had suspected, we had been let off lightly at "Reception." The usual routine, she told me, includes a vaginal examination as part of the search for contraband and a Lysol spraying of the head. She had found the experience horrifying, totally degrading. Furthermore some of the guards "get their kicks" from scaring the neophyte inmate by horrendous hints of what to expect from the "bull-daggers" (prison slang for lesbians). Is there actually much homosexuality, I asked? A certain amount, but not as much as the administration seems to think. "They are really hipped on the subject," she said. "They have bed checks all hours of the night, they come around flashing their bright lights, it's hard to get any sleep."

Della had been in the section for unsentenced prisoners for nine weeks waiting for her trial. In all that time she never saw her court-appointed lawyer, and her letters to him were unanswered. She met him for the first and only time in court on the day of her trial, where he advised her to plead guilty: "But he never asked me anything about my case, said he didn't want to hear. Said if we tried to fight it, the judge would be hard on me. But I don't see how he could have been any harder—six months for one count of soliciting!"

We wandered out into the crowded corridor to join the others. Because of the visitors, Della told me, everyone was on good behavior: "We *scrubbed* this place, girl!" And clean, though dreary, it certainly was.

Our group was there to learn, so we started asking questions. The Maryland legislator inquired about recreation facilities. "Re-cre-ation!" an inmate hooted derisively. "Come here, girls, I'll show you." She led us to one of the barred windows, through which we could barely descry a small concrete quadrangle entirely hemmed in by the building. On fine days, she explained, the entire population is sometimes taken down there for an hour or so if the correctional officers have time. Vocational training programs? "There's eight old broken-down typewriters somewhere in the building. I don't know if anybody ever uses them, though. Or you can go down to group therapy, but who wants it? A bunch of us bullshitting about our deprived lives?"

We had been told the authorities had arranged for the visitors to sample various aspects of prison life, that some would spend the night in sickbay, others would be brought before a disciplinary committee, accused of breaking the rules. To fortify myself against the latter eventuality I asked for a copy of the prison rule book. "No inmate shall engage in loud or boisterous talk, laughter, whistling or other vocal expression," it said in part. "Talking is permitted at all times except in church and in school, but talking must be conducted in a normal voice except on the recreation fields." One of the prisoners, a vivacious young black woman, confided to me that she was due to be disciplined that day for laughing too loud but had been reprieved because of our visit: "It's a dumb thing anyway to be punished for laughing. When you come to think of it, sometimes it's sort of a release to laugh out loud."

As in hospitals, food is served at unexpected times. At four thirty we went into the dining room to collect our trays of dinner. The food wasn't bad, but like most institutional cooking it was dull and starchy with a touch of wilted green. We ate tuna casserole, Jell-O, a choice of weak coffee or a puce-colored synthetic fruit drink. One of the few white prisoners came and sat beside me, a romantic-looking blonde in her early twenties; she reminded me vaguely of prison movies I had seen. Convicted of possession of heroin, she described her first days in the Detention Center as absolute torture: "You come down cold-turkey, they're not equipped here to treat addicts." She proved to be a discriminating connoisseur of the nation's prisons, and twinkled quite merrily as she rated them for me, one-star, two-star, as in a motel guide. "This joint's by no means the worst, but it's not the best, either." Her goal is to be admitted into one of the treatment centers for narcotics addicts, but so far she has been blocked because they are all full up. She has no idea when, or if, there will ever be an opening for her. What does she do all day? "I work some in the kitchen, just to keep from going crazy. There *isn't* anything to do here." Housekeeping jobs, she explained, are available on our floor but not for the unsentenced women on the floor below: "In some ways they're punished worse than we are, although they haven't even been found guilty of anything." Pay ranges from $5 a month to a top of $13, the higher rate being awarded on the basis of performance and "attitude"; there is no compensation for working part of a month.

"Jessica . . . Mitford . . . to the third . . . floor." The voice over the intercom was tinny and disembodied. I started to the door of our corridor and was at once intercepted by a correctional officer. "No, no, you can't go down by yourself," she said, shocked, and, seizing my arm, led me to the elevator. "You're wanted by the disciplinary committee," she said severely. Lock, double-lock all the way, from our fourth-floor abode to the elevator and down. A third-floor guard took over and led me to the small office where I was to be tried.

My prosecutors, jury, and judges (for the disciplinary committee incorporates all three functions) were the prison psychologist and two correctional officers. They were trying to look suitably stern, to make it all as "real" as possible. One of the officers read off the charges: "At 17.05 hours, Officer Smith opened the door to your cell and found you locked in a passionate embrace with Maureen [the reporter from the Washington *Post*]. As you know, this is an extremely serious offense. What have you to say?"

What, indeed. I could of course deny all (insist she wasn't my type?), but, mindful of my assignment for the ACLU, I decided to go another route. What if I challenged the whole legality of this "trial"? I took a deep breath.

"First, I should like to draw your attention to the prison rule book." (The trio seemed surprised; the rule book, it seems, is not generally available to prisoners.) "I see you have infractions broken down into two categories: *crimes* such as assault, theft, possession of narcotics, and failure to obey *rules*—wasting food, vulgar conversation, not making one's bed. Homosexual acts between inmates are listed here as a crime. Before I plead guilty or not guilty to the charge. I should like to see a copy of the statute under which homosexuality between consenting females is a crime. I don't believe it is a crime in any jurisdiction. I'm already in here for one crime. If you find me guilty of another, it will go very hard with me when my case comes before the parole board."

My inquisitors exchanged uncertain looks. "It's not a *statute*, it's a rule," said one.

"But as you've listed it as a *crime*, I want a lawyer to represent me. I want to cross-examine the officer who accused me, and to call witnesses who'll verify that I was in the dining room watching TV at 17.05 hours."

Nonplussed, the chief correctional officer said she thought they should send for Mrs. Patricia Taylor, the director of the Detention Center. This was done, and I repeated my request.

"Jessica, you must realize we're only trying to help you," said Mrs. Taylor.

"Well, thanks a lot. But I should still like to assert my right to the same procedural safeguards that should apply to any citizen accused of crime."

"You don't understand, Jessica, you are in an institution

now, you're an inmate, you haven't a right to a trial. *We'll* decide who's telling the truth. Now, if Officer Smith hadn't seen that, why would she say she had?"

"But I say she's lying, I'm not guilty and I want a chance to prove it. Why don't you bring her down here so I can question her, and clear myself?"

"Jessica, do you realize what would happen to discipline if we permitted the inmates to cross-examine the officers?"

We went over this a few times; I had made my point, but since it was only a charade (and I knew Maureen was waiting for her turn before the disciplinary committee) I soon gave up, and was duly sentenced to "ten days in Adjustment."

What if the situation had been real, I kept thinking? Instead of making this well-reasoned little speech about my constitutional rights I would have been shouting furiously, perhaps in tears. And instead of listening and answering calmly, would not my captors have responded in kind—put me down as a troublemaker or psycho for asserting my rights, and treated me accordingly? Now I was beginning to "feel." The governessy young criminology student would be proud of me!

Accompanied by the chief correctional officer, who firmly gripped my arm (did she think I might try to escape?), I traversed several corridors and those eerie wails gradually came closer. The officer in charge of Adjustment took me over. Here the stripping of individuality is turned up a notch. I am given a gray cotton shift in place of the patterned dress from the bin. Bra, shoes, cigarettes, wristwatch, wedding ring, paperback books are confiscated. To her chagrin, the officer discovers that all eight solitary cells are occupied (which means that about one in ten of the inmates is locked up there). I will have to double up with a thief who was put in Adjustment for beating up other women. Not a terribly reassuring thought. The door giving onto the corridor of solitary cells is immensely thick, opened by my keeper with several huge keys. Now we hear the screams full force—not just from Viola, they seem to be coming from several cells. *"Let me out!"* *"I want out!"* Women are moaning, shrieking, pounding with their fists against their doors. This is "Adjustment"? To what are they being adjusted?

"You have company," the officer announces tersely to my cellmate, and she double-locks the door behind us. Mindful of my companion's alleged infraction I flash her a conciliatory smile, but she is pleased to see me, makes me welcome, we sit on the bed (sole furnishing except for an open toilet that flushes only from the outside) and talk.

The Thief's Tale was well larded with fantasy, or so it seemed to me. A tall, attractive black woman about thirty years old, she was essentially "state-raised": orphaned at the age of eight, in and out of trouble, in and out of juvenile detention (but mostly in) until her middle twenties. "I tried to go straight for a spell, but I don't really dig it. On welfare, with two little kids to raise—what kind of life is that?" She turned to pickpocketing, a discipline in which she had received much theoretical instruction during her many years in reformatories. "The best place is near the Americana Hotel in New York, that's where lots of businessmen hang out." She told me she could clear upward of $500 on a good night and that once she netted $14,000 from the wallet of an unsuspecting passerby. Yet, in view of her expanding needs, she found it slow going: "My boyfriend and I wanted to start a nightclub in Atlantic City, we figured on $100,000 to open it. So I told him leave it to me, I'd raise it." The quickest way, she decided, was to travel around the country from motel to motel cashing bad checks in amounts of $500 to $1,000. She had got up to $40,000 of the needed capital when the feds caught up with her.

Our corridor had all but quieted down after the guard left. Now the screams started up again, coming apparently from the cell directly opposite ours, a terrible outcry of rage and misery, shrieks and obscenities interspersed with deep, racking sobs. We peered through the tiny grill in our door and could dimly see movement behind the opposite grill, hands clawing, head wildly shaking. My cellmate shouted soothing words across the corridor: "Now, honey, hush up, won't you? If you

349

be a good girl and stop all that noise, I'll speak to Mrs. Taylor, and I'll see that she lets you out of there. If I say to let you out, she'll do it."

"Who is she?" I asked.

"She's a juvenile, she's down here because she's too young to go upstairs."

"*Too young?* How old is she?"

"Seventeen."

Of course I didn't believe a word of it. Just another of her delusions, I thought, like the $14,000 wallet, the obliging motel managers who cash $1,000 checks for strangers, her role as confidante and adviser to Mrs. Taylor.

Soon—in an hour and a half, to be exact—my "ten days" were up. For further clarification I sought out Mrs. Taylor, a highly qualified black administrator with a long background in social work and Corrections. No longer an "inmate," I was formally ushered into her office, where we discussed what I had heard and seen that day.

First, as to the general prison scene, what are the women here being punished for? The great majority, about 85 percent, are in for a combination of prostitution and narcotics (as one inmate had told me, "They go together like salt and pepper; once you're hooked on the stuff, you have to hustle to support your habit"). Does Mrs. Taylor think prostitution is a crime? No, she believes many women are driven to it by circumstances outside their control. What about drug addiction? That's not a crime either, it's a sickness and should be treated as such.

Checking Mrs. Taylor's opinions against those of others in authority, from correctional officers to Mr. Kenneth Hardy, director of the department, I found unanimity on these points. *None* believed that prostitution and drug addiction are "crimes." Thus the patently crazy situation in which the keepers themselves, up and down the line, believe their mandate to imprison these women rests on a fundamentally unsound premise. But, they all point out, they are merely doing the job required of them by the courts, the legislature, the public: "We don't choose the inmates, we have to take whoever the judges send us."

In our discussion of the Adjustment setup, this sense of total irrationality deepened.

The case of Viola: she is a diagnosed schizophrenic, Mrs. Taylor explained. Because of a recent court decision, she cannot be transferred to a mental institution without a sanity hearing; but the courts are so clogged with cases that no date for such a hearing has been set. How long will she stay locked away in Adjustment? Nobody knows.

The screaming girl across the corridor? My cellmate was right after all, she really *is* only seventeen, she really *is* there because she is too young to go upstairs—in solitary because of a mistake of the Juvenile Court. Finding that she was incorrigible in the children's prison, the judge sentenced her to Women's Detention. But the law says that juvenile offenders may not mix with the adult prison population, so she was put in Adjustment. At first she was allowed "privileges"—mail, books, cigarettes. After several days of total solitude she set her mattress on fire (perhaps, Mrs. Taylor surmised, "to draw attention to herself?"). Consequently she is now considered a "disciplinary case" and all privileges have been withdrawn. How long will she have to stay there? For about three months, until she turns eighteen.

"Aren't you afraid she'll go completely insane by that time?"

"Well . . . there is that danger . . ."

Why, I wanted to know, is the inmate who is being punished for some infraction denied books, newspapers, games—*anything* that might make solitary confinement more tolerable?

"The idea is to remove her completely from the environment. You heard those women screaming in there. If we'd kept you in there for twenty-four hours, you would have been screaming, too."

"Then—is that your purpose, to destroy my self-control, to reduce me to a helpless, howling infant?"

"That's a risk we have to take," said Mrs. Taylor with a faint smile.

What of homosexuality, recognized by everyone in Corrections as an inevitable consequence of long-term segregation of the sexes? Having driven them to it, why punish for it? "Love affairs" between women inmates, born out of loneliness, longing for human affection, lack of male companionship—does Mrs. Taylor consider this sort of behavior criminal? "No, but if permitted it might lead to jealousy and fights. Besides, I am responsible for their morals while they are in here." *Their* morals? Yet Mrs. Taylor had something there, I thought. Is this not the essence of women's prisons, the punishment of unchaste, unwomanly behavior, a grotesque bow to long-outmoded nineteenth-century notions of feminine morality?

There is, Mrs. Taylor regretfully conceded, barely even the pretense of a useful trade or educational program for the women, most of whom she expects to see back again in her custody shortly after they are let out. They exit and reenter as through a revolving door, three quarters of those who are in now have been here before. Chances of getting a decent job when they leave, slim enough for ghetto women in any circumstances, are almost nonexistent for those with prison records, so inevitably they turn to their old ways when released.

This, then, is an American women's prison of the 1970's— and "not the worst," as my dinner companion said. A life of planned, unrelieved inactivity and boredom . . . no overt brutality but plenty of random, largely unintentional cruelty . . . a pervasive sense of helplessness and frustration engulfing not only the inmates but their keepers, themselves prisoners trapped in the weird complex of paradoxes that is the prison world.

And everyone passes the buck. The administrators protest they are merely carrying out the orders of the courts, in a setting they have inherited and are powerless to alter. The judges say they have no choice but to enforce the laws as given to them by the legislature. The lawmakers? With one eye on re-election they bow readily to mindless demands for ever "tougher measures" as a panacea for the nation's ills.

1. *In what way does Mitford's narration of events make it clear that she is not an actual prisoner confined in the jail for months or years? In what ways does her account differ from what you might expect to hear from someone who had served time in prison?*
2. *What does Mitford gain by writing about her personal experience rather than discussing the problem of prisons in more general terms?*
3. *Discuss the portraits Mitford offers of the prisoners she meets. Compare them in detail with her characterizations of prison administrators and other official personnel.*
4. *Mitford is not really writing an autobiography; she uses her personal experience primarily to examine the subject of penal conditions. How does her purpose affect the way she talks about her experience? Is her method different from that used by other writers in this chapter?*
5. *At what points and in what ways does Mitford introduce more general observations about prison life and the penal system? What issues seem particularly important to her? How does she present these issues? Does she suggest solutions?*

∾ Joan Didion ∾

(1934-   )

*Joan Didion was born and raised in California and educated at
the University of California at Berkeley. She moved to New
York, where she was an editor at* Vogue *magazine and a free-
lance writer who contributed articles, reviews, and pieces of
commentary to many national magazines. By the 1970s she
had returned to California, where she continues to write essays
and novels and to coauthor screenplays with her husband,
John Gregory Dunne. The selection here is reprinted from*
Slouching Towards Bethlehem *(1968); it presents Didion's reflections on a visit she and her baby daughter made to her
own childhood home in Sacramento.*

ON GOING HOME

I am home for my daughter's first birthday. By "home" I do
not mean the house in Los Angeles where my husband and I
and the baby live, but the place where my family is, in the
Central Valley of California. It is a vital although troublesome
distinction. My husband likes my family but is uneasy in
their house, because once there I fall into their ways, which
are difficult, oblique, deliberately inarticulate, not my husband's ways. We live in dusty houses ("D-U-S-T," he once
wrote with his finger on surfaces all over the house, but no
one noticed it) filled with mementos quite without value to
him (what could the Canton dessert plates mean to him? how

could he have known about the assay scales, why should he care if he did know?), and we appear to talk exclusively about people we know who have been committed to mental hospitals, about people we know who have been booked on drunk-driving charges, and about property, particularly about property, land, price per acre and C-2 zoning and assessments and freeway access. My brother does not understand my husband's inability to perceive the advantage in the rather common real-estate transaction known as "sale-leaseback," and my husband in turn does not understand why so many of the people he hears about in my father's house have recently been committed to mental hospitals or booked on drunk-driving charges. Nor does he understand that when we talk about sale-leasebacks and right-of-way condemnations we are talking in code about the things we like best, the yellow fields and the cottonwoods and the rivers rising and falling and the mountain roads closing when the heavy snow comes in. We miss each other's points, have another drink and regard the fire. My brother refers to my husband, in his presence, as "Joan's husband." Marriage is the classic betrayal.

Or perhaps it is not any more. Sometimes I think that those of us who are now in our thirties were born into the last generation to carry the burden of "home," to find in family life the source of all tension and drama. I had by all objective accounts a "normal" and a "happy" family situation, and yet I was almost thirty years old before I could talk to my family on the telephone without crying after I had hung up. We did not fight. Nothing was wrong. And yet some nameless anxiety colored the emotional charges between me and the place that I came from. The question of whether or not you could go home again was a very real part of the sentimental and largely literary baggage with which we left home in the fifties; I suspect that it is irrelevant to the children born of the fragmentation after World War II. A few weeks ago in a San Francisco bar I saw a pretty young girl on crystal take off her clothes and dance for the cash prize in an "amateur-topless" contest. There was no particular sense of moment about this, none of the effect of romantic degradation, of "dark journey," for which my generation strived so assiduously. What sense could that girl possibly make of, say, *Long Day's Journey into Night?* Who is beside the point?

That I am trapped in this particular irrelevancy is never more apparent to me than when I am home. Paralyzed by the neurotic lassitude engendered by meeting one's past at every turn, around every corner, inside every cupboard, I go aimlessly from room to room. I decide to meet it head-on and clean out a drawer, and I spread the contents on the bed. A bathing suit I wore the summer I was seventeen. A letter of rejection from *The Nation*, an aerial photograph of the site for a shopping center my father did not build in 1954. Three teacups hand-painted with cabbage roses and signed "E.M.," my grandmother's initials. There is no final solution for letters of rejection from *The Nation* and teacups hand-painted in 1900. Nor is there any answer to snapshots of one's grandfather as a young man on skis, surveying around Donner Pass in the year 1910. I smooth out the snapshot and look into his face, and do and do not see my own. I close the drawer, and have another cup of coffee with my mother. We get along very well, veterans of a guerrilla war we never understood.

Days pass. I see no one. I come to dread my husband's evening call, not only because he is full of news of what by now seems to me our remote life in Los Angeles, people he has seen, letters which require attention, but because he asks what I have been doing, suggests uneasily that I get out, drive to San Francisco or Berkeley. Instead I drive across the river to a family graveyard. It has been vandalized since my last visit and the monuments are broken, overturned in the dry grass. Because I once saw a rattlesnake in the grass I stay in the car and listen to a country-and-Western station. Later I drive with my father to a ranch he has in the foothills. The man who runs his cattle on it asks us to the roundup, a week from Sunday, and although I know that I will be in Los Angeles I say, in the oblique way my family talks, that I will come. Once home I mention the broken monuments in the graveyard. My mother shrugs.

I go to visit my great-aunts. A few of them think now that I am my cousin, or their daughter who died young. We recall an anecdote about a relative last seen in 1948, and they ask if I still like living in New York City. I have lived in Los Angeles for three years, but I say that I do. The baby is offered a horehound drop, and I am slipped a dollar bill "to buy a treat." Questions trail off, answers are abandoned, the baby plays with the dust motes in a shaft of afternoon sun.

It is time for the baby's birthday party: a white cake, strawberry-marshmallow ice cream, a bottle of champagne saved from another party. In the evening, after she has gone to sleep, I kneel beside the crib and touch her face, where it is pressed against the slats, with mine. She is an open and trusting child, unprepared for and unaccustomed to the ambushes of family life, and perhaps it is just as well that I can offer her little of that life. I would like to give her more. I would like to promise her that she will grow up with a sense of her cousins and of rivers and of her great-grandmother's teacups, would like to pledge her a picnic on a river with fried chicken and her hair uncombed, would like to give her *home* for her birthday, but we live differently now and I can promise her nothing like that. I give her a xylophone and a sundress from Madeira, and promise to tell her a funny story.

1. How does Didion suggest that life "at home" is different from life in her present home with her husband? How does her husband's attitude toward the family home differ from Didion's attitude?

2. In what ways does Didion regard herself as a member of a distinctive generation? According to her, in what ways will people younger than she is have difficulty understanding her?

3. Do the details we learn about life in Sacramento suggest that it is a flourishing way of life or not? Does Didion seem to have a special attachment to it, or does she feel it imprisons her, or does she have ambivalent feelings about it?

4. What differences do you see between the promises that Didion in her last paragraph feels she cannot make to her daughter and the promises she feels she can make? How are these final thoughts in the essay provoked by Didion's visit home?

∽ James Baldwin ∽

(1924-   )

Raised in Harlem, James Baldwin was a Pentacostal preacher while still in his teens and then embarked on a literary career. He lived in near poverty in New York and Paris until his first novel was published in 1952. Since that time, Baldwin has written fiction and drama, as well as a series of essays exploring the tensions and bitterness felt by the black man in a world controlled by whites. Through his writing, lectures, and television appearances, Baldwin has played an important role, both as interpreter and prophet, in articulating a black point of view. This selection is taken from his first collection of essays, Notes of a Native Son *(1953).*

STRANGER IN THE VILLAGE

From all available evidence no black man had ever set foot in this tiny Swiss village before I came. I was told before arriving that I would probably be a "sight" for the village; I took this to mean that people of my complexion were rarely seen in Switzerland, and also that city people are always something of a "sight" outside of the city. It did not occur to me—possibly because I am an American—that there could be people anywhere who had never seen a Negro.

It is a fact that cannot be explained on the basis of the inaccessibility of the village. The village is very high, but it is only four hours from Milan and three hours from Lausanne. It is true that it is virtually unknown. Few people making plans for a holiday would elect to come here. On the other hand, the villagers are able, presumably, to come and go as they please—which they do: to another town at the foot of the mountain, with a population of approximately five thousand, the nearest place to see a movie or go to the bank. In the village there is no movie house, no bank, no library, no theater; very few radios, one jeep, one station wagon; and, at the moment, one typewriter, mine, an invention which the woman next door to me here had never seen. There are about six hundred people living here, all Catholic—I conclude this from the fact that the Catholic church is open all year round, whereas the Protestant chapel, set off on a hill a little removed from the village, is open only in the summertime when the tourists arrive. There are four or five hotels, all closed now, and four or five *bistros*, of which, however, only two do any business during the winter. These two do not do a great deal, for life in the village seems to end around nine or ten o'clock. There are a few stores, butcher, baker, *épicerie*, a hardware store, and a money-changer—who cannot change travelers' checks, but must send them down to the bank, an operation which takes two or three days. There is something called the *Ballet Haus*, closed in the winter and used for God knows what, certainly not ballet, during the summer. There seems to be only one schoolhouse in the village, and this for the quite young children; I suppose this to mean that their older brothers and sisters at some point descend from these mountains in order to complete their education—possibly, again, to the town just below. The landscape is absolutely forbidding, mountains towering on all four sides, ice and snow as far as the eye can reach. In this white wilderness, men and women and children move all day, carrying washing, wood, buckets of milk or water, sometimes skiing on Sunday afternoons. All week long boys and young men are to be seen shoveling snow off the rooftops, or dragging wood down from the forest in sleds.

The village's only real attraction, which explains the tourist season, is the hot spring water. A disquietingly high proportion of these tourists are cripples, or semicripples, who come year after year—from other parts of Switzerland, usually—to take the waters. This lends the village, at the height of the season, a rather terrifying air of sanctity, as though it were a lesser Lourdes. There is often something beautiful, there is always something awful, in the spectacle of a person who has lost one of his faculties, a faculty he never questioned until it was gone, and who struggles to recover it. Yet people remain people, on crutches or indeed on deathbeds; and wherever I passed, the first summer I was here, among the native villagers or among the lame, a wind passed with me—of astonishment, curiosity, amusement, and outrage. That first summer I stayed two weeks and never intended to return. But I did return in the winter, to work; the village offers, obviously, no distractions whatever and has the further advantage of being extremely cheap. Now it is winter again, a year later, and I am here again. Everyone in the village knows my name, though they scarcely ever use it, knows that I come from America—though, this, apparently, they will never really believe: black men come from Africa—and everyone knows that I am the friend of the son of a woman who was born here, and that I am staying in their chalet. But I remain as much a stranger today as I was the first day I arrived, and the children shout *Neger! Neger!* as I walk along the streets.

It must be admitted that in the beginning I was far too shocked to have any real reaction. In so far as I reacted at all, I reacted by trying to be pleasant—it being a great part of the American Negro's education (long before he goes to school) that he must make people "like" him. This smile-and-the-world-smiles-with-you routine worked about as well in this situation as it had in the situation for which it was designed, which is to say that it did not work at all. No one, after all, can be liked whose human weight and complexity cannot be, or has not been, admitted. My smile was simply another unheard-of phenomenon which allowed them to see my teeth— they did not, really, see my smile and I began to think that, should I take to snarling, no one would notice any difference. All of the physical characteristics of the Negro which had caused me, in America, a very different and almost forgotten pain were nothing less than miraculous—or infernal—in the eyes of the village people. Some thought my hair was the color of tar, that it had the texture of wire, or the texture of cotton. It was jocularly suggested that I might let it all grow long and make myself a winter coat. If I sat in the sun for more than five minutes some daring creature was certain to come along and gingerly put his fingers on my hair, as though he were afraid of an electric shock, or put his hand on my hand, astonished that the color did not rub off. In all of this, in which it must be conceded there was the charm of genuine wonder and in which there was certainly no element of intentional unkindness, there was yet no suggestion that I was human: I was simply a living wonder.

I knew that they did not mean to be unkind, and I know it now; it is necessary, nevertheless, for me to repeat this to myself each time that I walk out of the chalet. The children who shout *Neger!* have no way of knowing the echoes this sound raises in me. They are brimming with good humor and the more daring swell with pride when I stop to speak with them. Just the same, there are days when I cannot pause and smile, when I have no heart to play with them; when, indeed, I mutter sourly to myself, exactly as I muttered on the streets of a city these children have never seen, when I was no bigger than these children are now: *Your* mother *was a nigger*. Joyce is right about history being a nightmare—but it may be the nightmare from which no one *can* awaken. People are trapped in history and history is trapped in them.

There is a custom in the village—I am told it is repeated in many villages—of "buying" African natives for the purpose of converting them to Christianity. There stands in the church all year round a small box with a slot for money, decorated with a black figurine, and into this box the villagers drop their francs. During the *carnaval* which precedes Lent, two village

362

children have their faces blackened—out of which bloodless darkness their blue eyes shine like ice—and fantastic horsehair wigs are placed on their blond heads; thus disguised, they solicit among the villagers for money for the missionaries in Africa. Between the box in the church and the blackened children, the village "bought" last year six or eight African natives. This was reported to me with pride by the wife of one of the *bistro* owners and I was careful to express astonishment and pleasure at the solicitude shown by the village for the souls of black folk. The *bistro* owner's wife beamed with a pleasure far more genuine than my own and seemed to feel that I might now breathe more easily concerning the souls of at least six of my kinsmen.

I tried not to think of these so lately baptized kinsmen, of the price paid for them, or the peculiar price they themselves would pay, and said nothing about my father, who having taken his own conversion too literally never, at bottom, forgave the white world (which he described as heathen) for having saddled him with a Christ in whom, to judge at least from their treatment of him, they themselves no longer believed. I thought of white men arriving for the first time in an African village, strangers there, as I am a stranger here, and tried to imagine the astounded populace touching their hair and marveling at the color of their skin. But there is a great difference between being the first white man to be seen by Africans and being the first black man to be seen by whites. The white man takes the astonishment as tribute, for he arrives to conquer and to convert the natives, whose inferiority in relation to himself is not even to be questioned; whereas I, without a thought of conquest, find myself among a people whose culture controls me, has even, in a sense, created me, people who have cost me more in anguish and rage than they will ever know, who yet do not even know of my existence. The astonishment with which I might have greeted them, should they have stumbled into my African village a few hundred years ago, might have rejoiced their hearts. But the astonishment with which they greet me today can only poison mine.

And this is so despite everything I may do to feel differently, despite my friendly conversations with the *bistro* owner's wife, despite their three-year-old son who has at last become my friend, despite the *saluts* and *bonsoirs* which I exchange with people as I walk, despite the fact that I know that no individual can be taken to task for what history is doing, or has done. I say that the culture of these people controls me—but they can scarcely be held responsible for European culture. America comes out of Europe, but these people have never seen America, nor have most of them seen more of Europe than the hamlet at the foot of their mountain. Yet they move with an authority which I shall never have; and they regard me, quite rightly, not only as a stranger in their village but as a suspect latecomer, bearing no credentials, to everything they have—however unconsciously—inherited.

For this village, even were it incomparably more remote and incredibly more primitive, is the West, the West onto which I have been so strangely grafted. These people cannot be, from the point of view of power, strangers anywhere in the world; they have made the modern world, in effect, even if they do not know it. The most illiterate among them is related, in a way that I am not, to Dante, Shakespeare, Michelangelo, Aeschylus, Da Vinci, Rembrandt, and Racine; the cathedral at Chartres says something to them which it cannot say to me, as indeed would New York's Empire State Building, should anyone here ever see it. Out of their hymns and dances come Beethoven and Bach. Go back a few centuries and they are in their full glory—but I am in Africa, watching the conquerors arrive.

The rage of the disesteemed is personally fruitless, but it is also absolutely inevitable; this rage, so generally discounted, so little understood even among the people whose daily bread it is, is one of the things that makes history. Rage can only with difficulty, and never entirely, be brought under the domination of the intelligence and is therefore not susceptible to any arguments whatever. This is a fact which ordinary representatives of the *Herrenvolk*, having never felt this rage and being unable to imagine it, quite fail to understand. Also, rage cannot be hidden, it can only be dissembled. This dissembling deludes the thoughtless, and strengthens rage and adds, to rage, contempt. There are, no doubt, as many ways of coping with the resulting complex of tensions as there are black men in the world, but no black man can hope ever to be entirely liberated from this internal warfare—rage, dissembling, and contempt having inevitably accompanied his first realization of the power of white men. What is crucial here is that, since white men represent in the black man's world so heavy a weight, white men have for black men a reality which is far from being reciprocal; and hence all black men have toward all white men an attitude which is designed, really, either to rob the white man of the jewel of his naïveté, or else to make it cost him dear.

The black man insists, by whatever means he finds at his disposal, that the white man cease to regard him as an exotic rarity and recognize him as a human being. This is a very charged and difficult moment, for there is a great deal of will power involved in the white man's naïveté. Most people are not naturally reflective any more than they are naturally malicious, and the white man prefers to keep the black man at a certain human remove because it is easier for him thus to preserve his simplicity and avoid being called to account for crimes committed by his forefathers, or his neighbors. He is inescapably aware, nevertheless, that he is in a better position in the world than black men are, nor can he quite put to death the suspicion that he is hated by black men therefore. He does not wish to be hated, neither does he wish to change places, and at this point in his uneasiness he can scarcely avoid having recourse to those legends which white men have created about black men, the most usual effect of which is that the white man finds himself enmeshed, so to speak, in his own language which describes hell, as well as the attributes which lead one to hell, as being as black as night.

Every legend, moreover, contains its residuum of truth, and the root function of language is to control the universe by describing it. It is of quite considerable significance that black men remain, in the imagination, and in overwhelming numbers in fact, beyond the disciplines of salvation; and this despite the fact that the West has been "buying" African natives for centuries. There is, I should hazard, an instantaneous necessity to be divorced from this so visibly unsaved stranger, in whose heart, moreover, one cannot guess what dreams of vengeance are being nourished; and, at the same time, there are few things on earth more attractive than the idea of the unspeakable liberty which is allowed the unredeemed. When, beneath the black mask, a human being begins to make himself felt one cannot escape a certain awful wonder as to what kind of human being it is. What one's imagination makes of other people is dictated, of course, by the laws of one's own personality and it is one of the ironies of black-white relations that, by means of what the white man imagines the black man to be, the black man is enabled to know who the white man is.

I have said, for example, that I am as much a stranger in this village today as I was the first summer I arrived, but this is not quite true. The villagers wonder less about the texture of my hair than they did then, and wonder rather more about me. And the fact that their wonder now exists on another level is reflected in their attitudes and in their eyes. There are the children who make those delightful, hilarious, sometimes astonishingly grave overtures of friendship in the unpredictable fashion of children; other children, having been taught that the devil is a black man, scream in genuine anguish as I approach. Some of the older women never pass without a friendly greeting, never pass, indeed, if it seems that they will be able to engage me in conversation; other women look down or look away or rather contemptuously smirk. Some of the men drink with me and suggest that I learn how to ski—

partly, I gather, because they cannot imagine what I would look like on skis—and want to know if I am married, and ask questions about my *métier*. But some of the men have accused *le sale nègre*—behind my back—of stealing wood and there is already in the eyes of some of them that peculiar, intent, paranoiac malevolence which one sometimes surprises in the eyes of American white men when, out walking with their Sunday girl, they see a Negro male approach.

There is a dreadful abyss between the streets of this village and the streets of the city in which I was born, between the children who shout *Neger!* today and those who shouted *Nigger!* yesterday—the abyss is experience, the American experience. The syllable hurled behind me today expresses, above all, wonder: I am a stranger here. But I am not a stranger in America and the same syllable riding on the American air expresses the war my presence has occasioned in the American soul.

For this village brings home to me this fact: that there was a day, and not really a very distant day, when Americans were scarcely Americans at all but discontented Europeans, facing a great unconquered continent and strolling, say, into a marketplace and seeing black men for the first time. The shock this spectacle afforded is suggested, surely, by the promptness with which they decided that these black men were not really men but cattle. It is true that the necessity on the part of the settlers of the New World of reconciling their moral assumptions with the fact—and the necessity—of slavery enhanced immensely the charm of this idea, and it is also true that this idea expresses, with a truly American bluntness, the attitude which to varying extents all masters have had toward all slaves.

But between all former slaves and slave-owners and the drama which begins for Americans over three hundred years ago at Jamestown, there are at least two differences to be observed. The American Negro slave could not suppose, for one thing, as slaves in past epochs had supposed and often done, that he would ever be able to wrest the power from his master's hands. This was a supposition which the modern era, which was to bring about such vast changes in the aims and dimensions of power, put to death; it only begins, in unprecedented fashion, and with dreadful implications, to be resurrected today. But even had this supposition persisted with undiminished force, the American Negro slave could not have used it to lend his condition dignity, for the reason that this supposition rests on another: that the slave in exile yet remains related to his past, has some means—if only in memory—of revering and sustaining the forms of his former life, is able, in short, to maintain his identity.

This was not the case with the American Negro slave. He is unique among the black men of the world in that his past was taken from him, almost literally, at one blow. One wonders what on earth the first slave found to say to the first dark child he bore. I am told that there are Haitians able to trace their ancestry back to African kings, but any American Negro wishing to go back so far will find his journey through time abruptly arrested by the signature on the bill of sale which served as the entrance paper for his ancestor. At the time—to say nothing of the circumstances—of the enslavement of the captive black man who was to become the American Negro, there was not the remotest possibility that he would ever take power from his master's hands. There was no reason to suppose that his situation would ever change, nor was there, shortly, anything to indicate that his situation had ever been different. It was his necessity, in the words of E. Franklin Frazier, to find a "motive for living under American culture or die." The identity of the American Negro comes out of this extreme situation, and the evolution of this identity was a source of the most intolerable anxiety in the minds and the lives of his masters.

For the history of the American Negro is unique also in this: that the question of his humanity, and of his rights therefore as a human being, became a burning one for several generations of Americans, so burning a question that it ultimately became one of those used to divide the nation. It is out of this argument that the venom of the epithet *Nigger!* is derived. It is an argument which Europe has never had, and hence Europe quite sincerely fails to understand how or why the argument arose in the first place, why its effects are so frequently disastrous and always so unpredictable, why it refuses until today to be entirely settled. Europe's black possessions remained—and do remain—in Europe's colonies, at which remove they represented no threat whatever to European identity. If they posed any problem at all for the European conscience, it was a problem which remained comfortingly abstract: in effect, the black man, *as a man*, did not exist for Europe. But in America, even as a slave, he was an inescapable part of the general social fabric and no American could escape having an attitude toward him. Americans attempt until today to make an abstraction of the Negro, but the very nature of these abstractions reveals the tremendous effects the presence of the Negro has had on the American character.

When one considers the history of the Negro in America it is of the greatest importance to recognize that the moral beliefs of a person, or a people, are never really as tenuous as life—which is not moral—very often causes them to appear; these create for them a frame of reference and a necessary hope, the hope being that when life has done its worst they will be enabled to rise above themselves and to triumph over life. Life would scarcely be bearable if this hope did not exist. Again, even when the worst has been said, to betray a belief is not by any means to have put oneself beyond its power; the betrayal of a belief is not the same thing as ceasing to believe. If this were not so there would be no moral standards in the world at all. Yet one must also recognize that morality is based on ideas and that all ideas are dangerous—dangerous because ideas can only lead to action and where the action leads no man can say. And dangerous in this respect: that confronted with the impossibility of remaining faithful to one's beliefs, and the equal impossibility of becoming free of them, one can be driven to the most inhuman excesses. The ideas on which American beliefs are based are not, though Americans often seem to think so, ideas which originated in America. They came out of Europe. And the establishment of democracy on the American continent was scarcely as radical a break with the past as was the necessity, which Americans faced, of broadening this concept to include black men.

This was, literally, a hard necessity. It was impossible, for one thing, for Americans to abandon their beliefs, not only because these beliefs alone seemed able to justify the sacrifices they had endured and the blood that they had spilled, but also because these beliefs afforded them their only bulwark against a moral chaos as absolute as the physical chaos of the continent it was their destiny to conquer. But in the situation in which Americans found themselves, these beliefs threatened an idea which, whether or not one likes to think so, is the very warp and woof of the heritage of the West, the idea of white supremacy.

Americans have made themselves notorious by the shrillness and the brutality with which they have insisted on this idea, but they did not invent it; and it has escaped the world's notice that those very excesses of which Americans have been guilty imply a certain, unprecedented uneasiness over the idea's life and power, if not, indeed, the idea's validity. The idea of white supremacy rests simply on the fact that white men are the creators of civilization (the present civilization, which is the only one that matters; all previous civilizations are simply "contributions" to our own) and are therefore civilization's guardians and defenders. Thus it was impossible for Americans to accept the black man as one of themselves, for to do so was to jeopardize their status as white men. But not so to accept him was to deny his human reality, his human weight and complexity, and the strain of denying the overwhelmingly undeniable forced Americans into rationalizations so fantastic that they approached the pathological.

At the root of the American Negro problem is the necessity of the American white man to find a way of living with the Negro in order to be able to live with himself. And the history of this problem can be reduced to the means used by Americans—lynch law and law, segregation and legal acceptance, terrorization and concession—either to come to terms with this necessity, or to find a way around it, or (most usually) to find a way of doing both these things at once. The resulting spectacle, at once foolish and dreadful, led someone to make the quite accurate observation that "the Negro-in-America is a form of insanity which overtakes white men."

In this long battle, a battle by no means finished, the unforeseeable effects of which will be felt by many future generations, the white man's motive was the protection of his identity; the black man was motivated by the need to establish an identity. And despite the terrorization which the Negro in America endured and endures sporadically until today, despite the cruel and totally inescapable ambivalence of his status in his country, the battle for his identity has long ago been won. He is not a visitor to the West, but a citizen there, an American; as American as the Americans who despise him, the Americans who fear him, the Americans who love him—the Americans who became less than themselves, or rose to be greater than themselves by virtue of the fact that the challenge he represented was inescapable. He is perhaps the only black man in the world whose relationship to white men is more terrible, more subtle, and more meaningful than the relationship of bitter possessed to uncertain possessor. His survival depended, and his development depends, on his ability to turn his peculiar status in the Western world to his own advantage and, it may be, to the very great advantage of that world. It remains for him to fashion out of his experience that which will give him sustenance, and a voice.

The cathedral at Chartres, I have said, says something to the people of this village which it cannot say to me; but it is important to understand that this cathedral says something to me which it cannot say to them. Perhaps they are struck by the power of the spires, the glory of the windows; but they have known God, after all, longer than I have known him, and in a different way, and I am terrified by the slippery bottomless well to be found in the crypt, down which heretics were hurled to death, and by the obscene, inescapable gargoyles jutting out of the stone and seeming to say that God and the devil can never be divorced. I doubt that the villagers think of the devil when they face a cathedral because they have never been identified with the devil. But I must accept the status which myth, if nothing else, gives me in the West before I can hope to change the myth.

Yet, if the American Negro has arrived at his identity by virtue of the absoluteness of his estrangement from his past, American white men still nourish the illusion that there is some means of recovering the European innocence, of returning to a state in which black men do not exist. This is one of the greatest errors Americans can make. The identity they fought so hard to protect has, by virtue of that battle, undergone a change: Americans are as unlike any other white people in the world as it is possible to be. I do not think, for example, that it is too much to suggest that the American vision of the world—which allows so little reality, generally speaking, for any of the darker forces in human life, which tends until today to paint moral issues in glaring black and white—owes a great deal to the battle waged by Americans to maintain between themselves and black men a human separation which could not be bridged. It is only now beginning to be borne in on us—very faintly, it must be admitted, very slowly, and very much against our will—that this vision of the world is dangerously inaccurate, and perfectly useless. For it protects our moral high-mindedness at the terrible expense of weakening our grasp of reality. People who shut their eyes to reality simply invite their own destruction, and anyone who insists on remaining in a state of innocence long after that innocence is dead turns himself into a monster.

The time has come to realize that the interracial drama acted out on the American continent has not only created a new black man, it has created a new white man, too. No road whatever will lead Americans back to the simplicity of this European village where white men still have the luxury of

JAMES BALDWIN

looking on me as a stranger. I am not, really, a stranger any
longer for any American alive. One of the things that distinguishes Americans from other people is that no other people
has ever been so deeply involved in the lives of black men, and
vice versa. This fact faced, with all its implications, it can be
seen that the history of the American Negro problem is not
merely shameful, it is also something of an achievement. For
even when the worst has been said, it must also be added that
the perpetual challenge posed by this problem was always,
somehow, perpetually met. It is precisely this black-white experience which may prove of indispensable value to us in the
world we face today. This world is white no longer, and it will
never be white again.

1. *Why does Baldwin give you so many descriptive details
about the Swiss village at the beginning of his essay? Do they
later help you to understand his own situation in the village?
How do they contribute to his more general argument about
the relationship between blacks and whites?*
2. *What significance does Baldwin find in the villagers' behavior toward him personally? In their collections for the African missions? Why does this experience in Switzerland
rather than some American experience make him contemplate
racial issues?*
3. *Once Baldwin has described the village, how much of the
rest of the essay refers to his own experiences in the village?
Where in the essay does he bring up these experiences and
why?*
4. *How broadly does Baldwin attempt to generalize on the
basis of his experience? How varied are the levels of generalization he introduces and how often does he clearly shift from
one level to another?*
5. *What gives Baldwin his authority when he speaks so
broadly of "people" or "white men" or "Negro Americans"?
How does he make you pay attention to his generalizations and
consider them seriously?*

373

∽ George Orwell ∽

(1903-1950)

See the biographical note on page 53. "Such, Such Were the Joys" was found among Orwell's papers after his death. It is based on his years (1911–1916) at St. Cyprian's (called Crossgates in the essay), a preparatory school where Orwell lived as a poor scholarship student among much wealthier classmates. Bingo and Sim, referred to in the essay, were the headmaster of the school and his wife; Orwell uses the nicknames they were given by the students. The selection here is the last of the six sections that comprise the essay.

SUCH, SUCH WERE THE JOYS

All this was thirty years ago and more. The question is: Does a child at school go through the same kind of experiences nowadays?

The only honest answer, I believe, is that we do not with certainty know. Of course it is obvious that the present-day *attitude* towards education is enormously more humane and sensible than that of the past. The snobbishness that was an integral part of my own education would be almost unthinkable today, because the society that nourished it is dead. I recall a conversation that must have taken place about a year before I left Crossgates. A Russian boy, large and fair-haired, a year older than myself, was questioning me.

"How much a-year has your father got?"

I told him what I thought it was, adding a few hundreds to make it sound better. The Russian boy, neat in his habits, produced a pencil and a small notebook and made a calculation. "My father has over two hundred times as much money as yours," he announced with a sort of amused contempt.

That was in 1915. What happened to that money a couple of years later, I wonder? And still more I wonder, do conversations of that kind happen at preparatory schools now?

Clearly there has been a vast change of outlook, a general growth of "enlightenment," even among ordinary, unthinking middle-class people. Religious belief, for instance, has largely vanished, dragging other kinds of nonsense after it. I imagine that very few people nowadays would tell a child that if it masturbates it will end in the lunatic asylum. Beating, too, has become discredited, and has even been abandoned at many schools. Nor is the underfeeding of children looked on as a normal, almost meritorious act. No one now would openly set out to give his pupils as little food as they could do with, or tell them that it is healthy to get up from a meal as hungry as you sat down. The whole status of children has improved, partly because they have grown relatively less numerous. And the diffusion of even a little psychological knowledge has made it harder for parents and schoolteachers to indulge their aberrations in the name of discipline. Here is a case, not known to me personally, but known to someone I can vouch for, and happening within my own lifetime. A small girl, daughter of a clergyman, continued wetting her bed at an age when she should have grown out of it. In order to punish her for this dreadful deed, her father took her to a large garden party and there introduced her to the whole company as a little girl who wetted her bed: and to underline her wickedness he had previously painted her face black. I do not suggest that Bingo and Sim would actually have done a thing like this, but I doubt whether it would have much surprised them. After all, things do change. And yet—!

The question is not whether boys are still buckled into Eton collars on Sunday, or told that babies are dug up under gooseberry bushes. That kind of thing is at an end, admittedly. The real question is whether it is still normal for a school child to live for years amid irrational terrors and lunatic misunderstandings. And here one is up against the very great difficulty of knowing what a child really feels and thinks. A child which appears reasonably happy may actually be suffering horrors which it cannot or will not reveal. It lives in a sort of alien under-water world which we can only penetrate by memory or divination. Our chief clue is the fact that we were once children ourselves, and many people appear to forget the atmosphere of their own childhood almost entirely. Think for instance of the unnecessary torments that people will inflict by sending a child back to school with clothes of the wrong pattern, and refusing to see that this matters! Over things of this kind a child will sometimes utter a protest, but a great deal of the time its attitude is one of simple concealment. Not to expose your true feelings to an adult seems to be instinctive from the age of seven or eight onwards. Even the affection that one feels for a child, the desire to protect and cherish it, is a cause of misunderstanding. One can love a child, perhaps, more deeply than one can love another adult, but it is rash to assume that the child feels any love in return. Looking back on my own childhood, after the infant years were over, I do not believe that I ever felt love for any mature person, except my mother, and even her I did not trust, in the sense that shyness made me conceal most of my real feelings from her. Love, the spontaneous, unqualified emotion of love, was something I could only feel for people who were young. Towards people who were old—and remember that "old" to a child means over thirty, or even over twenty-five—I could feel reverence, respect, admiration or compunction, but I seemed cut off from them by a veil of fear and shyness mixed up with physical distaste. People are too ready to forget the child's *physical* shrinking from the adult. The enormous size of grownups, their ungainly, rigid bodies, their coarse wrinkled skins, their great relaxed eyelids, their yellow teeth, and the whiffs of musty clothes and beer and sweat and tobacco that disengage from them at every movement! Part of the reason for the ugliness of adults, in a child's eyes, is that the child is usually looking upwards, and few faces are at their best when seen from below. Besides, being fresh and unmarked itself, the child has impossibly high standards in the matter of skin and teeth and complexion. But the greatest barrier of all is the child's misconception about age. A child can hardly envisage life beyond thirty, and in judging people's ages it will make fantastic mistakes. It will think that a person of twenty-five is forty, that a person of forty is sixty-five, and so on. Thus, when I fell in love with Elsie I took her to be grown up. I met her again, when I was thirteen and she, I think, must have been twenty-three; she now seemed to me a middle-aged woman, somewhat past her best. And the child thinks of growing old as an almost obscene calamity, which for some mysterious reason will never happen to itself. All who have passed the age of thirty are joyless grotesques, endlessly fussing about things of no importance and staying alive without, so far as the child can see, having anything to live for. Only child life is real life. The schoolmaster who imagines he is loved and trusted by his boys is in fact mimicked and laughed at behind his back. An adult who does not seem dangerous nearly always seems ridiculous.

I base these generalisations on what I can recall of my own childhood outlook. Treacherous though memory is, it seems to me the chief means we have of discovering how a child's mind works. Only by resurrecting our own memories can we realise how incredibly distorted is the child's vision of the world. Consider this, for example. How would Crossgates appear to me now, if I could go back, at my present age, and see it as it was in 1915? What should I think of Bingo and Sim, those terrible, all-powerful monsters? I should see them as a couple of silly, shallow, ineffectual people, eagerly clambering up a social ladder which any thinking person could see to be on the point of collapse. I would be no more frightened of them than I would be frightened of a dormouse. Moreover, in those days they seemed to me fantastically old, whereas—though of this I am not certain—I imagine they must have been somewhat younger than I am now. And how would Johnny Hall appear, with his blacksmith's arms and his red, jeering face? Merely a scruffy little boy, barely distinguishable from hundreds of other scruffy little boys. The two sets of facts can lie side by side in my mind, because these happen to be my own memories. But it would be very difficult for me to see with the eyes of any other child, except by an effort of the imagination which might lead me completely astray. The child and the adult live in different worlds. If that is so, we cannot be certain that school, at any rate boarding school, is not still for many children as dreadful an experience as it used to be. Take away God, Latin, the cane, class distinctions and sexual taboos, and the fear, the hatred, the snobbery and the misunderstanding might still all be there. It will have been seen that my own main trouble was an utter lack of any sense of proportion or probability. This led me to accept outrages and believe absurdities, and to suffer torments over things which were in fact of no importance. It is not enough to say that I was "silly" and "ought to have known better." Look back into your own childhood and think of the nonsense you used to believe and the trivialities which could make you suffer. Of course my own case had its individual variations, but essentially it was that of countless other boys. The weakness of the child is that it starts with a blank sheet. It neither understands nor questions the society in which it lives, and because of its credulity other people can work upon it, infecting it with the sense of inferiority and the dread of offending against mysterious, terrible laws. It may be that everything that happened to me at Crossgates could happen in the most "enlightened" school, though perhaps in subtler forms. Of one thing, however, I do feel fairly sure, and that is that boarding schools are worse than day schools. A child has a better chance with the sanctuary of its home near at hand. And I think the characteristic faults of the English upper and middle classes may be partly due to the practice, general until recently, of sending children away from home as young as nine, eight or even seven.

I have never been back to Crossgates. In a way it is only within the last decade that I have really thought over my schooldays, vividly though their memory has haunted me. Nowadays, I believe, it would make very little impression on me to see the place again, if it still exists. And if I went inside and smelt again the inky, dusty smell of the big schoolroom, the rosiny smell of the chapel, the stagnant smell of the swimming bath and the cold reek of the lavatories, I think I should only feel what one invariably feels in revisiting any scene of childhood: How small everything has grown, and how terrible is the deterioration in myself!

1. This selection is the final section of a six-part essay based on Orwell's own experiences as a scholarship boy at an English preparatory school. How does Orwell's method make clear that he is concluding the essay?

2. What sort of perspective has the passage of thirty years given to Orwell as he writes about school? How does he organize the selection to reflect his mature experience?

3. Since Orwell's own schooling occurred so many years earlier, how is he able to make use of it as support for his present views of the school situation? When and how does he refer to his own experience for illustration?

4. How much of what Orwell sees as the difficulties children experience does he relate to flaws in schools, how much to the condition of childhood itself? Do you think Orwell's primary purpose here is to encourage educational reform?

∿ V. S. Pritchett ∿

(1900-   )

V. S. Pritchett typifies the English man of letters. He has writ-
ten in virtually every form: novels, short stories, travel books,
essays, literary criticism, and reminiscences. He has also been
remarkably consistent as well as prolific, publishing a volume
every year or two, each one showing the mark of a skillful and
thoughtful writer. His autobiographical volumes, A Cab At
the Door *(1968) and* Midnight Oil *(1971) are portraits of a*
genteel and eccentric English world that no longer exists.

WRITING AN AUTOBIOGRAPHY

On the face of it, to write one's autobiography is the easiest and
most grateful task in the world. No search for anti-hero or
hero: he is you. No search for material, it is all there: your
own life. No imagination is necessary; the question of structure—one of the most difficult problems in writing—is automatically solved by sticking to chronology, year after year.
The first person singular seems to be the perfect camera-eye.
Unless you suffer from a neurotic block, your childhood and
early youth have long ago crystallized. This is the most vivid
and certain part of your life.

So you set out. You write 20 pages and suddenly you stop.
Why is it you are bewildered? Why do you have the sensation
of being in a rowing boat in the middle of the ocean and having lost your oars? Who is this "I," you wonder, which of my
many selves is writing? And what kind of autobiography did

From V. S. Pritchett: "Writing an Autobiography," reprinted from *Page 2*, ed.
Francis Brown. (New York: Holt, Rinehart & Winston, Inc., 1969). Copyright by
V. S. Pritchett. Reprinted by permission of Harold Matson Co., Inc.

you mean to write? What is its theme? There is nothing to do but start again.

Let us suppose you are a famous statesman or general, a great bull fighter, opera singer, a surgeon or sportsman, or that you have been very close to the famous, a valet of the eminent. You have made your career; you have had adventures; you have known crowds of people. You will have kept notes, letters and diaries all your life. The public will expect that you reveal what you know and will hang upon your indiscretion. You will be writing your reminiscences or a memoir; you will not in the strict sense be writing your autobiography at all. Your truth will be a contribution to social history or anecdotage. Or suppose you have been the witness of a great event and put that down: the event and not yourself is the subject. You will be only a collection of enviable glimpses. What if you are a natural diarist—say, a Pepys or an Amiel—and inevitably reveal yourself? Does that make you an autobiographer? Rarely.

The born diarists are the snails of life: they are secretive and enclosed in their shells, and their whispering contributes either to history or—as in Amiel's case—to a case history. The pure autobiographer is concerned with shaping a past from the standpoint of a present that may be totally unlike it. That is why you tore up those 20 pages and paused to consider who your first-person singular is and what "truth" you intend to state.

For there is no absolute truth. You will be unable to tell all or you will be incapable of it. Or let us hope that you are, for one definition of a bore is that he is a man who tells you everything. The writer who has—and quotes—his diaries or preserved letters is in great danger here: this has been the bane of Victorian autobiography and is a continuing danger in America where keeping records has been enjoined almost as a historical obligation. The Boston memoir is the classic example.

Your difficulties with truth-telling arise from the fossilization of memory. Perhaps hypnosis could dissolve a trauma that has become sacred; but I cannot see what can be done about the fact that it is easier to remember things that happened 40 years ago than those that occurred in the last 10. Our lives are really a collection of adroit generalizations which enable us to push on from the present minute. The longer one lives, the less certain one is of who one is. So many people and events have swarmed in that the sense of a self—Gray's "pleasing anxious being"—who lives an hour, a day at a time and not in collections of years, is dispersed and even vulgarized. One begins to think there was no "I" after all.

And, in fact, the "I" is a relatively new invention. To start with, it is exclusively European in origin. Asia and Africa have no autobiographers. About seven years ago I read an excellent if severe book called "Design and Truth in Autobiography" by Roy Pascal, who pointed this out and added that in Europe there are no autobiographies in the classical period.

The genre can be said to have started with St. Augustine, but centuries passed before a Cellini, a Geronimo Cardano, a Saint Theresa appeared in the Renaissance. Unlike ourselves these writers are not recreating a past from the standpoint of the present; Cellini casting his statue, Saint Theresa in founding her convent, are proclaiming new selves in a new world and are conscious of themselves in the act. They differ from us in being very little conscious of their society as an overwhelming influence.

It is not until we reach the 18th and early 19th centuries that the confidence a man has in his society and his belief in the pleasure and interest of his private tastes and habits give him an avid concern with himself in relation to it. It is the age of the great autobiographers—of Rousseau, Gibbon, Franklin, Goethe and Casanova. Later, the strenuous effort towards self-realization among the new middle class, urged on also by the idea of the Romantic movement, gives us Harriet Martineau, John Stuart Mill, John Ruskin, even Henry Adams, and still later Wells and Beatrice Webb. Leonard Woolf's recent volumes are written as a valediction to a civilization determined on suicide.

In our own time, Mr. Pascal says, a writer like Koestler shows the self passing through historical calamity and asking why it was so chosen. One offers oneself as a sample of the historical process in one's own life time. And here, I wonder, if the present vogue of autobiography has not something dubious about it. Doesn't calamity really make nonsense of the distinctive individual; doesn't its stamp make us all alike?

What reason have I to believe that I have more than the common interest? I may be only a type. Am I dramatizing myself because I am lonely? The "I" in Cellini or Goethe, Newman and Henry James is a pronoun of pride; isn't it a badge of wistful desperation for us, the only thing left so that it has to "do" for everything we have lost? Fortunately for the autobiographer the social process still goes on even if it runs down, and the individual still asserts himself, but frantically now in the midst of it.

I have myself written an autobiography and can speak of the practical difficulties. I was forced to reject the official sounding family memoir. Unlike Bertrand Russell, I am not a great man or a public figure. I cannot draw on distinguished, public-spirited ancestors or famous family connections. I have visited Society, but, like most writers, only for a minute or two. That kind of life is no good to us. I have belonged to no celebrated set, and although I have met many celebrated people (for, as they say of London life, everyone knows everybody), I have not been very intimate with them. My most intimate meeting, I think, was with Georges Carpentier, the French boxer, who accidentally stepped back and trod hard on my toe on the Channel boat when I was off to France in my twenties. He walked away without saying a word.

As for my literary reminiscences or my reflections on literature in the past 45 years, they must wait. I am not fond of shop talk. But, being self-centered I could not resist writing about the unlikely background that made a writer of me. I confined myself to my prewriting years. At 21 they ended; after that, being a writer, I found myself being met by what I had already written.

After 21, unless one is a note-taker, a letter keeper or diarist —which I have rarely been—memory blurs, years and phases telescope. What about my inner life? I have not so far shown any talent for the confessional. That requires a certain temperament. In one sense all writing is a confession. But after 21, whether he is confessional or not, the autobiographer who writes intimately is in the difficulty that many people who were important to him are still alive. As a storyteller I have no consideration for people; nor should I have. But I cannot involve the living in my "truth" (though I have to admit that the discarded mistresses of great artists have not hesitated here).

The odd thing is that sitters will often tolerate a portrait done "warts and all" by a painter, but do not care for the same thing in print. They ring up their lawyers at once; and even praise offends, for one has not praised them for what they would like to be praised. From the autobiographer's point of view, people live far too long. Society asks too much of the "truthful" autobiographer when it obliges him to live on to his nineties before he can speak. By that time, as Somerset Maugham's nonagenarian revelations showed, one is apt to be vinegarish.

I can think of no vainglorious autobiography since Cellini, unless Frank Harris counts. There have been dedicated believers in imaginative lying like Ford Madox Ford. Goethe spoke of his "poetry" but also of his "truth." There have been exploiters of self-accusation like Rousseau. The three main difficulties of autobiography are one's self-pity, one's shames and one's self-justifications. It is also difficult to write exactly about chastity in a period like the present when it is regarded as ridiculous. Only the Turgenevs can write about early love; only the Pushkins can tell with a poet's brutality of how and why it ends. To feel is to tire. So much of love is love of love.

It is also hard to record one's early opinions truthfully: one has forgotten their force. Self-pity is fairly easy to deal with now for we have been toughened. As for shame, one must not wallow. The youth you are ashamed of was, among other things, an engaging fellow; if he was a prig and pompous ass most of his contemporaries were pompous asses and prigs too. It was part of the general charm. The French who have an extreme regard for the solemnities of adolescence miss this romantic Anglo-Saxon worry. The real problem is how to avoid subtle and secretive self-justification, especially when one is recording discarded emotions or beliefs. Here one's standpoint of a present totally unlike the past is liable to bully or skillfully deceive.

Roy Pascal points out. that Tolstoy's "A Confession" like other confessions of religious experience, has the fault of devaluing earlier experience, so that the unity of personality is broken. The sinner and the reformed sinner are, in fact, inseparable, and it is hard to admit this. We usually cover up by one or two eloquent but hollow passages. Schweitzer makes his development too logical. Henry Adams was attached to democratic ideas for longer than he admits in the "Education." We are so anxious to show that our blatant errors did not last a long time.

This common dilemma would vanish if we saw that it is normal for many of us to hold one belief or emotion and its opposite at the same time. And here it is hard to admit that one was swayed by snobbery, self-interest or the influence of persons now despised. It is hard not to convey that only the highest considerations really weighed with one. The phlegm and coolness of a Gibbon with his "I sighed as a lover but obeyed as a son" is beyond most of us. And it is dangerous even to be too good at candor; it may be nothing but vanity which was Valéry's criticism of Gide (Again I take this from Mr. Pascal): "To spin words to one's confessor is a serious matter: it will make him forget to absolve you."

For myself I had long ago recognized that, like my story-telling mother, I was an inventive person. I was one of those, I had to see, who invents himself and had not much capacity for self-analysis or introspection except of the dreariest kind. I would be less interested in myself than the story I saw in other people: the most boring part of my autobiography described my early literary efforts. I could only be careless, so that my character, for good or ill, would become plain in what I said about others. I novelized and was, no doubt, inaccurate in this or that, but I told my truth. I never cease to be startled by the fantastic interior of most lives. I inherit a good ear and memory for what is spoken: I swear by the dialogue I have written.

My judgments are another matter. A more earnest, more detailed and documented narrative might have been more accurate. I think it would have been tedious. A tragic interpretation could have been made. Either would have been "true." I would find it impossible to continue the story of my life in the same vein. This suggests to me that where modern autobiography so often fails is that it tends to be written in the same key throughout.

1. Do you have the impression from this essay that Pritchett would be an interesting writer of autobiography himself? Why or why not?

2. To what extent does Pritchett make this essay autobiographical? In what ways does he enlarge upon his own experience to give a more general view of autobiography?

3. What use does Pritchett make of history in his essay? Does his discussion of the tradition of autobiography strike you as particularly scholarly? If not, how does he make you take his point of view seriously?

4. How does Pritchett organize his different observations about autobiography? Does the separation of the essay into two sections have some organizational basis that makes sense to you?

5. Summarize what you think Pritchett sees as the most important problems for the autobiographer. Can you identify selections in this collection that reflect one or another of these problems? Have you found any of these problems causing you difficulties in your own autobiographical writing?

Possibilities for Writing

1. Look back at some experience that covered an extended period of time in your life and is now over—for example, your senior year in high school, your last year in a high school club or on an athletic team, your summer job, a vacation trip you took that lasted several weeks. Write an essay in which you interpret and evaluate that experience, showing what it meant in the overall pattern of your life.

2. After you have read V. S. Pritchett's essay in this chapter, write your own essay on the subject of autobiography. Draw on the experience you have had during the semester to help you explain the special characteristics or the special difficulties of autobiographical writing.

3. Write an essay in which you use your personal experience as part of an argument for some specific social or institutional changes. For example, you could relate your own school experiences to some larger argument for changes that would make schools better or your own experiences as a driver to more general views of transportation problems.

4. After reading the selection by Richard Rodriguez, write an essay in which you discuss some circumstances that cause you to act or speak or think differently, depending on whether you are in public or in private surroundings. Analyze what causes

these differences and decide whether they would lead to the same results for other people in a similar situation.

5. Choose three of the Orwell essays in this anthology and show how they reveal themselves to be the work of a single writer. Concern yourself with Orwell's attitudes, his way of characterizing himself, and his way of presenting events and people.